OPERATION PSEUDO MIRANDA

A Veteran of the CIA Drug Wars Tells All

Kenneth C. Bucchi

Penmarin Books
Granite Bay, California

Editorial Offices:
Penmarin Books
2011 Ashridge Way
Granite Bay, CA 95746

Sales and Customer Service Offices:
Midpoint Trade Books
27 W. 20th Street, Suite 1102
New York, NY 10011
(212) 727-0190

Penmarin Books are available at special discounts for bulk purchases for premiums, sales promotions, or education. For details, contact the Publisher. On your letterhead, include information concerning the intended use of the books and how many you wish to purchase.

Visit our Website at **www.penmarin.com** for more information about this and other exciting titles.

Printed in Canada
1 2 3 4 5 6 7 8 9 10   04 03 02 01 00

Library of Congress Cataloging-in-Publication Data
Bucchi, Kenneth C.
     Operation Pseudo Miranda : a veteran of the CIA drug wars tells all / Kenneth C. Bucchi.
       p. cm.
     ISBN 1-883955-17-3
     1. Bucchi, Kenneth C. 2. Narcotics, Control of—United States—Case studies. 3. Cocaine industry—Government policy—United States—Case studies. 4. Cocaine industry—Colombia—Case studies. 5. Undercover operations—Colombia—Case studies. 6. United States. Central Intelligence Agency—Officials and employees—Biography. I. Title

HV5825.B79   2000
363.45′0973—dc21   00-049156

This book is dedicated to

the memory of my sister

Deborah Ann Bucchi-Haigh

Her jubilance and youthful nature brought joy to all who knew her. Her inviting character transformed everyday encounters into lasting friendships. Although her life was cut short at 37, she found eternal salvation in Jesus Christ, and it is with that knowledge that I persevere.

Acknowledgments

I would like to thank my wife, Joanna, for her love and devotion, and my children, Jack and "The Bean" (Noah), for making us a family. And to my mom and dad (Dorothy and Ben) for supporting and loving me through thick and thin.

I would also like to thank my agent, Jason Scoggins of The Gersh Agency, for treating me as though I were his only client. His unwavering belief in my abilities infused me with the confidence that I needed to successfully navigate the rather circuitous Hollywood studio system and eventually sign deals with Atlas Entertainment, Universal Studios, 20th Century Fox, and NBC.

Thanks also to my publisher, Hal Lockwood, and Atlas Entertainment's Doug Segal, for immediately grasping the synergistic, multimedia potential of my work and for having the faith in me to realize that potential. Finally, I would like to give special thanks to my editor, Virginia Ray, for providing clarity to the work itself.

OPERATION PSEUDO MIRANDA

A Veteran of the
CIA Drug Wars Tells All

Despite my second identity as an undercover agent, I drove a flashy gull-winged Delorean from my home in San Antonio, Texas, to the airfield at Kelly Air Force Base, where I then climbed into an unmarked, six-passenger, single-engine Cessna 210 piloted by a man I'd never seen before. Although I was a first lieutenant in the Air Force by occupation, I now wore casual civilian clothing, as did the pilot and the three other passengers—also strangers to me—who the Agency had teamed together for a new assignment. I would never see any of them again. Central Intelligence compartmentalizes its people in such a way that they can never be linked to one another.

During the flight I was briefed on the assignment. My group was to intercept a newly arrived drug shipment from South America at an un-disclosed destination. We were to confiscate the entire shipment, which represented half of the Medellin cartel's export for a seven-day period. We'd been doing this for years now, working in tandem with such global major cocaine distributors as Manuel Noriega, Fabio Ochoa and Pablo Escobar, and preventing tons of drugs from reaching American streets.

It was basically a dangerous business, but we'd become accustomed to that and learned to work around it . . . well, mostly. But on this May morning in 1987 I was feeling a special tension, somehow sensing that something was going to go terribly wrong this time. I decided it was because I now had enough experience to know realistically how probable such an outcome could be.

As we approached Hondo Airport, located about ninety miles west southwest of San Antonio, a usual gathering point for us, we swept by a barren and cracked runway where grass grew through cracks in the tarmac and gravel filled aircraft grounding points. The facility was used only to refurbish aircraft and to accommodate CIA missions such as ours. Aircraft hulls and smaller parts were visible behind hangars. Outside the fenced-in containment was a golf course.

Having landed, and now in one of those hangars where vintage World War II fighter aircraft were stored, I joined five people with whom I'd worked during the past few years, all of them using aliases. Mine was Anthony Vesbucci.

The one person I relied on most, however, was missing. Boxer, nicknamed Box, had been my handler (the euphemism for a thirty-something CIA agent whose sole function was to chaperone inexperienced field agents) from the beginning. A good-looking, six-foot two-inch, smoothly muscled black man, Box loved rock-and-roll, and he was a moralistic person who could always be counted on to do what was necessary. From the outset we'd worked shoulder to shoulder on every assignment, but this time he'd been required to accompany the rest of the team to another interception in southern Florida.

Joey was going on the mission, though, and that meant a lot to me. He only stood five feet nine inches tall and had a slender build and a detectable feminine air about him, but his gung-ho attitude and arrow-splitting marksmanship made him a formidable surrogate for Box. Quick and strong, Joey startled those who mistook him for anything but their physical equal.

On the other hand, Quinn was a woman who wore her masculinity and, for that matter, her sexual predisposition, on her sleeve. She had a stout body and dirty blond, tightly cropped hair, and she could produce a real muscle. More at home in a fist fight than a conversation, she hid her innate sentimentality very well.

I called the next guy Fossil because of his apparent age and because he was too big a prick to reveal his name. In his middle fifties, perhaps five feet nine inches tall and gray-haired, he spoke in a distinctively raspy voice. He immediately proclaimed himself in command of the assignment and was at once demanding and authoritative, to the point of being dictatorial. He was a new addition to the team, which had never happened before. To say the least, I was a bit concerned about that.

Jesus Rivas was a Hispanic of medium height with long, wavy hair and a splendidly groomed mustache. He was extremely cocky, but tempered it with a good sense of humor. When bad things happened, which they often did, you could always count on Jesus to overextend himself, and yet he would somehow come through unscathed.

Lourdes was a blond-haired, emerald-eyed Latina with smooth, tan skin. She had shapely legs, a washboard stomach and a face so adorable I had to constantly fight the urge to pinch it. She was extremely honest and direct, which I decided was probably due to naiveté. Her sweetness made her seem almost out of place on our hardscrabble team. Although she, too, had a sense of humor, she was slow to show it. She never grasped any sort of complex political or social issue, which, for the most part, was refreshing for the rest of us jaded agents.

Ming was a six-foot, athletic Asian who spoke three languages. Although he'd trained with us in Tonopah, he usually worked out of our sister operation in Thailand. He worked for Lance Motley, Box's counterpart in Asia. He was disciplined and reserved but lacked the ability to improvise.

When not feeling extreme stress, we were usually a talkative bunch. But today near silence prevailed. I thought that the others, for whatever reasons, were perhaps having the same premonition I was.

We collected weapons in the hangar. I attached a side-holstered Colt .45 automatic pistol and two grenades to my belt. We boarded two small Bell helicopters for the flight to our interception destination.

We landed in a clearing densely surrounded by live oaks at about three o'clock in the afternoon. As we walked cautiously through the thickly wooded Texas hill country, we occasionally crossed dirt paths leading to small residences, many of which were mobile homes. One that caught my eye featured an exotic collection of what appeared to be pet cougars and peacocks. As we moved into the farthest part of the forest, the homes fell away, leaving nothing but an endless expanse of trees.

We finally came to a house standing by itself on a lonely hill, and we hunkered down at the mouth of the trail leading up to it. The building was a white, two-and-one-half-story, frame structure with a wooden deck contoured around it. A four-foot iron fence enclosed a treeless area at the rear where windows spread across the entire upper floor. Through a large picture window at the front of the house, we could see several people milling about.

We hunkered down and waited tensely.

After what seemed an interminable silence, I said to Fossil, "It'll take a hell of a pilot to make a successful drop in this terrain, especially with the drop zone limited to that cleared space in the backyard."

He said, "The intelligence report indicates that the shipment has already been made. The mules inside transported the drugs from the drop zone to here and should be waiting for a second-level transfer. That's why we need to move swiftly and precisely."

"Whoa, whoa, whoa," I replied imposingly, my arms stretched out before me. "What kind of bullshit is this? Look. I don't know exactly what's going on here, but I do know this: We don't get involved with the affairs of the DEA. If this coke has already been received by Escobar's mules, then we're getting our asses outta here."

"I don't give a rat's ass what you think. And I don't personally give a flying fuck what you do or don't want to get involved with. I'm running the show, and you'll do exactly what you're told to do! Not that you deserve an explanation, but you were told at the start of Pseudo Miranda that first-level interceptions would be made, and a code word would be used to facilitate it." He paused, altering his tone dramatically. "Oh, which reminds me, the code word is 'Shangri La'."

We were both talking in low, angry whispers. I said, "Oh, that *reminds* you? Well, let me tell you something. And forgive me if I don't sound as perfunctory as you, but if so much as one shot is fired here today, the next one'll separate your head from your shoulders. So go ahead and run your fuckin' show."

He hesitated, a bead of sweat running off his forehead. Then he said, "When I'm convinced those guys in the house have got the message that we're here to take their drugs, you'd better be ready to move!"

"Okay," I said. "Joey, you and I'll go right up the pipe." Joey knew that this meant we were going straight through the front door. "Lourdes, you and Rivas flank us. Quinn, you and Ming stay positioned right here."

Quinn said, "Any particular marching orders?"

"Yeah," I told her. "If he . . . ," motioning toward Fossil with the Colt in my hand, " . . . does anything but support us, do that head 'n' shoulders thing."

After waiting another forty-five minutes, Fossil picked up his megaphone and rasped, "Shangri La!"

Joey and I got on our feet and started walking up the path toward the house. It seemed to take an eternity, and I could feel muscles tightening all over my body as we approached the building. I reached out with my left hand, embracing Joey's right arm. He glanced back with heavy eyes and struggled to smile, as if telling me good-bye. He knew, as I did, the fate that lurked on the other side of the door.

When we climbed the stairs to the deck, the front door opened, and we stormed inside. The room we entered was split level. On my left, it rose another level, which led to another room. On the wall facing us was a large mirror; to our rear a spiral staircase ascended to a corridor and smaller adjoining rooms. We saw a huge amount of drugs on the floor— probably 500 kilos—lined up neat and tidy. This made it look like a legitimate and sizable interception. I was feeling a touch better.

Half of the people standing in the room in front of us looked to be American, the other half Hispanic. Because the drugs were stacked more on the right side, I told the people to move to the left and signaled in that direction for the benefit of the Latinos who didn't speak English.

They all shifted to the right.

A dreadful feeling came over me.

In my peripheral vision, something flashed in the mirror and I looked to the left. There were more mules, and they had guns—very big guns. With my pulse racing, I realized why the first group had moved right instead of left.

I yelled, "Grenades!"

Joey immediately pulled one off his belt, yanked the pin, and lobbed it toward the unexpected threat. There was a big explosion.

Debris flew at us, and, because it funneled out from a smaller room to a bigger one, it was as though it blew through a wind tunnel. The blast struck with tremendous force. I ducked. But then I looked back, and the scene became surrealistic as debris flowed slowly toward me like snowflakes on a gentle breeze.

Our ambushers had only to fire in our general direction and Joey and I would be dead. So we started shooting at anything. There was a confusing melee of explosions, shouting and debris splattering about. I didn't know what was happening in the other room. I didn't know what was happening outside. And I was thinking, "My God, is Joey still alive?"

Then, suddenly feeling a strange detachment in the midst of all of that, I found my mind turning back to that earlier time when I was younger and more naïve—just an easygoing student on a peaceful campus in Murray, Kentucky.

Chapter 2

It was early 1984, and I was a twenty-one-year-old senior at Murray State University, majoring in criminal justice and minoring in sociology. The rustic little campus with its ten thousand students was the principal industry in the small, tranquil village.

I was an Alpha Tau Omega, but I didn't live in the fraternity house with the rest of the "frogs," as we called ourselves. Instead, I preferred 208 Poplar Street, a compact, three-bedroom house that I rented in a quiet neighborhood where everyone kept to themselves. I sublet two of the bedrooms to fraternity brothers. There was a tiny front yard and a larger backyard bordered by tall brush, which concealed it from outside view. On one side, at the street corner, was a repair business. On the other side was a house occupied by an elderly deaf woman. In other words, it was a very private place to live.

I had many friends in the fraternity and good friends in the community as well. I dated a lot but rarely had what might be called a relationship. My buddies and I spent a good deal of time partying at Kentucky Lake. We often traveled to Tennessee and occasionally as far as New Orleans for the same reason. That was pretty much the scene at the time: sports, women, partying and cramming as much studying into the remaining few minutes as fraternity life would allow.

The last thing I would have ever considered happening to me was being recruited by the CIA. But that is exactly what happened. Only it had begun a year earlier, and I was totally oblivious to it. As with most things, I might add. Looking back on it, I can now see why the saying "Ignorance is bliss" became a cliché. I only wish now that I had remained ignorant and gone to law school.

*   *   *

Mike was a part-time student who commuted from Paducah, a good-looking guy who really attracted the women, and an interesting character. We started hanging out together. And there was this weird game, suggested by Mike, that we started playing.

Both of us would kick anywhere from ten to a hundred bucks into a pool. The object was to convince someone—a stranger—of some crazy thing we just pulled out of thin air. If you could get away with such things, you collected the pool. If you couldn't, you owed double. As an example, I once posed as a health inspector dedicated to enforcing hygiene statutes. In a bar one time, I was so convincing that I got one young lady to show me her underwear and another to confess that she was not wearing any. "Do I have to leave?" she asked, sincerely convinced she had broken the law. Of course, there was no way I was letting her leave the bar.

The whole thing was rigged so that Mike could observe how I handled people, including when they turned antagonistic. But I had no idea he was doing this, even a year later when Mike dropped by my house and said, "You're really interested in what you're studying, aren't you? The criminology?"

"Yeah. Corrections. Various agencies."

"CIA?"

"Well . . . I don't know. I never thought about it."

"They're testing in Chicago."

"How the hell do you know that?"

"It was in the *Louisville Courier-Journal* yesterday."

I was amazed. "You tryin' to tell me they're actually advertising in a newspaper?"

"Yeah."

"That doesn't make any sense. They're . . . they're . . . what, what is that word? Clandestine. They're too clandestine for that. Aren't they?"

"No. They've got a lot of jobs that have nothing to do with that. Logistical things, secretaries, map people, positions like that. But maybe they hire for a lot of their secret jobs that way too. Who knows? There are a series of tests you have to go through, I think."

"How the hell do you know so much about it?"

"It was in the paper."

He showed me the cover. It was in the paper, all right. Taking those tests seemed like the promise of a good time. We drove to Chicago.

* * *

The Federal Building was at the southern part of the Loop, on Dearborn. The offices that we were searching for were on the seventh floor. To our surprise, however, the signage on the front door announced them as belonging to the FBI. Needless to say, I was very confused and a bit frustrated. We were then directed to a room where I had expected to see hundreds of people.

There were, instead, just two. Both were in their middle thirties, mustached, trim, neatly dressed and cordial. One of them, who introduced himself as Salter—the one who would do all of the talking—showed me a badge that identified him as belonging to the Department of Defense. I noticed that he had a Chief Master Sergeant's insignia on his pen, which indicated that he must have served in the Air Force. But what he did and said now identified him as State Department.

He started out by saying, "Tell me a little bit about yourself."

I gave him a short autobiography, the type you give when you stand up on your first day of class.

He then took a file from a briefcase. I was the subject. Although they shouldn't even have known that I was coming, I suddenly realized they had been expecting me.

Salter started talking about an old high school friend of mine named Jim. Jim dabbled in the cocaine trade primarily to rebel against his parents, who he felt treated him badly. As an example, he'd once told me that his parents took the rest of the family to Europe and left him behind. Looking back on it now, I realize that he was probably full of crap, but the effect such a story had on me was nonetheless effective. Although I never involved myself in drugs—my father would have shoved a tightly coiled hundred-dollar bill up my nose if he ever found out—I sympathized with Jim's purported situation and therefore his response to it.

One night in 1978, when his parents were away, Jim threw a really big cocaine party at their house. He basically gave away his profits for an entire month. It turned into a mess, and people ended up trashing the house.

He disappeared and I went looking for him. When I finally found him, he was nearly passed out—Lord knows how many drugs he'd taken. People were playing with him, throwing him back and forth. I broke that up. But I didn't know what to do with him. I didn't want to call an ambulance. The minute it arrived, he'd be locked up for the rest of his life, I thought. He had more than a kilo of cocaine stashed in that house.

What I finally did was call the police and report a disturbance on the street at another address. I figured that when the cops showed on the street, people would discreetly get the hell out of Jim's house. It worked. People left, and I was able to get Jim to vomit up the pharmacopia he had ingested.

Now, in Chicago, I found out how all of this got into my file. Back in my high school days I'd known someone named Levine a little better than casually. He'd been at Jim's party. I guessed that he was either DEA or FBI and had created a file on me. Apparently neither of those agencies had use for someone with my peculiar talents. But now the file had found its way to the CIA. And what had happened the night of Jim's party and in numerous other tight spots with Jim meant to the CIA that I was a guy who could get close to drugs and deal with the people involved and yet not get dirty myself. In the CIA's estimation, I'd done a lot of things in 1978 that were good for a guy my age.

It was a surprise to me.

The interviewer talked to me about my father's stepfather being in the Mafia. I didn't know that. Then the CIA agent, Salter, told me that Jim had been selling cocaine for a guy named Delvechio, who was doing it for a guy named Hood, who was doing it for a guy named Patriarca, who was the head of the Mafia in all of New England.

The chain was there, and I was thinking I was in big trouble.

But then Salter said, "How would you like a job?"

It wasn't as though I had a lot of leeway to say no. But at the same time he made it sound nice enough and good enough so that I became really interested. And I was thinking, "What the heck, it's going to pay an inordinate amount of money, it's going to be in my line of work, it's a clandestine organization," which, as all men can appreciate, offers the perfect pick-up line.

But all I really knew was that it involved drug interdiction, that the organization was called Central Intelligence Drug Enforcement, abbreviated CIDE (but pronounced "city"), and that, if I went for it, I would be contacted.

I went for it by nodding yes.

* * *

Basically I went back to college and played "school." I'd met Boxer, my training agent, for the first time in Chicago. Now he appeared at my house several times. He put me through scenarios involving drug deals. I didn't know if they were real or not. I'd work a week in that fashion, then there was nothing for a month or so.

I pretty much broke away from the fraternity and hung around with a group of older friends. I just was no longer interested in being with the younger Alpha Tau Omega guys . . . the preppies.

Then, in the spring of 1984, I attended my first secret meeting. It was to be held in Cumberland, Maryland. I had no idea, at the time, that Bill Casey would be there. I went to Chicago because I would be driving down to the meeting with Box. The Agency made cars available to us there, and I chose a black Pantera DeTomaso, a sports car with European curves yet with the distinct roar of an American pedigree created by the power of its 351-cubic-inch Cleveland engine, Ford's greatest creation. As we drove down to Maryland in that car, I detected enough from Box's conversations to believe that he was married and had kids. I also discovered that my choice of the flamboyant Pantera was something he worried about every mile of the way.

* * *

We paused at a small town near Cumberland that still had hitching posts along the storefronts and gas stations with old-fashioned pumps. After we'd stopped and gotten out at the town center, some little girls came up selling cookies. We bought all they had because we figured they would then go home. We realized all the while what a contrast there was between the children's innocence and our reason for being there. When we arrived in Cumberland, we checked into the Holiday Inn on George Street, a street I remembered because it was the name of my late, favorite uncle, George Buckley.

The next day we showed up for the meeting at a house that had been confiscated by the Drug Enforcement Administration, I learned. These meetings were jokingly termed Commission meetings, in reference to the Mafia commission meetings. They included mid-level officials from all of the different government agencies, including the DEA, the Defense Intelligence Agency, the FBI, the Department of Defense, the CIA, and one high-ranking official from one of these major agencies who was technically the chairperson.

The reason to have all these officials there was to achieve more cooperation between the various agencies than would otherwise happen. The meetings took place in remote locations in order to avoid the embarrassment of public knowledge about the petty conflicts that seriously hindered individual agencies from functioning as they should. And so those meetings, I would eventually discover, basically cultivated finger pointing and ass kissing among the agencies.

Before we went into the house, I found out that Box wasn't the only one worrying about my choice of the Pantera, which I'd parked outside. Two men, one of them wearing a very loud sports shirt, approached Box and me. The one with the shirt said angrily, "Why didn't you just announce your arrival to the whole damned neighborhood?"

"I thought I'd let your shirt do it instead," I replied.

"You're one of those funny guys. You must be with the Central Ignorance Agency."

"You have no sense of humor whatsoever. You must be with the FBI."

"DEA, asshole!"

"I thought you had to pass a test to get in the DEA."

Said the second man, "What kind of an idiot drives a Ferrari to a meeting like this?"

"You need to get out of your office more often," I said. "That's a Pantera, not a Ferrari. Anyhow, who dresses like that to go hunting?"

Said the one with the shirt, "Hunting? What the hell makes you think I'm going hunting?"

I nodded toward the second one. "You brought your dog, didn't ya?"

We walked away from them, toward the house, and Box finally relaxed, laughing and saying, "How could anyone have fallen for that old joke?"

I was acting like any twenty-two-year-old college kid. I'd decided that if that were the person they'd wanted to hire, then this was the way I would continue to act. But now, stepping into this top-secret governmental meeting where Bill Casey was indeed in attendance, I became acutely aware of the dramatic shift my life had taken.

Chapter 3

The meeting was held in a room that had been enlarged by taking out a wall. At one end was the speaker's platform with a large screen in the center flanked by an easel on either side. In front of the platform and perpendicular to it was a long, veneered table that narrowed at both ends. Seated along its sides were the two DEA men, two from the FBI and one from the Defense Intelligence Agency. Box and I sat near the end of the table most distant from the speaker's platform. To our immediate right, at the head of the table, Bill Casey presided. The chairs swiveled and were comfortable, even though covered with plastic, except Casey's, which was upholstered in black leather and had a high, executive-style back. Security guards were positioned on both sides of the single door leading into the room.

Casey, of course, dominated our attention. He was a gray-haired man about six feet tall, with two and a half chins on a sagging face, which featured large, round glasses. His shoulders had slumped forward in a rounded posture, and he wore a large school ring on one finger. It was obvious that he was highly intelligent, but he mumbled a lot. In fact, you couldn't understand most of what he said—except when he wanted you to. Then he became wonderfully coherent. He was also easily agitated. He wanted absolute control and focus on himself.

Nevertheless, several of the others at the meeting got up and spoke. One of the DEA representatives described an individual named Carijuana and the man's partner, Bolero, a Massachusetts attorney. Appropriately, Carijuana dealt marijuana in Florida. He was literally thumbing his nose at the DEA because they'd been unable to stop him. The DEA wanted cooperation from the CIA because they'd discovered that Carijuana had connections to Cuba. The CIA also had connections to Cuba and, as a result, could perhaps facilitate his apprehension there.

When the discussion about Carijuana ended, Casey called a short break. We went outside and walked around the house and ate doughnuts and chatted. Box and I found ourselves reunited with the two DEA agents. We joked with them again. Then the DEA men again brought up the problem they'd been having capturing Carijuana and Bolero.

I finally said, "Why do you people waste countless tax dollars building a case against a guy you know is a drug dealer and arrest him only after you've allowed him to dump tons of drugs onto the street? The moment you throw him in jail, someone's there to step in and take over without skipping a beat. It's the people on the next level below him who make it difficult for you. They're like assembly line workers. Their jobs don't change, regardless of who's at the top. So if you arrest Carijuana, they'll simply replace him."

I could see that what I was saying bothered the DEA pair, which was exactly what I'd intended in response to the way they'd jumped on me earlier about the car. I went on, "Why don't you just suspend Carijuana's Miranda rights? Don't give him any of his constitutional guarantees. When you know he's done something illegal, simply kick his door in. Take all his money. Take all his drugs. Then let him go on his merry way."

I knew they were getting heated, but I kept on, saying, "What's he gonna do? Go to the media and say, 'They stole my five million dollars worth of marijuana?'" I could hear Box chuckling. "You know Carijuana's not going to do that. So eventually you'll run him out of business. All right, it's illegal. But you're not making any arrests. No one's hurt. No one's going to complain. And you accomplish more. Because if you just have these long-term investigations costing millions of dollars, when you finally nail the guy on some stupid hokey charge, all that'll happen is someone else will take over. You don't really interrupt the business. But if you interrupt it by taking money and drugs, no one else will take the business over because it won't be profitable. Call the operation Pseudo Miranda."

The DEA men were genuinely angry now. Both Box and I were laughing. We went back to the meeting.

* * *

The next speaker was one of the FBI agents. He was entirely professional. But he was so boring that I didn't pay attention. When he finally finished, I was just staring into space. That was when Bill Casey leaned past Box and slapped my shoulder. He said something that was hard to understand, but it was clearly in reference to the Miranda thing I'd talked about outside. I realized that he'd probably overheard the conversation Box and I had had with the two DEA guys at break time.

"Get up and tell us about it, Mr. Vesbucci," Casey said to me.

"It was a joke," I replied.

"No, no. Give us a briefing on the merits of it."

"There aren't any merits. I was just kidding."

He was becoming agitated again and snapped, "Do what I'm telling you!"

I went to the podium thinking that as long as I sounded intelligent, I was going to be all right in this job. "Sound smart," I thought. "Don't sound realistic." So I talked, delivering what I decided he wanted to hear.

When I finished, Casey said in his mumbling fashion, "All right. Fine. But it's not practical. It can't be done. There are too many complications. You can sit down, Mr. Vesbucci."

I returned to my chair thinking, "Well, good. It's gonna be okay." The whole thing was over. The meeting ended. We went back to the Holiday Inn. Box was obviously relieved, thinking, too, that everything was going to be all right now.

We decided that what they'd been trying to do was bleed us for anything we had, figuring that Box and I had been talking about the Miranda business for months, which we hadn't, and that we had drummed up a number of great ideas, which we hadn't.

But there was nothing to worry about now.

Five hours later we got a call that definitely indicated there was. Box hung up and looked at me accusingly. "Good going, Ace. Guess who has to return to the Commission. Gooood going!"

"Are you serious? What do you think it means?"

"Our asses, you moron!"

"Take a chill pill, Box. I can handle this."

"You can, huh?"

"If Case Face wanted to tear me a new asshole, he would have done it earlier."

"I hope you're right. And drop the Bill Casey pet names before you accidentally use one in front of him!"

"How in God's name have you survived a decade in this line of work?"

"Mostly by not associating with people like you."

"Thanks for the support and encouragement."

"I'm not being paid to pad your ego, Bucchi!"

"What exactly are you being paid to do?"

"Let's just go. And I'm driving!"

"Which obviously means you're in no hurry to get there."

*　　*　　*

When we again arrived at the house, we found that all kinds of people were waiting for us—computer types, logistic types, communication types. By this time I had decided that some of the stuff I'd presented had made sense to Casey. The reason he'd dismissed my ideas earlier was because he didn't want the DEA guys and everyone else in that room to know that he intended to go in the direction I'd indicated, something he'd probably been considering for years.

Casey asked me to repeat the plan. This time I tried to present it both smartly and realistically. In essence you wanted to isolate the biggest cocaine distributors in the world, predominantly in Peru, Bolivia and Colombia. You would then empower them to destroy their smaller competitors, of which there were many, giving the whole market to those few big distributors.

At that point you wouldn't have increased the overall market size. Instead, you would have concentrated that market in just a few hands, which would give you more control. Then, because you would have increased the markets of these select few perhaps tenfold, you would have them turn over half of their drug shipments to you.

Now you're stopping fifty percent of the cocaine coming into the country. And the biggest distributors still have fivefold the profits they would have had previously. On top of that, you wouldn't make any arrests. So they would no longer have any fear of that.

You would set up corridors where the distributors could fly into the country safely under the umbrella of the radar systems that aided the DEA and Customs. Because the flights would be undetected by anyone else, you would be the one to stop half the shipments and let half go on through. There were other, minor details we'd concocted as well.

Driving back to Chicago, I got the impression that Box was feeling a little jealous. He kept insisting we'd still get in trouble over my speech. However, as a trainer, he had rules to follow that I didn't. Besides, we were basically very different people. For example, he liked Pink Floyd and Led Zeppelin. I hated both. It was funny, though, because we didn't worry about bigger differences such as color or religion or where we came from. We never looked for trouble that didn't exist. Not once did he and I have a discussion about any of those things.

*　　*　　*

In Chicago we took a break and stayed at a yacht club on Lakeshore Drive. We stayed there two days and a night in a cabin on the *Down Easter,* wondering what would develop next. In the evening, Box broke out the Wild Turkey. I was listening to Alice Cooper's "Only Women Bleed." Box was at last getting over his trepidations and small jealousies and ventured, "Can you believe that we could soon be involved with this new operation? We could really make a difference in the war on drugs. Of course, the downside is that we could easily get ourselves dead doing it."

"Just a few days ago you were calling my ideas loony tunes."

"I was afraid to admit I believed your ideas made sense for fear that people would think we thought alike."

"Think, thank, thunk . . . let's get to the booze and crank some more tunes."

We did that, with building optimism and excitement. We eventually worked our way to chairs on the deck of the ship, and eventually got honest and serious.

"Believe it or not," Box said gravely, "it's the reason I originally became an agent."

"*It,* meaning to consume grotesque amounts of alcohol?"

"No, you bonehead. To make a real and tangible difference! You know. To live a little on the edge for a real purpose. God, I hope I'm not getting too enthused about the possibilities! I hate being let down when my expectations get too high. By God, I'm glad I hooked up with you. Although you'll probably end up getting me killed. Aren't you going to say something?"

"You're doing fine for the both of us. Anyhow, I don't like to mix important discussions with alcohol."

"Me neither."

"You don't drink much, do you?"

*   *   *

In late June, Box joined me again, this time at my place on 208 Poplar Street in Murray.

"Well," he said, enjoying himself, "you wanted to be part of something really big. It looks like you're going to get your chance."

"So tell me everything. Do I get to carry a gun? . . . I'm just kidding."

"Actually you will be carrying a gun. But not before you finish training. It looks like you and I will be going to a remote and undisclosed locale. Here's a complete list of the things you'll need. Don't bring any of your Big Daddy Cane clothes with you!"

"I'll have you know women love the way I dress."

"I've seen the women you go with. Okay. You'll be departing from Paducah Airport. You know where that is. You won't be able to tell anyone what you're doing. You'll simply tell your family and friends in Massachusetts that you'll be attending the summer semester here. Tell your friends in town that you've graduated and you'll be keeping residence here while you travel periodically around the country looking for a job. Are you following me?"

"I think so," I said with deliberate moronic sarcasm.

"Look, I know this may sound condescending. But it's just that I want everything to go smoothly. So please bear with me. Believe it or not, I actually think we'll make a good team. Atypical, but effective nonetheless. The big news is that we're going to be participants in Pseudo Miranda."

"You mean they're actually going to use the name I came up with?"

"I forgot to mention that."

"Hey, wow! I can't believe they named it that! That's great! Can you believe they did that? Holy shit! How long have I been working for them? And now they've named a program after my idea!"

"Enough already! The name's insignificant. What's important is what we'll be doing."

"You're jealous, Box. You've been working for the Company for over a decade. And they've never named a program for one of your ideas."

"Company! Nobody calls it that. Don't get too cocky. So they named the program Pseudo Miranda. The idea's been kicked around by Mr. Casey for a long time. It just happens that you, by sheer luck, happened to express some views and ideas that he liked."

"Jealous!" I exclaimed.

* * *

Paducah Airport was located in extreme western Kentucky, far from populated areas. There were no terminals. Security was pitifully lax. Years later, a nut case ran out to a departing aircraft and grabbed onto a wing, not letting go until he was several hundred feet in the air, and fell to his death, demonstrating how bad the security was at this place.

Looking back with the wisdom of hindsight, I wonder if I was just as much a nut case for getting into this so deeply and forgetting my personal security. But on that day I felt no such misgivings. A T-39 aircraft flown in from Wright Patterson Air Force Base in Ohio stopped on the runway. I walked out onto the tarmac to board, feeling only excitement that I was heading for my training in Tonopah, Nevada.

Chapter 4

The T-39 that flew us to Tonopah appeared to have made several stops before picking me up in Paducah, as evidenced by the three passengers already on board who seemed as unfamiliar to one another as they were to me. We continued to land at various places to board and drop off passengers as we lethargically proceeded to Nevada. Although Box was too tense for conversation, he instructed me not to speak to anyone concerning the purpose of our journey. I guessed that this was the same directive given to all the passengers. After all, this was Flight 007. It certainly made for some ridiculous conversation though.

"So, what's your name?" I inquired of a woman sitting opposite me.

"Davarra. How 'bout yours?" she replied with a revealing grin. I knew that she was lying. We all lied. It was the nature of the business to lie about anything dealing directly with your background. I responded, "Davarra. That's a beautiful name. Any significance?"

"Yeah. Quite a bit, actually." She snickered, then regained her composure. "It's *Arravad* spelled backwards."

"Arravad! That's Turkish, isn't it?

"Turkey! Yeah . . . right. Turkey." She knew perfectly well that I knew she'd made up the name Davarra, but this was a game she wanted to play. "Well, actually it's Greek. At least it was at the time . . . when my parents were in Davarra . . . Cyprus. It's the most beautiful town in all of . . . yeah, extremely small town in all of Cyprus. Almost microscopic. You can't blink. You know what I'm sayin'? So . . . you never told me your name. Mister . . . ?"

"Tuscadero. Levon Tuscadero."

"Your parents Elton John fans?"

"No," I said abruptly, concealing my ignorance of rock and roll history. "My mom just wanted a *novel* name, I guess."

"And Tuscadero?" She picked up on the reference to a "Happy Days" classic. "Was your father a demolition driver partial to women's pink clothing?"

The rules of engagement were being developed as we went along, and she was very much on her game. The conversations were amusing because they were all fake. We had decided, without ever verbalizing it, that we had to develop the story wherever it led. Box wasn't nearly as entertained with the game as we were, however.

"How 'bout you? Yeah, you." She nodded her head toward Box. "What's your name?"

"No thank you," Box snapped, pointing to his head, as if indicating that he had a headache.

"I think he's telling us that his name is Head. Is that his name, do you think?" she said tauntingly.

"Yeah, I do. Come on, Richard. Why don't you wanna play?"

"Very funny, asshole," Box moaned, with his head tucked beneath a newspaper. "You're a damned dick head."

*   *   *

By the time we entered a landing pattern over Nellis Air Force Base, Nevada, it was approaching midnight. The city below sparkled angelically, projecting a softened image of the pagan vulgarity that is Las Vegas.

Davarra parted company with us at Nellis. The plane taxied to the end of the tarmac where two military policemen of the 4450th (a top-secret squadron) met Box and me and escorted us to a secure staging area. From there we were hastily shuttled to a helicopter under armed guard. I no longer felt reflective or amused. The blood in my brain hammered at my temples. I analyzed Boxer's reaction to the changing events in an attempt to gauge our present state of health. He was expressionless, almost catatonic. Realistically, I knew that he had no more information than I, but there was a certain comfort in knowing that I wasn't in danger alone. I decided to engage in a conversation with one of our escorts.

"Is it always this hot out here?" I asked. No response. "So . . . where's Tonopah?"

"No talking, sir," the Chief Master Sergeant shouted over the noise of the helicopter rotor blades.

Needless to say, I scratched that idea. The fact that he called me *sir*, though, alleviated a lot of the stress that I was feeling. "After all," I thought, "You don't call someone *sir* and then kill 'em." My ignorance served me well back then. In this instance, it gave me a comforting but false sense of security.

Tonopah was just a jaunt away. Located northwest of Nellis, Tonopah is engulfed by mountains. My sense of direction was distorted by my inability to see outside the aircraft. Once on the tarmac in Tonopah, we were blindfolded and loaded onto a bus with blackened windows. After everyone was inside, we were allowed to take the blindfolds off, but it was so dark we could barely see anyway. The driver was a vague figure wrapped in shadow. Security was paramount, but it was humbling to literally be kept in the dark.

When Box and I exited the vehicle, we were struck by an incredible sight: a 600-foot by 300-foot crater. It stood as a beacon in the darkness. My initial impression was that I was standing on the butte in the final scene of *Close Encounters of the Third Kind*. The enormity of it was startling, but its contents were even more impressive. It was like a massive Hollywood sound stage, replete with temporary buildings, alleyways, running water and electricity. The structures were supported at the rear by wood scaffolding bonded to beams that ran along the perimeter of the crater. At either end were long metal staircases, also temporary, with armed guards from the 4450th posted at the bottom. The fact that the guards were at the bottom of each staircase and not the top told me they were there to keep people from leaving, not entering. The rim of the crater where we presently stood was supported by reinforced concrete bracings that swept downward from the top and functioned as dirt retainers.

Looking out over the edge, I now saw several people below in civilian clothing gathered around a few men in camouflage fatigues. One of the men in fatigues signaled with a sweeping motion for us to come down. This was immediately followed by a radio transmission to the guard telling him that we were cleared to enter.

Descending into the arena, I felt a sense of importance. I couldn't help but wonder if much of what I was seeing came by way of the Commission meeting I attended in Cumberland, Maryland.

The staircase clanged and reverberated from our footfalls as we gradually made our way downward. Buildings slowly gained depth and dimension, appearing to have more substance than just facade. The world fell away, leaving only one reality: This was now real, and all that mattered.

Box began to advise me on the appropriate protocol for such an alien environment. In a low, raspy voice, he said sternly, "Listen first. Speak only when asked to. And for God's sakes, no grandstanding!"

"What'd I say?"

"This is some serious shit! Look at this place . . . this is some serious shit," Box nervously repeated.

"Yeah, I gotta agree with you on this one. This . . . this is some *real* serious shit."

"Just no repeats of Maryland. Okay?"

"Yeah. No repeats." I spoke as if in a trance.

*   *   *

The stairs continued below ground level some sixty feet to the center floor, where a man about six feet five inches tall, with an athletic build, greeted us with a welcoming handshake. "Vesbucci and Boxer, I presume," he said, correctly identifying us. "You'll refer to me heretofore as Instructor Jones."

"Do I look that Italian?" I said sarcastically.

"No, you don't." He stood between us, placing his hands on our shoulders. "But this guy looks a lot like a dog I once ran over." He cackled and then continued, "You two gentlemen have a meeting with the commandant. After that, I'll show you where you'll bunk."

"So. What's this meeting about?" Box asked.

"Don't know. What I do know is that there's forty-plus people scheduled to arrive here this evening and only two scheduled to meet with the man." He stepped to the front and spun around to face us. Now walking backwards, he pointed his index fingers like a cameraman cueing the actors of a live television show. "You two."

Box and I looked at one another, his face filled with accusation, mine with guilt. Box uttered, "Now what?"

"Why you looking at me? We've been together all day! This has been one of my better days. . . . It has."

Instructor Jones, dressed in desert fatigues and jungle boots, led us up a short wooden staircase to the smallest structure on the block, located exactly halfway up the gravel street. The commandant excused our escort and invited us to sit down. The commandant was without a doubt a CIA refugee. I recognized what once had been a strong and invincible man. Little more than a shell of his former self, he seemed to come with a disclaimer, as if he wanted those he met to know of his infamous past, but was held in check by his pride. His hair, gray and groomed tight, was full and thick. A long scar curved in an elongated S from the top of his left cheek to the base of his chin. I wondered how he could have received such a wound. I was always paranoid about facial deformities. I knew that I would prefer a bullet to the stomach than a cut to the face. My vanity would eventually rank much lower among the priorities in my life.

The commandant began, "You two were specifically remanded to this assessment program by Director Casey. Before you get all puffed up, realize that my only instructions are to evaluate you with the others. You'll get no preferential treatment from me or my staff, I assure you. You'll mention the nature of what you're being evaluated for to no one. You're the only ones who know what the selectees will be involved with at the completion of training. This obviously places a special burden on you to succeed." He paused, exhaled deeply, and concluded tersely, "Well, good luck. That'll be all."

As Box and I departed, I wondered aloud, "What do you suppose he meant by 'a special burden to succeed?'"

"I'm not sure. I just hope it doesn't mean what I think it means."

"Yeah? What's that?"

"Nothing. Just . . . just work hard, that's all!"

"No. Tell me. What do you think it means?"

Instructor Jones interceded, "Oky doke, gentlemen. Let me show you where you'll be bunking and introduce you to the others."

"How did the commandant receive that scar on his cheek," I asked bluntly.

"No one around here really knows. There are a whole shitload of theories, though. I personally think it happened in Nam during the Phoenix project."

"Really!" I pretended to be impressed. Leaning toward Box, I whispered, "I think it's where the coat hanger nearly snagged his ass."

"What's that?" Jones asked with a bewildered grin on his face.

Box was snickering over the frustration he was feeling toward me when he responded, "Nothing. He was just saying how they probably tried to coat . . . hang . . . him." Boxer's voice diminished as he floundered for a plausible answer that sounded a lot like *coat hanger*. He was pathetic. "You know. In Vietnam . . . *Nam*! When they would hang people by their . . . their coats . . . to publicly humiliate them. He was just talking about that."

"And you found that funny?" Jones probed.

"Yeah, Box. What's funny about a man being tortured for his country?" I said, stirring the proverbial pot. Box just grunted in frustration.

*   *   *

Instructor Jones led us to the barracks, where several other trainees were already asleep. Forty of us slept in a barracks built for twenty. Everyone who would eventually become Pseudo Miranda team members were present, but for now they were just anonymous faces in a crowd. Except for Box, of course. He bunked in the cot next to me. The clothing we wore when we arrived was replaced with military drab, which our gracious hosts provided. Our toiletries were the only items they allowed us to keep. The trainers secured all personal belongings and identification. Jones told us to anticipate a 5:00 A.M. wake-up call, then left. That was in three hours. Everyone else was asleep, so introductions would have to wait.

*   *   *

I expected a rude awakening, with banging trashcans and cold water poured on us. What I got, however, was a friendly, "Okay, ladies and gentlemen . . . time to get up."

"Ladies," I thought out loud. "Holy shit! Hey, Box, man, check out the ladies."

"Yeah. I've seen women before, asshole. You mean to tell me you didn't smell the perfume last night?"

"Not over that shit you're wearing," I said as I signaled to the instructor who awakened us. "Instructor . . . ?"

"White. That should be easy for you to remember, huh?" He was ironically referring to his African American ethnicity.

"Yes, Instructor White. The men's shower?"

"It's in the same place as the women's. Next building over. Five stalls."

"Thank you, Instructor White!" As he left, I said in a voice loud enough for all to hear. "White. Ten bucks says his middle name is Ain't." Everyone chuckled.

Instructor White stood about five feet eleven inches tall and suffered from rounded posture. Too much neck and shoulder development had forced his shoulders to fold around his chest, while his forearms and calves showed neglect, a sign of vanity. He had apparently developed only those muscles that conveyed the essence of strength, but not those muscles that had any real practical application. With a freckled face and dimples, White seemed almost cartoon-like.

Everyone was anxious to know what the training would encompass. Would it be predominately classroom instruction, or would it concentrate on physical activity and conditioning? And how about weapons training and defense techniques?

I met my first training mate on the way to roll call. He introduced himself as Joe and attempted to give me advice on everything from handling people to hand-to-hand combat. I shared little more than my name. Then we were instructed to form up in military fashion outside the barracks.

As we gathered, the commandant stepped forward, as if to address us on what to expect over the course of our training. "Everything that happens here is real!" he began, but he then paused, as if about to deliver a lengthy speech, and retreated back to his office.

"That's it?" I thought.

A stocky man of Spanish descent stepped to the fore and introduced himself as Mr. Smith. His sleeves were rolled to the elbow, displaying a string of tattoos that flowed up his forearm into his fatigues. A wide mustache squarely covered his upper lip but stopped abruptly at the corners of his mouth. Hairs grew wildly out of his nose and ears, completing his rogue image. He began calling out names of potential trainees.

"Charlene Gregory!"

"Yes, sir. Here," Charlene acknowledged.

"Charlene, you're cut from the program. Step out of formation please."

"What? Why? What'd I do?"

"Stop babbling and move your ass, damn it," Smith said furiously.

"Mike Alvarez . . . Mike Alvarez!" He searched about, scanning faces. "Is there a Mike Alvarez here? Speak up, damn it! We don't have all day."

"Here! I'm right here," Alvarez muttered.

"You're gone, asshole. Step out."

"Anthony Vesbucci! Vesbucci!" He waited for an answer. "Come on, people! This isn't a name you'd forget. . . . Anyone! If I don't get an Anthony Vesbucci real soon-like, everyone's gonna pay a dear price," Smith screamed.

Box looked over at me in a manner that told me he understood and agreed with my decision not to speak. Neither of us knew what was going on, but we knew that to answer meant certain dismissal from training. I waited anxiously for some sort of explanation of what was happening when Joe raised his hand.

"Yes, sir. Are you our Vesbucci?" Smith inquired.

"No, sir, but I do know a guy named Anthony. I met him a few minutes ago."

"Point his deaf ass out to me," Smith said angrily.

"Right there. He's right there, sir."

He pointed to me. Smith walked over and faced off with me. He spoke softly, saying, "Are you Anthony?"

"Yes, sir."

"You're dismissed," he said routinely.

"Not Anthony what's-his-face, though," I quickly followed.

"Anthony who, then, might I ask?"

"Just Anthony."

Smith then motioned to Joe to join our conversation. Joe approached with artificial confidence, acting as if he knew something the rest of us didn't. Smith placed his arm around Joe and began to gently interrogate him.

"Is this the guy you met, ahhh . . . ," Smith snapped his finger a couple times as if hunting for Joe's name.

"Joe, sir!" Joe asserted.

"Joe ahhh . . . "

"Joe Thompson. Joseph Thompson!"

"Joe . . . Joseph . . . you have a nice trip home. Now move your chump ass!"

Instructor Jones grabbed Joe by the fatigue collar and hauled him away. Smith retreated to the front of the formation and continued his psychological hazing.

"Okay, people. *Just* Anthony has decided your collective fate for the next twenty-four hours. While the staff and I are sleeping on our Posturepedics, you'll be resting in these." Smith pointed to a single wooden box that stood seven feet tall by three feet wide. "We'll provide as many of these as necessary in just a few minutes. Now let me continue this roll call. A simple answer to a simple question will prevent you from having to endure this agony. So listen up!" He called out the remaining names and only four people bowed out by responding in the affirmative.

He then continued, "Everyone will be going to bed now except for Vesbucci. Let me correct that . . . except for *Just* Anthony." While everyone looked on, Smith asked me another simple question. "Do you like walnuts, Anthony?"

"On brownies. Not so much on hot fudge sundaes, though."

"You know, the Vietnamese love their walnuts. Take your fuckin' shoes off, smart ass."

I shot back, "Bring your little pint-size ass over here and take 'em off for me."

With his 9mm automatic raised and pointed at my skull, he countered, "Keep three things in mind when making your next decision: I work for the CIA. No one, *but no one*, knows where the fuck you are at this moment. *And* . . . I'll take exceedingly great pleasure in shooting your hairy ass." Smith then fired a round at my feet.

I took my shoes off.

White escorted me to the front of the group, cuffing my hands to my back with a thick plastic tie. Jones proceeded to pour hundreds of walnuts on the ground before blindfolding me. Smith called out for my apology in exchange for not having to endure this torture. I vacillated for a short period, concluding finally that I had to resist. I wished I hadn't insulted Smith, but I realized that there was no turning back. To acquiesce now would only demonstrate that I could be manipulated with threats of violence. I couldn't let that happen. Before I was led barefoot over the nuts, Box cried out in support with tension-breaking humor, "Attica! Attica! Attica!" Everyone soon chimed in.

White struck a baton blow to the back of my knees without warning. Crashing face first into the walnuts, I came to the frightening conclusion that torture was more art than science. I attempted to regain my feet, but discovered that there existed no position among these walnuts that wasn't excruciatingly painful. The genius behind this torment is that the tormented inflicts more agony upon himself with every attempt to relieve pain from another part of his body. When my back became overwhelmed with pain, I would roll to my stomach in an effort to regain my feet, shocking my knees in the process. My feet would soon become agonized, forcing me to fall backwards into my tormentors.

The chants of support diminished as reality set in. No one wanted to follow in my footsteps. I heard murmuring from the audience as I grunted in distress. The nuts sent daggers of pain up through the arches of my feet to the rest of my sensory system. Smith asked coldly, "What is it you know about us?"

"What?" I screamed out in dismay.

White struck another blow to the back of the legs, sending me crashing onto the walnut shells again.

"What have you learned?"

"I've learned that you're all lifetime members of the Ferrari Club!"

"Come again?" Smith seemed confused.

"If you own a Ferrari, you don't need a big dick," I said, wincing.

"Lift him," Smith demanded.

White and Jones lifted me by my arms and tossed me back down onto the nuts.

"You're CIA. Ahh . . . ahhh. Oh, shit! I don't know! What the fuck do you wanna know! Animal, vegetable, mineral! Shit! Give me a damn clue!"

"Anything you know to be true about us," Smith said calmly.

I tried to replay all that had happened over the last eighteen hours. Nothing seemed salient. "What doesn't fit?" I repeated to myself. The pain my body was enduring seemed remote as my mind raced. Then, as I felt a pair of hands grip my shoulder blades, it struck me. "You're Vietnamese!" I rolled around on my back and laughed because I didn't get a negative response. "That's it! You're the fucking Cong! I was right. You do have small dicks!"

* * *

With everyone looking on, my captors carried me to the demonstration box and placed me inside. The cuffs and blindfold were removed, providing me with a claustrophobic view of the sarcophagus that was my new bedroom. The first thing I noticed was that I could neither straighten up all the way nor squat all the way down. My six-foot stature and calcified left knee restricted my mobility, and they would soon cause me great pain. Slits in the wood provided adequate air, which was a blessing in the heat of the afternoon, but a curse when the frigid evening air set in.

After a while, my legs and back collapsed under the strain. As I folded into painful angles at the base of the box, I could feel the bones grinding in my bad knee, which had continuously deteriorated since high school, when I irreparably damaged it during a football game. I knew that I would not be able to endure that pain for long, so I decided to trade off standing and squatting positions periodically. Standing was as autonomic as breathing, but squatting was another thing altogether. I simply couldn't deliberately bend my leg beyond the threshold of pain.

Screams for clemency from other trainees snatched my mind away from my own hardship. I felt no empathy for their pleas. Begging for exoneration only served to validate our tormentors' methods and exacerbate the situation further. Through a narrow crack in my casket, I witnessed the parade of rejects who attempted to negotiate their way out of the box. Instead, they negotiated their way onto the next flight home. There were now twenty-four candidates left.

As the day became evening, panic subsided. Those who remained understood the sacrifice they needed to make. We received water intermittently, but only enough to prevent dehydration. The sweat our bodies had shed by day turned chilly in the cool night air. Pain and discomfort gave way to fatigue as we stole what little shuteye we could.

When morning broke, I awakened to the faint moans of stiffened bodies attempting to regain their natural form. Only now could I appreciate the full extent of the abuse from the day before. Oddly enough, yesterday's wounds distracted me from the aches I suffered from sleeping all cramped up. I wondered how Box was holding up. I worried because he was too old for this physical abuse. He was in his mid-thirties, which seemed ancient to a twenty-two-year-old like myself. I wanted to call to him, but I couldn't risk our adversaries knowing his name. It occurred to me that he may have forgotten that he could safely call me *Just* Anthony. I addressed him innocuously, hoping that he would immediately recognize my Massachusetts accent. "Hey, home! It's *Just* Anthony! Are you all right, bubba?"

"Yeah, I'm okay. How 'bout yourself? You must be dying from that heinous shit yesterday."

"Look, we probably can't talk long. From now on, everyone will refer to you as Number One. When we all get out, we'll assign everyone a number. I'll have to go by *Just* Anthony, I guess. Do you copy?"

"Roger that," Box whispered hastily.

"There'll be no talking," Smith hollered as he pelted the sides of our coffins with his baton.

"Screw you!" Box began. "Three hours sleep! Standing all night in a box! Freezin' my black ass off! Come down here and tell me to shut up! You candy ass, can't get a real job, Ferrari-driving, nut-sucking, mothafucka! Rap your stick against my bed? Shiiiit."

"Number one. Chill out, dude. Shit ain't worth it, man," I advised.

"Oh, shit," Box said nervously.

"What? What's goin' on? What's happening?" I pressed anxiously.

"I don't know! But I hear 'em behind me!" Box began to panic. "Damn!"

"What's happening?" I shouted.

"It's cool, it's cool! They just doused me with H_2O! It'll dry. I'm okay!"

"Water? Oh, shit," I said quietly.

"What's that?" Box asked with uneasy anticipation. "Ahhhh! Ahhhh! Shit! Ahh, shit!" Box screeched in pain. His shrieks turned immediately to sighs of relief when he realized he hadn't been electrocuted to death.

"They shocked me!" he said incredulously. "Holy shit! The sons of bitches fried my ass!"

"Are you okay, bubba?"

"Shit! Thank God my hair's naturally curly," he said flippantly.

"Quiet," Smith interrupted.

Box and I heeded the warning. However, the same could not be said of one of our fellow trainees. At the opposite end of this Stonehenge of caskets, I could hear the dampened cries of an angry woman. She insisted on getting "the immediate release of all prisoners." Although I absolutely agreed with her demand, I couldn't help but feel she took the POW stuff way too seriously.

Soon thereafter I heard a number of voices mingled in discussion. Unable to make sense of the precise words, I knew they were nevertheless deciding her fate. An ominous calm fell over the crater, broken only by the frightened screams of a woman being stripped of her clothes by three frenetic men. The cracks in our individual boxes allowed unobstructed views of her humiliation. I couldn't watch beyond the initial tearing. I repeated endlessly the words "God, no" to myself, and laid my head against the ventilation cracks. The men quickly tossed her back into her box without having violated her, although I sensed that they wanted to assault a woman and were looking for a reason. The brutality of this conveyed that there were few boundaries they would not cross.

Several hours later we were released from our boxes into the late afternoon heat. The naked woman was not given any clothing, and she stood sobbing by herself as the rest of us formed up a line. No one dared assist her, fearing that it would only provoke further reciprocities. We seemed to have an unspoken collective mind not to look at her.

Smith, now flanked by several armed guards dressed in North Vietnamese clothing, ordered us to reveal our true identities to him. He insisted that our treatment would only worsen if we resisted.

Five more trainees, all women, departed. No one condemned them for leaving. To our astonishment, however, the woman who was viciously assaulted was not among them. Instructor White handed her some new fatigues and instructed her to go back to her box to dress. Her name was Christina Dawn Wells.

Nicknamed "Seedy" for her first two initials and her soiled past, she was a walking dichotomy. She had an innate wholesomeness that veiled the hard knocks she had endured in life. Her California hair, soft and naturally blond, flowed thick and evenly across her face, shadowing the sockets of her drawn and darkened eyes She seemed older than she probably was. Fortunately for her, she had a plump face that smoothed out the wrinkles, high cheekbones and puffy lips. She stood five feet ten inches tall, with visible muscle definition in her stomach and legs. Her arms were remarkably thin and feminine, yet strong, and her figure was the type that was physically molded by work rather than exercise. Seedy's violet eyes were without a doubt her greatest asset; I saw them range the full gamut of expression.

"Come on, people. I know you must realize the hopelessness of your situation. If you don't bug out now . . . ," Smith said in a fading voice. "How 'bout you, spic?" He taunted Jesus Rivas. "Shouldn't you be home in the barrio, cruising in your purple, raked Cadillac with the furry dice, curb feelers and leopard skin seat covers? Huh, Beaner?"

Rivas stared back in disbelief. He then countered by pointing to his own chest and, in a befuddled manner, stating, "I'm Lebanese."

"Good. 'Cause I hate the dune-coon, camel-jockey, rag-headed motherfuckers more than I do the spics! *Comprende?*"

Smith, who had been plastered nose to nose with Rivas during his verbal assault, stepped back and regained his composure. He eyed the lot of us standing in formation. Now casually strolling down the line, he randomly jabbed trainees in the abdomen or swiped their chests with his club. He laughed sinisterly as he returned to the front of the formation.

"People! People! Is this shit really worth it? Huh?" He bent at the waist and swirled his trunk in a circular direction as he spoke. "One last time before I torture the ever-livin' shit outta ya. Who wants to give me their name? I'll give you ten minutes to mull it over. After that . . . I'm gonna hurt ya. I'm gonna hurt ya real bad." Smith turned on his heel and stalked up the stairs and into the commandant's office.

"So, what do ya think, Number One?" I asked Box as I knelt to tie my boot.

"Fuck that shit, man! My name's Box. Damn!" Box knelt alongside me and grabbed a stone. As he was about to give it a toss, he continued, "Damn it! I'm a training agent. I don't make a good prisoner of war." He then proceeded to heave the stone, accidentally shattering the commandant's window. "Tell me that didn't happen," he said in disbelief. "I'm a dead man. You're looking at a dead man. I'm dead. That's all there is to it."

Smith returned abruptly. Baton in hand, he scampered down the stairs. As he once again moved briskly down the line, he poked us gently in the chest and spoke in cadence. "So-do-we-have-a-prank-ster-a-mong-us? Huh? Do we? Do we? Huh? Huh? Huh? Well, people? Well?!" Smith then calmed down and stalked back to the front and faced the formation. "You people don't seem to be getting the message." Smith suddenly became animated. Using a full range of physical gestures, he continued: "This is a prisoner of war camp! You're in Viet-Fuckin'-Nam! You're all gonna talk! It's only a question of when. So. To hasten the process . . . you know . . . because we're pretty busy fellas . . . we're gonna kill one of you. . . . So! Before we get this little formality out of the way, do we have any more names?"

"Don't! He's bluffing! They'd never go that far!" Debara Allen cried out.

Debara (pronounced De-BEAR-a) was a strikingly beautiful woman. Standing almost five feet eight inches tall, she commanded attention. Her thick, milky brown hair ran rich and straight. Her emerald green eyes simply drew you in. My eyes lingered on her chiseled face and brush-stroked brows. Debara was without question the most attractive woman I had ever laid eyes on.

"And you would be?" Smith inquired softly and deliberately. When Debara refused to respond, Smith continued, "Jane Fonda! Oh! That makes it all complete. Okay, Jane. You decide who we should *not* kill next." A desperate pause ensued. "How about this bitch!" Smith grabbed a woman by the hair and dragged her forward as she pleaded for her life.

"My name is Fawn Sanders," the woman shouted in hopes of being spared what appeared to be a certain death.

"Sorry, bitch. Jane says there's no mistreatment of prisoners at this camp." Smith yanked Fawn in front of the formation and stepped back a few paces behind her. He pointed his 9mm automatic at her chest. Fawn continued to beg for her life. He then fired two shots. Fawn fell backwards, blood spewing from her chest. "Now, who would like to give me their name?"

I stared transfixed at her limp, bleeding body. Her saliva mingled with dirt and blood and collected on her chin. Her limbs twisted in a lifeless manner. There is something about a dead body that leaves you feeling cold and empty. Something that can't be reproduced or faked. I suppose it's the lack of a soul.

Whatever it was, however, this body didn't have it. I sensed life in her. At that moment, it also occurred to me that at the moment of death people frequently lose control of their bowels. I drew a deep breath but smelled nothing and said with a smile, "Yup! Hers are intact."

I thought I would simply tell everyone that it was all a fake. "But what if I'm wrong? And if I'm right, do I really want this many gullible people working with me?" I thought. "Shoot me next, butthead," I hollered instinctively.

"How 'bout I blow apart your fat friend here," Smith said with a smirk. He took Box by the back of the head and placed his gun to Boxer's throat. "Blow his brains . . . what little he has . . . all over the . . ."

Box snapped back at him, "Fat?! Little brain?! Go ahead, asshole. SHOOT!"

My confidence waned as I pointed to Smith's gun. "Uhhh, Box, I don't think that's such a good idea."

"Whatta ya mean? What? What was all that 'shoot me' bullshit? What . . . what the hell have ya gotten me into this time?"

"No, no, no . . . there are blanks in the gun. That's for sure. They're blanks all right. But a blank will blow your skull apart at that range." I paused for a moment. "Back up! Then yell at him!" I told him, while simultaneously signalling with a clenched fist that I really meant he shouldn't yell at him but hit him.

Box said, "Ohhh. Riiiight." He then whipped around suddenly and clocked Smith with an overhand right, knocking him unconscious. "Now go wake that bitch up," Box added, motioning to the woman who was still sprawled on the ground.

Rivas shook the woman violently and turned quickly toward Box with a look of horror in his face. "She's dead! Oh, my God, Number One. She's really dead."

"What?" Box gasped.

"Oh, shit," I said. Everyone gasped.

"Just kidding. She's a fake!" Rivas shouted joyfully.

The commandant reentered the picture. He walked to the bottom of the staircase and informed us that the prisoner-of-war portion of the curriculum was over. He dispelled our skepticism at his announcement by calling out our names in the order in which we stood, acknowledging us each with a nod of his head. He went on to say, "I count eighteen. That's good. Better than I expected. My boys are slippin'." After pause, he said, "We'll now begin the main training portion of our program. You won't see any more of Smith. I'm certain that'll break all your hearts. But before we go any further, let's fill those guts of yours. Chow time! Oh! One more thing. Congratulations so far."

* * *

The training became much more conventional and structured after that. We met our new trainer when we reassembled the next day in front of the barracks. His name, Instructor Black, was in keeping with the others. Black was the quintessential athlete. A formidable figure at six feet four inches tall and 210 pounds, his body was one big muscle.

At first he seemed quite reasonable. Black's job was to lead us through a crash course in self-defense. He had to dispense pain to make us learn quickly. As with all the training we would receive, I couldn't imagine its applicability. Nevertheless, I did what was asked.

After Black demonstrated the use of a long, hollow, wooden pole, he proceeded to batter a few trainees into submission. Not the least of which was myself. We trained with him off and on over the next few weeks. He would knock us around and then indulge himself in a dissertation about how pathetic we were and how "the enemy" wouldn't show us any mercy. Through all this, I noticed a conspicuous few whom he never chose to do battle with, namely, Briant Boxer, Rick Chavez and Jeremiah Robinson. The common denominator? Their brute strength.

Rick Chavez was a tall Native American with the razor-sharp facial features and skin tone that reflected the melting pot of his ancestry. He wore his long hair, which was black and silky, in a pony tail. His legs were disproportionately larger than his upper body, and his feet were big. Above all, his strength and courage harkened back to an era of greatness he would never let us forget. Rick laid no false claim to his heritage, though. He never claimed to have insight that we lacked or that the Indian way of life was better than ours. Chavez lived very much in the present, merely offering historical perspective when it seemed appropriate. His subtle melding of past and present was epitomized by his favorite song, "Cheyenne Anthem," by the rock-and-roll group Kansas.

Jeremiah Robinson was an imposing figure, and arguably the most physically capable of all us trainees. A darkly complected black man, he was tall, with elongated limbs. He wore his hair in a flat top. Like Chavez, Jeremiah was sculpted from head to toe. Unlike Chavez, he would remind you of his ancestral suffering whenever it suited him. Although his lineage included Caucasian influences, he asserted that all people of African American descent had a claim against those who had practiced slavery. As intelligent as he was powerful, it amazed me that he never let the facts get in the way of any discussion dealing with the history of oppression and the wrongs that still needed to be righted. In spite of this, he was at the center a very decent and caring individual.

*   *   *

Instructors White, Jones and Black handled our training from this point on. Jones conducted weapons training, while White gave classroom instruction on logistics and field training on precision drug interdiction and deadly confrontation.

The weapons training ranged from handguns to assault rifles and included the use of explosives such as C-4 and grenades. Our resident expert on the use of explosives was little Joey Bali. On our first day of live fire, we handled a wide range of assault and hunting weapons. I preferred the 30/06 and 45mm automatic to all other weapons, including the M-16, MAC-10, Uzi and AK-47, to name a few. Once we found weapons that suited us, we began to strive for proficiency. When the final scores were tallied, Joey was crowned the king of marksmanship. Lourdes (this was her complete name) ranked only a hair's breadth behind him, qualifying as an expert in all weapons except handguns.

Chapter 5

I'd been in training now for a couple weeks and had become acclimated to the routine. We learned to anticipate scratches and bruises, and most of us accepted the inevitably sleepless nights as normal. One particularly uneventful day (which was fine by me), Christina was called into Instructor Black's "Circle of Death" for another sadistic lesson in self-defense.

"Hands up! Watch your adversary's eyes!" Black directed. "Why you looking at my feet? My eyes, damn it! My eyes!"

Personally, I always watched his feet. He never once struck me with his eyes. Black was pretentiously absorbed in the philosophy of Kung Fu and, for that matter, all forms of martial arts. I wasn't under the impression that he'd ever had to apply his craft in real life, however. Of course, I lived with the understanding that he could kick the crap out of me any time he pleased.

Black laid a side kick into Christina's trunk, collapsing her rib cage like so much Silly Putty. She buckled over in agony, and then he struck her again unmercifully with a roundhouse kick to the temple. Christina flew in the direction of her broken ribs, crashing hard to the earth. Black knelt at her side and bellowed:

"Ooow, Milly, that felt good!"

"Lay off her! She's had enough," Box demanded.

"Why? 'Cause she's a woman? She'll let him know when she's had enough," Debara said defensively.

"She's gonna have a difficult time speaking with her skull fractured! Get off your damn Gloria Steinem kick, Jane! This is the real world. And this asshole doesn't give a hoot about equality," I said, livid and confrontational.

"And I don't need your and Box's macho bullshit!" Debara said, disgusted, as she leaned into the circle and asked, "Can you get up, Seedy? Do you need help? Just say when you wanna quit, okay?"

"Gee, Jane. She doesn't seem too responsive," I said sarcastically.

"Call me Jane one more time and I'll see how responsive your nuts are to my boot."

"If you two love birds are through, I'm gonna finish what I've begun here," Black said matter-of-factly. He then took a hop step toward Christina, who had gathered herself to her knees, and lashed a fluid drop kick at her face. His shoe landed right on the bridge of her nose, crushing it like an aluminum can. Everyone leaped to her aid, restraining Black from committing further damage.

An alarm sounded. It wailed loud and constant, then trailed off suddenly and continued with another blast. The training ground became a melee. Armed agents scrambled to support Instructor Black. In response, we spontaneously formed a circle around Christina and assumed a defensive stance. Although Instructor White threatened to kill us if we didn't step away from Christina, we held firm in our common defense. We were protecting a fallen team member, but more importantly, we were standing together.

The commandant interceded in the dispute and ordered immediate medical attention for Christina. He then told everyone to disperse to their respective quarters.

Instructor Black was feeling pretty good about himself at this point and couldn't resist demoralizing Christina one more time.

"Every time you look in the mirror, you'll be reminded of how you couldn't cut it."

"I don't recall her begging for mercy, asshole!" I retaliated.

"What did you call me, you little prick?" Black hollered combatively.

I knew he was bent on making me cower, so I sought to gain the psychological edge. I had a bad habit of initiating such things, so I could always see them coming before they arrived. I said, "Do you only beat up on women? No, don't. . . . I think I know the answer to that question."

"You just wrote your epitaph, buddy." Black asserted as he spread his arms, warning everyone to back off. The commandant withdrew to watch from his staircase. I interjected one last comment to ensure that Black understood the ground rules.

"If you start this, realize it ain't over until someone begs for mercy."

Box took hold of my shoulders as he faced me. "This guy's psychotic. *I* can kick your ass, and this guy can kick mine. Use your fuckin' head. That's why you're here, damn it! Not because of your damn fighting skills. Now tell him you didn't mean it."

I stared coldly through Box, directly at my adversary, hardly noticing what he was saying. I walked robotically through Boxer's grip and into the dreaded circle. Initially, I stood in an appropriate martial arts pose. Black fired off several misdirected kicks and punches before landing an effective kick to the back of my head. I collapsed after a few more assaults to the legs, chest and head. Inexplicably, the pain momentarily subsided and I regained my focus. I staggered to my feet and observed Instructor Black withdrawing from an aggressive stance. He was taken aback by my lucidity. Without hesitance, I attacked with flailing appendages. He swung ineffectively back at me, as I made an ever changing target, and then I tackled him around the waist. I knew that I would be victorious the moment I felt my shoulder make firm contact with his gut. I twisted and contorted my body in an effort to cast him to the ground and fall on top of him with all my weight. It worked. Once I had him on his back, I proceeded to unleash a barrage of punches to his side, face and head. As he tried to roll away from me, I kept up the onslaught and planted several good punches on his nose. Before I could extract a plea for mercy, however, the commandant ordered us separated.

At best, it was a draw. We were both feeling the painful aftereffects of flesh pounding flesh. It then occurred to me that I'd made a promise. I'd told Instructor Black that the fight would end only when one of us pleaded for mercy. With my right arm slung around Box as we walked toward the barracks, I shuffled to a halt. Spinning reluctantly in Black's direction, I reminded him of the ground rules.

"Hey, Black! This ain't over! Don't fall asleep!" I warned.

I knew that Black had to go through his daily ritual of meetings and briefings, but I'd be able to grab a brief rest. Christina was taken for medical attention somewhere within the confines of Sandia. By the time I awakened, Christina had returned, her nose now reset. The physical pain she braved was far less anguishing than her belief that she somehow didn't measure up. As the cobwebs in my head began to fall away, I could make out patronizing words of consolation directed toward Christina—words designed to bolster her failing morale. The words were contrived, and Christina knew it. Realistically, she would fail the program if she didn't excel in all major evaluations, and she knew this, too.

"Seedy, don't get down on yourself," Lourdes began. "You just need more practice. We'll help you."

"Yeah, Christina. We're here for ya," Chavez added.

"You're here for her? Where the hell were you when she was getting her face mangled?" Lourdes asked. "Why weren't you *here* for her then? She doesn't need you now! She needed you out there! That's where we win and lose this game! Out there! Not here! They don't give a crap about our support for one another in here! It's out there! They only care what we do when the chips are down and there are no rules! You're here for her. Right."

I got up from my cot and walked over to where Christina was lying. Chavez was steaming but remained seated on an overturned trash can at the foot of Christina's cot as I continued, "Face it, Seedy. You're gone if you don't do well. All the mincing we do with the facts won't change that simple truth. You're not gonna beat that Nazi son of a bitch. I don't care how long you train. Now what are we gonna do about it?"

"Oh, I suppose one of you big strong men will protect her," Quinn said acerbically.

"Watch it, Quinn. Or he'll be calling you Gloria Allred. And blaming you for the disintegration of the American family," Jeremiah embellished.

"Who?" everyone said in virtual unison.

"You're kidding me. Right?" Jeremiah responded in dismay.

"She must be a radical feminist. I'm surprised Debara doesn't know who she is." I shifted gears slightly. "Anyhow, so you think there are no inherent differences between the sexes? Give it a rest for Pete's sake. Ahh, the hell with it. You'd never understand what I'm saying anyway. And even if you did, I don't have the time or the inclination to persuade you in the first place." I then tried to persuade him, saying, "It's not about our individual talents and abilities. It's not about that at all." I turned back in the direction of the door and began to walk away with Box trailing after me.

"Where you goin', man?" Box asked

"What the hell's it about then?" Debara barked.

I looked over my shoulder and said simply, "It's about giving your word." I walked out to the front of Instructor Black's personal quarters. He had just laid down for the evening when I rapped on his door and shouted, "Sleep tight, Adolf! I'll be waiting for your snore!"

He charged out of his quarters and ordered me back to the barracks.

"I'm sorry, sir, but I can't accept that order until our verbal contract is resolved."

"What! You wacko! Get your ass out of here, or else."

"Or else what? Come on! You want some of this? I'm ready! Let's settle this now! Let's do it! Come on! Come on!" I yelled in a crazed manner. I really didn't want to fight, and I was betting that he didn't either.

"You're mental. That's it. You're . . . you're . . . you've lost your mind. Pack your bags, nut case. You're gone tomorrow," Black said bewilderedly.

"That's tomorrow. Tonight I'm gonna camp outside your door and wait for you to fall asleep. Sweet dreams."

"Suit yourself. But you better be ready tomorrow at oh-five-hundred."

I waited patiently by his door for the distinct sounds of slumber. As he dozed off, I banged on his door and awakened him. Black then stumbled to the door in a rage, hoping to find me standing there. I fled into the still, dark night with Black in pursuit. I was surprised to find that no one attempted to stop me as I crouched behind some structural bracings that supported the front side of a fake night club. Instructor Black cried out in frustration, "Damn it! Where are you? You pussy! Where the hell are you? Where the hell is security?"

This routine continued throughout the evening. Neither of us got any sleep, but it was easier on me because I'd stolen a little shut-eye earlier that day. The commitment I felt to fulfill my promise and demonstrate my leadership also provided me with the extra adrenaline I needed to stay one step ahead of him.

The following day I found myself waiting outside the door to the commandant's office while Instructor Black implored him to drop me from the program. The commandant did not waver as he lectured Black on the importance of integrity.

"Didn't he tell you yesterday that if you fought him it wasn't over until somebody officially surrendered?" the commandant said sternly.

"No!" Black replied in a crackling voice.

"Integrity! I was there! He told you! And now he's sticking to his guns!" The commandant paused, then continued in a lower voice, "I like this. What do you suppose his goal is?"

"To beat me senseless! Look, sir, I've got to get some sleep."

"Oh, you'll be fine. Who's the teacher here, anyhow? Nooo. I want to see where he's goin' with this. This could get real interesting." He paused, then added, "It's pretty obvious why Casey sent him here."

"With all due respect, sir, this guy's certifiable. I know where he's goin' with this. And to be perfectly honest, I don't find it all that interesting," Black whined.

"You brought this on. Now let's see how it's gonna end. Go on. Get back to work. Send in Vesbucci."

"Hey! Amerigo Vesbucci. Get your ass in there," Black said caustically.

"Don't sit. You won't be here that long," the commandant began. "Run with this. Realize, though, you'll attend all forms of training, and any sub-par performance will not be tolerated. You have a special burden to succeed here. Now get out of my office."

That "special burden to succeed" thing reared its ugly head once again. "What the hell does that mean?" I wondered. Over the next day and a half, I floundered wearily through training. Luckily, my teammates supported me in every manner possible. For example, during a stationary target shooting test, Joey fired a few rounds into my target. This detracted from his own results, while supplying me with a sufficient number of points to receive a passing grade.

Instructor Black and I had endured two consecutive sleepless nights. As evening set in on the third day, I initiated the same harassment I'd inflicted the two previous nights. This time, however, I allowed him to drift into a deep sleep only a few hours before dawn.

I gently picked the unsophisticated lock to his door with a knife given me by our trainers. When I stood over Instructor Black, who by this time was drifting in deep R.E.M. sleep, I struggled with a decision: Should I beat him into submission and in the process make good on my word? Should I show compassion, and in doing so demonstrate that I was above his level of morality and remain true to my father's credo, which, in part, forbade throwing the first punch? I vacillated for about ten seconds. Then, starting with a barrage of punches to the face, I proceeded to beat him to a pulp. He was unable to resist. He passed directly from asleep to comatose.

"Whenever you look in the mirror, you'll be reminded of how you couldn't cut it," I said with melancholy.

After regaining my composure, I found myself staring at his mangled face for what seemed an eternity. The odd thing was, I was never unaware of the damage I was inflicting. I suppose that's what frightened me the most. I felt for a pulse. I hurt him so badly it seemed logical to check if he was still alive. It was there. "My God," I said aloud. I thought I knew my limits. Only now did I realize that there were boundaries I would cross, given the right circumstances.

Three hours later, Instructor Black was discovered semiconscious in his blood-drenched bed. He was immediately shuttled to a hospital as I lay sleeping in my cot. Everyone except me watched his departure.

* * *

I woke to find that I was the only team member left in the barracks. I glanced outdoors and noticed that the sun had almost run its course. I frantically searched until I found a set of clean fatigues. Grunting in frustration, I clumsily attempted to draw them over the fatigues I still wore from the night before. With combat boots in hand, I flew outside into the gray of early evening. I was certain that I was now through here.

"Ahhh!" I shouted, as I was tackled from the rear and pressed to the ground. "What the . . . Quinn! What the hell are you doin'?"

"Shhhh! Shush. Everything's cool. You're not in any trouble. We're in the middle of . . ." Quinn quieted sharply. "Oh shit." She looked up. Her eyes bulged. "Damn it! Not again." The team was in the midst of a game called Interdiction, and an adversary had electronically wasted her.

Interdiction was little more than us running a gauntlet of CIA paramilitary agents from one end of the "pit" (the long street with buildings lining both sides) to the other. The CIA agents and we were both armed with electronic guns called amplitude module weapons. Everyone wore receivers on their chest and abdomen and partial receivers on their head. This limited the kill zones to those areas; wounds were disregarded. Our mission was to get at least one person to the opposite end of the arena without being extinguished. Considering that they saturated the area with agents, this task of getting one of our people to the end of the street was monumental at best.

Many of the structures along the street had first floors, and therefore came complete with four fake walls, furniture, and a temporary ceiling as well. Consequently, we couldn't race down the backside of the buildings toward the opposite end. We had to climb over the scaffolding above the first floor and precariously run across the connecting beams of each structure. The only major flaw in this plan was that a guard was posted at the base of each staircase, which, to my chagrin, was located right next to the only beams leading to the top of the scaffolding on either side of the street. Eliminate the guard at our end of the street, I thought, and we could position two shooters above the street. This would give us a clear firing zone and enable us to triangulate any target drawn out into the open. Of course, it was another matter getting the enemy out in the open.

"Sorry, Quinn," I said, feeling a bit stupid.

"Oh, it's all right. They'd have won anyhow. I just hate the humiliation of the Dead Room." Downcast, Quinn meandered to the Dead Room. This was the place where anyone from either side went once eliminated from play, or killed. The "dead" would watch the game being played out on several 27-inch TV screens. It was always the same. We would watch solemnly as our comrades were knocked off, then have to listen to the taunts and jeers of our battle-tested opponents.

Every day as part of our training we had to jog five miles (countless laps up and down the pit). One day, we were allowed to finish our run and then knock off training a few hours early. We dedicated this free time to getting to know one another—as much as our trainers allowed us— and brainstorming ways to beat our adversaries at Interdiction. I remained on the sidelines and just enjoyed listening to the discussion. It eventually came around to the subject of developing a strategy for Interdiction. Many ideas were suggested but were later dropped. I listened intently, considering the pros and cons of each, but never offering my opinion. It became apparent that none of us had any practical experience in military strategy. Squabbles soon broke out concerning who was most qualified to lead the group. I still held my tongue. Chavez sarcastically baited me, saying, "We couldn't shut you up earlier, and now you're quiet as a monk?"

"Yeah, right. Like ol' pretty boy, frat-brat over there could give us pointers on battlefield tactics. Maybe if we were gonna drink 'em to death or somethin'. But not strategy. Please!" Jeremiah prodded.

"He's Italian. He's gotta have more to offer than you guys. So shut the fuck up an' let 'im talk," Joey said with exaggerated gestures.

Jeremiah responded, "Was that racist, you little guinea prick? I'll fuck your gay ass up. Little guinea mothafucka." He attempted to pull Box into the argument with a combination of high- and low-fives, but Box remained reticent.

"Yeah, let 'im speak," Rivas chimed in. "Oh. And before you start with any Hispanic jokes, I'll slit your African American throat in your sleep."

"Well?" Debara prompted. Then, after a moment of waiting, "Obviously he hasn't a clue either."

"Told ya he's full of shit," Jeremiah contended.

"He may be full of shit," Box began, "but this operation was sorta his idea."

"Good goin', Ace," I said in disbelief.

"Your idea? Give me a break. No friggin' way. Your idea? Is that true? Tell me that ain't true," Debara babbled.

"With the CIA who knows?" I answered. At least they made us feel like it was my idea.

"So what exactly have we gotten ourselves into? Joey inquired gingerly.

"We can't say," Box rifled in response, preempting my own.

"Well? Do you know anything that'll help us get through this war stuff?" asked Debara.

"As a matter a fact, I have been giving this some thought," I began, getting up from my cot and signalling for everyone to gather around. "The way I see it, we need to get two people up on the I-beams that run across the top of all the buildings, parallel to the street. Then . . ."

"Who?" Box inquired.

"Who what?" I answered.

"Who goes up top?"

"It doesn't matter." I shrugged, agitated by his interruption. "Me and you. Anyhow, where was I? Oh, yeah . . ."

"Bullshit," Box said in a monotone.

"You'll be fine. Trust me."

"Nope. Pick someone else." Box remained calm but determined. I took him aside and asked, "What are you doin'? I'm tryin' to sell this over here and you're making me pick up the prison soap."

"I'm not going up there with you. Pick someone else. That's all I'm saying on the subject. Pick someone else. How 'bout your buddy Jeremiah. You should get a big kick outta seeing him break his stinkin' neck."

We returned to the group, and I laid out my plan. "Me and Box will situate ourselves on the roof. Four people—Debara, Christina, Joey and Jesus—will make their way halfway down the street and form a circle. They never begin shooting until we reach that point, because it's the point of no return."

"So we're decoys," Debara interjected, disappointed.

"Sort of."

"Why us? Why not you and Box?" she persisted.

"Because you're good marksmen and tough targets to hit. Small stature and all. Oh, excuse me. Markspersons. But don't worry, because I've got a few ideas about delaying your inevitable deaths."

"I'm sure we're all comforted by that thought. But who's gonna run the gauntlet?" Debara questioned.

"The cheetah, Lourdes, of course."

"Wooo!" Lourdes shouted with jubilation. She began prancing up and down the room, assuming the position of a runner in the starting blocks and simulating a sprint in super slow motion while humming the theme to *Chariots of Fire*.

Joey asked, "So what's to prevent the four of us from being instantly dissolved?"

"This," I replied, and then fell to the ground, lying on my back. Folding my legs in a yogalike position, I crossed my calves and laid my hands atop my ankles, as if gripping a gun between my legs. In this fashion I could fire my radio wave weapon and simultaneously protect my kill zones.

"What's to stop them from shooting your legs and ass?" Jeremiah countered.

"Nothing. There aren't any receivers there, so don't worry."

"But if these were real guns . . . ," Jeremiah started.

"But they're not, and that's all we need be concerned with. Don't you see? This is about winning, plain and simple. This isn't the real world. This is our only world. Let's adapt to it and win. Now. I've noticed a couple things everyone is doing wrong. When a target is fleeing, don't fire behind them and try to catch up. Aim ahead of them and direct your fire backwards into their path. When shooting around a corner, don't expose your kill zone by using the incorrect hand. Around right corners, use your left hand. Around left corners, use your right hand. When in motion, bank on your opponent missing with his first round. Wait out his first shot as he changes direction, and steady your weapon before firing.

Now, we're gonna need to take a few preemptive measures. Lourdes, tomorrow during live fire I want you to liberate a handgun. I don't care what kind."

"Why?" Lourdes began.

"Because you're the last one they'd expect." I continued, "We'll also need some mirrors. Decent-sized ones."

"Mirrors?" Joey questioned, brushing back his hair with his fingers.

"Later. Just get 'em."

"Consider it done," Rivas promised.

"Why weren't we privy to this brilliant shit before, when we needed it?" Jeremiah wanted to know. "Why now?"

"The way I figure it, whenever we beat them, or perform a task at the highest level, we're through with it. I gotta figure it all culminates with Interdiction. If we try something new and it fails, we won't get a second chance with it. They'll be even more prepared—if that's even possible—the next time. I wanted enough time to analyze what we were doing wrong. More than that. If we hit 'em all at once with a synchronized plan, they won't know what hit 'em. They're not expecting any metamorphic changes. That's why I didn't want any piecemeal adaptations. All at once. One chance. That's all we'll get before they bring the next candidates in."

"You know this? That they'll bring in new people if we fail?" Lourdes wore a look of sadness. "Because I don't wanna go back to where I was. I belong here, damn it. I can do this. One chance is all we'll need. I'll be ready. I'll get to the end. Just make me a path. That's all I ask."

"No, I don't know that for sure. But I sure liked your speech. Anyhow, Lourdes, you'll secure us a gun tomorrow. Without that I'm afraid everything else is moot."

* * *

The following day was fraught with anxiety. Lourdes' overt nervousness drew unwanted attention. She placed far too much pressure on herself.

Her strength was that she desperately wanted this job. Her weakness, however, was that she desperately needed this job. Everyone deliberately avoided her on the range in an effort to not draw attention to her nervousness. The result, of course, was the opposite.

All the weapons were laid in shadow cases, or boxes imprinted with the shape of each particular weapon. To steal one meant taking a weapon from an unused case so as not to draw attention to an open shadow case with a glaringly empty space. Weapons that were fired or seen removed from their cases were inventoried on the spot. A complete inventory was only conducted before each live-fire exercise. This would buy us enough time to use the weapon during the Interdiction exercise before it would be discovered missing prior to the next live-fire training. At least that was the plan.

"Freeze! Take one more step and I'll blow your fuckin' head off!" hollered one of the security men. He placed a 12-gauge shotgun at the base of Lourdes' head. "Instructor Jones, sir! Instructor! Sir!"

"What've we got here?" Jones responded as he approached calmly.

"She's stolen a weapon, sir!"

"She has. Tisk, tisk. Shame on you," Jones said and reached around the front of Lourdes, inserting his hand into her trousers and removing a .22-caliber automatic pistol. Jones stared closely at the gun and said, "Hey, everybody! I've resolved the dispute! She's a natural blond!" He leaned in and said gently in her ear, "Now what in the world were you intending to do with this?" Stepping back, he waved his arm in a circle and said, "Take her away for questioning."

"I think your plan just fell apart, Ace," Jeremiah commented.

"You got it?" I asked softly.

"Uh-huh," Steven Hall answered.

"Good. We're in business."

Steven was our resident communications expert. In his mid-thirties, he was balding and overweight. He wore glasses and, almost always, a fishing hat. He seemed to know instinctively the orbits of certain satellites but, ironically, had no sense of direction otherwise. Steven rarely spoke, but when he did he commanded attention. He had a good sense of humor, although he used it sparingly.

As we walked back to our quarters, unescorted, the questions flew. "She was a decoy?" Debara asked in a concerned manner. "Did she know she was a decoy?"

"Before you go off the deep end . . . ," I said, moving to the front of the group. Now directly in front of our billet, I held my hands out, palms facing forward, and hastily explained. "I knew she'd be a wreck, so I used it to our advantage. But I also knew that she'd be the last to crack under pressure, because it means so damn much to her. Anyhow, we got the gun. That's what's most important here."

"You used her," Jeremiah said judgmentally. "How 'bout *her?*' Did ya ever consider her?"

"She is *us*! And we're *her*! And if you don't see it that way then maybe you're not *us*. You think I liked making this decision? Why don't you try taking some risks for once? You think it's easy deciding people's fate. Well, I'm here to tell ya it ain't. It sucks! But someone better damn well do it! Sacrifices have to be made, buddy, and someone has to decide where and when! You're welcome to the position. Because I sure as hell don't want it. When she returns, I'll suffer any consequence she deems fair. So take your holier-than-thou attitude to the N double A C P, because I personally don't give a flying fuck what's fair! I'm here to win. And anyone who isn't can join another game. Our country isn't paying us to lose."

"Win at all cost, right?" Jeremiah persisted.

"No, no. But I'll spend every last dime to stop from losing. Then, if I still lose, I can live with myself. My father taught me that. Winning at all cost . . . no. But don't concede until you're spent." I reached into my pocket. "It appears I've got a couple nickels left yet to spend. Oh, look. Here's a coin with your name on it. In fact, there's a coin here for everyone. Are you in or out? That's all I'm asking."

"I'm in. Another smart-ass NAACP comment, though, and I'm gonna spend your nickel." Jeremiah smirked and threw one of his arms around me, placing me in a head lock. As he released me, I casually asked,

"Doesn't the CP in NAACP stand for 'colored people'?"

"Yeah, what about it?"

"Shouldn't it be N quadruple A P? Then we could simply refer to it as Nappy."

"I'm just happy they didn't form the alliance back when we were referred to as Negros," Jeremiah laughed. "Then it'd be Nanny."

We entered our barracks and gathered around Steven to see what he had swiped. "So what'd ya boost? And please tell me it isn't a pea shooter like Lourdes grabbed. Well?" I queried.

Steven acted coy and then unsure. "Well, you said just grab a gun. Any gun. That's what ya said. So I grabbed one that looked cool."

"What do mean by *cool,* exactly?"

I became uneasy. "My only instructions were to grab a gun that was small and coated in bluing for concealment purposes. How in tarnation could you screw up those directions?"

"It was that bluing part that confused me."

I rubbed my forehead in frustration. "Just show us what you've got. Lord, please don't make this a flare gun."

Steven reached into his pants and removed a nickel-plated .357 magnum revolver. Everyone's jaw fell to the floor. Rivas was especially impressed. "You ever been to Miami? Let's start planning our vacations together, my friend."

"She's beautiful," Joey admired, pretending to cry joyfully.

"I did good?" Steven asked knowingly.

"You did real good. Real good," Box said, bolstering Steven's confidence. "Okay, boys and girls. Let's get some rest. Tomorrow's 'D Day'."

*   *   *

We began the day with a little morning jog. Lourdes had rejoined us. She had a split lip and a black eye, but that in no manner deterred her. One thing was for sure; she was resilient. As we passed by the structures at the far end of the pit, we surreptitiously placed mirrors at key locations. Beneath the clothing of a few of our team members, we fastened smaller mirrors to the chest. We did this only to a select few because I knew that they would be immediately disqualified once the infraction was detected by the observers watching on closed-circuit television from outside the compound. I decided that these people would travel along the perimeter of the street and strafe the buildings as they went along in an attempt to terminate as many of the enemy as possible. The mirrors would reflect any signal fired at them back in the direction it came from and, in doing so, cause the signal to be absorbed by the assailant's receiver. Once turned off, units could not be turned back on without a key. The key was controlled by the commandant outside the compound. If we were able to run the gauntlet before he could reactivate those units, we would win.

"It's time, Box," I informed him, heart racing, full of energy. "They'll be calling us to the staging area in ten minutes. Remember, don't wait for us. Scurry along and conceal our absence. Oh, boy," I said, and sighed tensely. "I appreciate all the cooperation, guys. Good luck."

Box and I meandered to the side of the compound opposite the end we would attempt to gain. The guard had grown accustomed to us doing this. You see, I'd been dragging Box to this end of the compound every morning for weeks, under the guise that I needed privacy when conferring with him. This is why I needed his assistance at this juncture and no one else's. The guard was relaxed and nonchalant, just as I'd expected. We neared the post and I mumbled to Box, "Get ready with the gun."

"What gun? I thought you had the gun."

"You better be kidding."

"You didn't think I had a sense of humor, did ya? This thing sure is cold. My nuts are in my throat."

"I told you to put it behind you."

"You ever had a bazooka in your butt? Oh wait. You don't have a butt, do you? Sorry."

"You picked a peculiar time to suddenly be funny." We approached the staircase where the guard stood.

"Okay, let me distract 'im," I said to Box.

"Sergeant Walker! Shot anyone today?"

"No, but it's still early yet. Lots of daylight left," Walker responded with wit.

"There's always spotlighting," Box joined in, referring to the practice of placing a spotlight on a deer and freezing it in its tracks.

"That would be illegal," Walker rebutted authoritatively.

"Yeah, Box," I added. Turning now toward Walker I said, "You can set 'em free, but ya can't give 'em a sense of humor." Walker burst out laughing and then began to slap me in the chest like buddies often do. I signaled Box with my eyes. He reached into his pants and pulled out the .357 magnum. The hammer snagged his shorts on the way out, exposing boxers decorated with red hearts.

"Hey, buddy. Put your racist arms in the air," Box demanded. The guard turned with dread. He immediately surrendered his weapon. His fear turned to laughter, however, when he noticed Boxer's shorts.

"Maybe there's hope for your sense of humor yet," I declared, a grin still on my face.

"Get your hands up too!" Box yelled without conviction. "What kind of a crack was that?" He looked down at his shorts. "They're all I had clean. They were for my birthday. My wife. You know. Damn. I didn't want to ruin 'em."

"So you're married, huh?"

"I don't think we have time for this. The roof. You know," Box reminded me.

"See ya in the victory circle, home."

We gagged the guard, cuffing him to the exposed framing at the back of a building. I figured that by the time he was discovered missing, we would already be on the roof and the game would be underway. I scaled the angled truss to the top and crawled on hands and knees to a point halfway down the street. I poked my head over the top to see if the game had begun yet. The four who would form the circle were to go first, so I looked for them. Nothing yet. I searched for Boxer's head but saw nothing. I didn't know it at the time, but he was unable to make the climb.

"Where the hell is he?" I whispered loudly, perturbed. I was ecstatic, however, to find that I could see at least five opponents clearly. I stole another peek. There they were: Christina, Jesus, Joey and Debara formed a perfect circle and then sat down in the dust. I got goose bumps. Silence hung over the arena. I knew that our opponents must have experienced a sinking feeling when they saw the circle team perform this nonsensical act. I turned back to the rear of the building and fired several perfectly placed shots at the five adversaries I had spotted, sending them to the Dead Room. The circle team had yet to fire, and our strafers blitzed the sides of the street. Screams of frustration rang out as a few more of our adversaries died after firing directly at the chests of our runners, who wore the hidden mirror. One of those runners, Tina Parker, got cornered by the freshly dead, and they physically assaulted her when they discovered the hidden mirrors. I hadn't considered this possibility. Steven broke rank and started down the street to assist her. He was immediately shot with a radio wave. This didn't matter much to Steven, but it certainly affected the overall picture. I realized that the opposition's numerical superiority was a calculated advantage, designed as a fail-safe in case we somehow gained the upper hand.

"The guard's M-16," I thought. "That's it. Oh, shit. I left it at the base of the beam." My mind went into overdrive. "Box. He's got a gun. But if I call to him, I'll give away my position." I could hear calls from the rest of the team. They weren't going to be patient while I considered our options. "Box! Box!" I screamed, but couldn't be heard over all the other yelling.

"Everyone shut up!" It became remarkably quiet.

"Only Box and me! Box!"

"Yeah!"

"The gun! You got it!"

"Roger that!"

All I could think was that I wished it was Joey, the best marksman on the team, who had the gun. "Joey," I said to myself.

"Box!" I called out once again.

"Yeah!" Box replied with impatience.

"Run it to Joey!" I directed him. "Joey! Stay put! When you get it, do your thing!"

"Fuckin' A!" Joey responded with jubilation.

Box ran unobstructed to Joey, sliding head first into the circle. Joey took the .357, pointing it like an extension of his arm, and fired a couple rounds at the guys who had Tina pinned down. Deadly force was avoided by mere inches. Tina's assailants fled in a frenzy up the staircase. Steven, who was disqualified along with the runners, assisted Tina to safety.

"Okay! Nothing's changed! Continue the course!" I shouted encouragingly. Nothing seemed to be happening, however. The defenders remained entrenched, waiting for us to advance. I looked down and caught a glimpse of one of the enemy in one of our hidden mirrors. He was otherwise sheltered from view, and satisfied that he could not be hit by our fire. He did not, however, detect the mirror located only thirty or so feet from him in which I could see him. I fired several beams into the mirror as he came in and out of sight. I nailed him. He became enraged at having been eliminated, throwing a temper tantrum. Seeing him hit from an undetected quarter, his teammates suddenly felt vulnerable and began to act individually and without discipline. This created a target-rich environment, and the circle had a field day. Our battle-tested opponents were falling apart at the seams, and we were ready to rip them in half.

"Send Lourdes!" I hollered. Then, on the periphery, I witnessed a very disconcerting development: ten additional men entering the game from the floor of a building below me.

"Wait! Don't send her!" I countermanded. "Has she gone?"

"No! Not yet!" Chavez called back. "Why! What's happenin'? What's goin' on? We should send her now! No one's around."

I would come to find out that these were the men we had extinguished illegally. They were returning to the game in a similarly illicit fashion.

I could never take out ten men and expect to survive. I crawled back for the M-16. As I did, I asked everyone to hold steady and described what I'd just seen. I didn't know what, if anything, I would do with the gun once I retrieved it, but I decided I'd be better off with it than without it, so I made my way back and seized the weapon.

Crawling back up the scaffolding, forty-plus feet in the air, I once again made my way toward the center of the street. I was startled by a thunderous crashing noise above me and by screams of distress. Box had smashed his way through the adjoining building's thin, plaster walls and assaulted the enemy. With surprise in his favor, he was able to eliminate eight adversaries before meeting his own end. Although his electronic gun was rendered inoperative after his figurative demise, it didn't prevent him from physically attacking our opponents and pounding them into submission. The rules of the game changed radically as the situation evolved.

Returning to the two-foot ledge, I observed the havoc the circle had wreaked on our foes as scores of walking human carnage made their way to the Dead Room. Deciding when to send Lourdes to the opposite end of the compound to sound the magical horn that signalled an end to the exercise became my paramount concern. I couldn't very easily confirm that we had eradicated enough of the enemy to ensure a high probability of success.

Suddenly, a man appeared on the horizon, and he appeared to be heading for the staircase we had attempted to gain. At that very moment, several of the dead who had been hidden from view for a time walked expectantly into the street. We fired on them, but our weapons indicated that their systems were already inoperative. When the man on the horizon placed his foot on the first stair, I heard Joey scream out, "Key!"

"Stop him!" I answered. I knew that we would meet certain death if that key fell into the hands of the men we had killed illegally.

Joey sprang to his feet and took careful aim with the .357 magnum. Eerily, the man stood stock still while Joey squeezed the trigger, but nothing happened. "I'm spent!" he cried out.

"I'm not!" I replied, rising to my feet, the M-16 pointed squarely at the man on the staircase. The man took another timid step.

"Shoot him!" Joey urged me.

"Do it!" Debara added nervously.

I could feel all eyes upon me. I was center stage, front. "Does this man understand the risks involved here?" I wondered. I could sense my breathing, and then stillness. I became almost insentient—cold—as I had before the fight with Instructor Black.

"No! Don't!" Box screamed at me. He said to all those who were coaxing me on, and by now, that was everyone, "He'll do it, damn it. He'll really do it."

"He's right, Booch! This isn't that important!" Debara argued, now frightened.

"Come on down! Hey! I knew my gun was empty before I pulled the trigger!" Joey explained. I knew then that they had only been trying to scare the man into backing down by yelling for me to shoot him. But I also knew that Joey truly believed he had a shell remaining when he fired. He felt confident in his own ability to turn back the intruder but seriously doubted mine. This was likely what everyone else believed too. I fired.

The man cringed in fear as the bullet traveled to destinations unknown.

"He's not gonna do it, you stupid shit! Bring us the damn key! Hurry!" one of the undead eagerly yelled.

Several thoughts struck me simultaneously: I knew that the key holder was not significant in the command structure; I saw that the dead could not go to the key, but rather that the key had to come to them; I felt that the opposition doubted my resolve; and I found that my aim stank.

The key holder stood up and took two more steps. I aimed three steps below him. Anticipating a slow descent, I waited to fire until he made a motion as if to start walking. He walked quicker than I anticipated he would, and I fired short of where I thought I would. The bullet missed his leg by three inches. He retreated like an extra in a *Godzilla* movie, stopping only momentarily to heave the key to the dead, who were gathered at the base of the staircase.

They swarmed to the key, not deterred whatsoever by several carefully placed bullets I delivered in a tight pattern around the spot the key had to have fallen. I stopped firing. I knew I couldn't send Lourdes through live fire, and I also knew I lacked enough information about the enemy to risk sending her through the gauntlet.

The dead then took a calculated risk. They formed a solid mass and methodically shuffled their way to the stairs to pick up the key. I couldn't fire from such close range at such a large target without risking a real casualty. My options suddenly narrowed.

"Send her!" I called out.

"Now?" Lourdes responded.

"Now!"

She bolted, hitting her stride in the first ten yards or so. Her feet struck the dirt in a rhythmic beat, like Secretariat on the home stretch of Churchill Downs. Her determination brought a lump to my throat, as she bobbed and weaved her way down the street, avoiding the few enemy that remained. She was alone. We simply couldn't risk laying down covering fire, for fear of hitting her with a stray beam. We were now armed only with cheers of support.

"Go! Go! Go!" I belted out, then to myself I said, "Go, Lourdes. Do it for us."

Everyone chimed in with their own words of encouragement, and then, as if on cue, fell silent. We watched wordlessly as she ran serpentine down the length of the street.

The dead found the key. One by one they reactivated their weapons and, realizing that we would not come to Lourdes' defense, they briskly stepped forward into plain view, attempting to get a clear shot at Lourdes before she reached the horn. Lourdes unharnessed a hidden reserve of energy and sped between her attackers before they could intercept her. I watched in amazement, never really believing she would succeed. When the horn sounded, I leaped from my crouch, threw my arms into the air, gun in hand, and screamed in elation. The horn resounded across the desert.

I watched the other team members, except Box, charge toward Lourdes. My attention slowly focused on Box standing in front of a building forty feet below me and directly across the street. He looked up at me, then toward the jubilation at the end of the street, then once again at me. He raised one hand high in the air, thumbs up in a salute, and then let it drop to his side as he stared, transfixed, at the sight of the trainees celebrating wildly. Lourdes took a victory climb to the top of the staircase, humming loudly the music to *Rocky*. Debara stepped back from the knot of celebrants and waved to me. I acknowledged her with a short wave in return, not quite sure what I was feeling. It was over.

* * *

When the final tally was made, only sixteen trainees remained. Two of our teammates had been spies for the opposition, although apparently not very good ones. This final group of sixteen became our unit, nicknamed "4PM" because 1600 hours is the military terminology for four o'clock in the afternoon. Conveniently, Pseudo Miranda shared the same abbreviation as *post meridian,* hence 4PM.

During our final days in Tonopah, we learned about our first mission in detail and about the larger scope and plan of Pseudo Miranda. We were to intercept Colombian cocaine coming into America by posing as the Coast Guard. Once we secured the vessel, we were to send the crew back to its port of origin with a message for the drug lord to send a representative to Zurich, Switzerland, to meet with other *cocaleros* and discuss an operation of mutual benefit to themselves and the U.S. government.

This coterie of drug lords would be given the means to destroy the numerically superior but smaller drug traffickers in Latin America and the Caribbean; specifically, they would receive U.S. intelligence on the exact locations of competitors' cocaine laboratories and be given weapons to destroy the labs and any collateral resistance. This was designed to centralize Colombian drug-trafficking operations and to give the CIA more control over them.

The Peruvians and the Bolivians would be partners with the Colombians in the drug trade. They would remain the primary growers of the coca and would process the raw material into coca paste, which they would supply to the Colombians, but they would essentially be excluded from the distribution network into North America. The deal would also exclude affiliates of Shining Path or other revolutionary movements.

Although the CIA initially tried to get Cuba involved in Pseudo Miranda, the attempt misfired, and Cuba was neutralized as a participant by Carlos Lehder. From Norman's Cay, his personal Bahamian island, Lehder facilitated the distribution of Cuban cocaine to America. This cocaine originated in Colombia, but was already included in the amount authorized for importation under Operation Pseudo Miranda, therefore prohibiting any additional shipments of cocaine from Cuba as part of the deal.

I was awed by the logistical complexity of the operation. Pseudo Miranda aircraft taking off from Colombia and carrying large quantities of cocaine would lock onto CIA long-range navigation (LORAN) radar, descend to a low altitude, and fly below U.S. Customs and Defense Department radar systems. This became known as Operation Light House. If this was not feasible for some reason, another approach was to use an aircraft with a scheduled flight plan—typically a U.S. Air Force flight—to conceal the radar signature of a drug aircraft flying in close proximity. This shadowing ploy was termed Olympic Victor for the OV-10 reconnaissance aircraft outsmarted by the maneuver. Once over American soil, the drug planes would be intercepted by a CIA chase plane. Identify Friend or Foe (IFF) transponders, which were installed on both the drug planes and the CIA aircraft, would establish positive identification. After taking the helm, the CIA chase plane would conduct the drug plane over a drop zone. The pilot of the drug plane would then track on an inertial landing system (ILS) radar beam, usually used for instrument landings, and release his cargo to agents on the ground.

We were those agents. Once we gathered up the cargo, we would transport it to a predesignated area and fly it to Mena, Arkansas. Immediately after our departure, a special team would arrive at the drop zone and hastily tear down the ILS radar system. The cocaine would eventually arrive at its final destination in Tonopah, Nevada, where it would be stored securely several stories underground.

*　*　*

I was proud of what I'd accomplished in training, but I worried whether I had the ability to carry this success into the real world. At the time, though, I just wanted to tell someone of my accomplishment. That of course was impossible. I settled instead for a telephone call to my parents to tell them that I'd finally graduated from college. They were quite complimentary, and it made me feel good, so I pretended they were congratulating me on what I'd really done. This worked well, and I would look back on these days fondly. They seemed safe; there were boundaries.

Chapter 6

After completing the training in Nevada, I returned to Murray, where I awaited further instruction from Box and attended a few summer classes at Murray State. I had enrolled there before going to Tonopah as an instrument of my cover. When I got back, I found that the course in Italian I had signed up for had begun weeks earlier, but I was confident in my ability to excel in my ancestral tongue.

My girlfriend of a couple years, Andy (short for Andrea), who also attended classes at Murray, was under the impression that I had been in Massachusetts visiting my family for the past month or so.

Box paid me a visit at home one afternoon in the latter part of the summer. "You alone?" muttered Box at my door, then poked his head over the threshold.

"Not any more. How you doin', partner? You look good! Wife must be treatin' ya well. Come on in!"

"No, I'm not asking for myself. I brought a few people with me. Are you expecting anyone soon?"

"Why?"

"We're gonna install a STU III (pronounced *Stew Three*) secure phone in your bedroom."

"Oh. Oh, shit. My girlfriend. Umm, yeah. I'll call her and tell her that we're goin' to the lake together or something."

"Good. Do that." Box removed a hand radio, known as a "brick," from his jacket and summoned the installation team. "This won't take long, believe me. These guys installed one at my place in a snap." Box walked into my bedroom and, appalled at its condition, added, "Well, maybe 'a snap' was a poor choice of words."

"What? Oh. You're just not used to seeing a bedroom that gets a lot of use."

"Right. Hey! I'm gonna need to demonstrate the proper use of this puppy."

Before I departed for the lake with Andy, Box told me that I would be flying to the Florida Keys in a week. Specifically, a tiny island called Islamorada. Box and I would take off from Paducah, Kentucky, and arrive that same day at Homestead Air Force Base, Florida. From there, we would go directly to the Drop Anchor Hotel in Isla Morada, where the 4PM team would receive a detailed briefing on its first interception: a drug shipment from Colombia.

"What do you think about . . . um . . . What would you say to . . . You know, driving instead of flying?" Box tentatively suggested.

"Excuse me?"

"It's a simple question! I thought it was something you'd prefer to do. But if it isn't, then fine. We'll fly."

"Chill out. We'll drive. But tell me the real reason."

"Ah, shit. I don't know. They've got me in charge of the mission. I really thought they'd give us someone who'd done this sort of stuff before. I don't know, I guess I thought we'd talk about it for a couple days before we get there. I don't know why they didn't just give the damn job to you."

"Yeah, right. They're gonna have *me* lead us? Take your head outta your ass. I'm an impromptu kind of guy. I don't much go in for this planning stuff."

"Impromptu is what we need! At least that's the way I see it. Look what you did in training," Box offered.

"That was training. Anyhow, don't worry. I'll be right with you. Shoulder to shoulder. We're a team, right?"

*   *   *

We drove my 1982 Corvette to Florida, stopping along the way for the essentials: gas, food and beer. Near midnight on our first day on the road, we were passing through the great state of Georgia and Box was fast asleep when I spotted them. I slammed on the brakes, bringing the car from seventy-five miles per hour to a screeching halt. Box, having road tested his seat belt, sprang from the automobile, gun in hand, and took cover along his side of the vehicle.

"Stop playing around, Box," I teased.

"What the hell's goin' on?! Where the hell are we?! Why did you slam on the brakes?!"

"The beef's prime for tipping."

"What?"

"You ever tipped a cow?"

"That's it? That's why you almost killed us? Cows? First chance we get, we're getting you some mental help." Box paused for a moment as if considering what he had said, then spluttered, "Cow tipping? He almost kills me for cows."

"Come on. It'll be an adventure."

Box holstered his weapon and reluctantly followed me. I had never done this before, so I wasn't quite sure what to expect. I did know, however, that Box needed something to distract him from his anxiety. He also needed to know that we were of one mind.

Most of the cows were sprawled on the ground, something I hadn't anticipated.

"Hey. It appears that someone has already tipped these cows. Now can we get the hell out of here?"

"Over here," I said eagerly. I had found one cow sleeping upright. At least I thought he was sleeping. I had Box line up his shoulder on mine, as I explained to him the importance of slamming into the cow simultaneously. We were about to attack when Box commented, "This cow has horns."

I responded, "Cows have horns."

"They do?"

"City boy?" I joked.

We slammed our bodies into the side of the bull, only to rebound immediately backwards. The bull remained momentarily unmoved, and then lost its balance, crashing to the ground. It butted its head spasmodically into the dirt numerous times before returning to its feet. As it looked around, confused, we wondered aloud whether the bull thought it was dreaming or that one of the other cows was playing a trick on it.

Our gut-wrenching laughter caught the bull's attention. It charged with malice. I ran directly for the barbed wire fence that we had crossed earlier, launching myself over it like a football player diving for the end zone. Box played ring around the cows with the bull before eluding the beast and heading for the fence. He leaped but failed to clear it, snagging his leather coat on the wire. The bull collided with the fence, just missing Box, who decided then and there to forget about his prized possession and spare himself the wrath of the bull. Later on, after he finished complaining, Box admitted that the experience was worth a leather jacket.

"If I'd remained sleeping," he said, "the day wouldn't be remembered. But I promise, I'll never forget this one."

The following afternoon we stopped for lunch at a burger joint in northern Florida. Box was visibly tense, and he confided that he was quite scared about the mission.

"It's all you can drink, you know."

"Huh?"

"The soda." I pointed to the self-service fountain. "Free refills."

"I know that! I'm talking about something real important here," Box remonstrated, but he couldn't maintain the look of outrage. "Okay. So it's free refills. What's your point?"

"You bought a large?"

"I didn't feel like running back and forth for refills."

"So you pay a buck more. The ultimate in lazy."

"Is there a point to all this?"

"You're settled. Only a married, settled person would do that. Look around. Do you see any young people with large drinks? You've gotten to the place in life where convenience is worth paying a higher price for. Settled."

"Because I purchased a large? You're serious?"

"An unsettled person wouldn't worry so much about the possibility of dying."

"Maybe I have reason to stay alive. Maybe I have people who would be just a bit concerned that I tipped cows at the stroke of midnight. Yeah. Maybe I'm a bit conservative and a touch cautious, but I have more than myself to think of here."

"Exactly."

As we began the last leg of our trip, I slurped down the final drops of my drink. Box, never one to pass up an opportunity to gloat, said,

"Nothing so quenching as a large soda on a hot day. Yup! This puppy ought to last until next stop. Aren't you glad we got . . . Oh, no. I'm sorry. I forgot. You got a small soda, didn't ya? Oh, well." Box sat back in his seat, full of himself.

*   *   *

The Drop Anchor Hotel sat right on the ocean, separated from the water by a narrow dock. A swimming pool and a few shuffleboard courts occupied the center of the U-shaped structure. Coconut trees provided shade and added a sense of serenity. The elderly couple who ran the facility were also the owners, and they treated us like family. On this first mission, as with all of our missions, the entire team was not present—just the core: Christina, Jeremiah, Rivas, Joey, Rick, Steven, Lourdes, Quinn, Debara, Box and me. The eleven of us would form the backbone of 4PM.

The evening before, Box had read a detailed list of instructions, assigning specific responsibilities to each of us. Steven would provide constant updates on the exact location of the target ship and warn of any approaching U.S. drug interdiction craft. Debara was in charge of piloting the boat, a 1984 Hatteras, and Joey's expertise with explosives would be invaluable in case of a tumultuous interception. Christina came mainly as a Spanish interpreter, but like all the others on board, she was expected to hold her own with a weapon. Jeremiah and Rick supplied the physical strength necessary to lift the large bales of drugs we frequently found. Lourdes' marksmanship made her a must, but her devotion to Pseudo Miranda was sufficient reason to have her accompany all missions. Rivas and Quinn were expert divers, and would be called upon if we had to go below the waterline of the target craft to search for hidden drugs. As for me, Box simply said, "If there's trouble of any sort or if they refuse to cooperate, your job is to make it happen."

The Hatteras would anchor a few hundred yards off the hotel dock, and a smaller boat would come in to pick us up there. After taking us to the Hatteras, the crew would quickly vanish.

*   *   *

I suggested we all have a couple drinks poolside somewhere around 9:00 P.M. Box reluctantly agreed, and kept a vigilant eye on all of us. Although it seemed quite innocent, he had serious reservations about the team arriving hung-over to start our first mission. The atmosphere was relaxed, however, and Box, after consuming a screwdriver, seemed more at ease. I took advantage of the changing mood and introduced a few more fifths of vodka. Soon thereafter, Rick challenged everyone to a contest to see who could consume the most alcohol under water, at the bottom of the pool. The party went downhill from there.

When I awoke, I realized that I was stark naked. In fact, everyone was. The pool cleaner was busy removing bottles and cans from the water. I slithered on my belly, gathering my clothes and my humility. Everyone awoke to the same awkward realization, not quite sure if laughter was the appropriate response.

"So what the hell happened here last night?" I innocently asked the pool cleaner.

"Oh, some young men and women got drunk and stupid. Kept up a lot of folks. Retired people, you know. Yeah. We cater to the retired. Anyhow, before I threw 'em out, I went around to our guests to apologize for the disturbance." The old man pulled a bottle from the pool and poured the water at my feet. "Everyone said the same thing. Said it was the most fun they'd had in years. So I guess I'll let 'em stay." The old man owned the place.

*   *   *

The Hatteras arrived. I watched silently as it bobbed forbiddingly on the vast sea. The smaller craft came into view and my head immediately cleared. "We're really going through with this," I thought. We were all dressed as tourists, attempting, with hearts racing, to remain inconspicuous.

We boarded the transfer craft, and shortly, the Hatteras. Debara took the helm and was directed by Steven to set a course bearing 71 degrees longitude by 22 degrees latitude. Our approximate destination was the southern tip of Andros Island in the Bahamas. Steven was hooked up directly with Mena, Arkansas, the hub of all CIA-run missions into South America, which in turn had a direct link to an Air Force reconnaissance aircraft. All courtesy of Equatorial Communications, a daring company run by the CIA. If everything went as planned, we would intercept the drug vessel approximately seventy-five miles off our shores.

We had been at sea for some three hours and had had no visual contact with the target. Box was feeling the pressure and said, "Steven. Steven. I don't wanna end up in the Bay of Pigs. Where the hell are they?"

"Oh, don't worry about that. The Bay of Pigs is on the southern coast of Cuba. We should hit Havana long before that," Steven responded sincerely.

"God. Tell me he's kidding. Just tell me where the hell they are."

"Apparently we're headed right or I'd have received an update."

Box became a bit agitated. "Could ya please check?"

Steven radioed Mena and got a prompt response. "We're right on course. Should see 'em within the next twenty minutes or so."

"It's a pretty big ocean. Are you sure?"

"Neither of us have altered our course one iota."

*   *   *

Course changes now came in quick succession as we neared the intercept. It was as though Debara and Steven had worked together for years. We skipped about the ocean at a rapid rate, altering course erratically as we closed the gap. As in so many aspects of Pseudo Miranda, the many had to rely heavily on the few. In this case, Debara and Steven controlled our destiny, and they performed beautifully.

Our hearts quickened as we listened to the changes in course and updates about the target. We sat shoulder to shoulder, leaning back against the sides of the ship. I began to yawn repeatedly, something I did whenever I sensed myself feeling nervous. Jeremiah pounded his elbows against the side of the boat psyching himself up for action. I remained quiet, never one to use artificial means to prepare myself. Joey, sitting to my right, vomited quickly and violently over his rifle.

"Nerves?" I asked.

"No," he answered, bouncing his head back and forth.

"Something you ate?" Box inquired further.

"No, just something I do," Joey replied, never acknowledging us with eye contact.

"So, how do you feel?" Box asked me, almost as if he knew before he asked that I felt all knotted up inside.

"Nervous. But I'm always nervous. I think I do better that way," I responded.

"I'm countin' on ya." Box grabbed my knee, cracking a tense smile.

We became distracted by a sudden change in cadence in the dialogue between Debara and Steven, which until now consisted of Steven calling out course changes and Debara echoing his calls. The only voice heard now however, was Debara's. "We should've seen the damn thing by now! Where are they! Where the hell are they!"

"They should be right in front of us," Steven said.

"Well, they're not! Whatta we do now?" And then, "Wait. There! Hold on, everyone!" Debara said, and veered hard left, pulling our craft ahead of the target. She vectored a cutoff like a trap shooter leading a clay pigeon. She was a predator closing in on the kill.

Debara throttled back abruptly and called out, "They're stopping! Is everybody ready?"

It was time. We snugged our bulletproof vests tight and prepared our weapons. With two magnetic signs placed on either side of the ship, signifying that we were the United States Coast Guard, everyone except Box, Debara and Rick hid from view. Dressed in Coast Guard uniforms, they guided our boat within a short distance of the other vessel, and Rick, yelling on a bull horn in fluent Spanish, directed them to chop their motors. They did, and attempted no resistance.

I knew the next thing I did would change my life forever. Once I bore down on this ship with my gun, there would be no turning back. I was bombarded with thoughts, but one stood out: "What would it feel like if these people actually fired bullets at me?"

As our Hatteras pulled alongside the drug craft, a large Bayliner, we snapped from our prone positions, pointing eight assault rifles at the occupants. The apparent leader yelled, "No Coast Guard! Coast Guard marauders!" They became extraordinarily friendly, welcoming us aboard. Box looked confused, doubtful of the man's sincerity. I didn't wait for Boxer's directive, fearing that hesitation would make him appear indecisive. I knew he was frightened that one of us might get killed under his command.

"I'll go first," I said. "Turn this tub into Swiss cheese if they try anything. Oh, yeah. Jesus! I'm gonna need a translator."

"I'm there!" Rivas volunteered. "Do you want me to tell him about the 'Swiss cheese' thing?"

"As a matter of fact, yeah." I climbed aboard the Bayliner with him and immediately placed the barrel of my gun to the leader's skull. With Rivas simultaneously translating, I demanded, "The cocaine. Where is it? And don't waste my time or I'll splatter your brains across this deck!"

"No need for threats, he responded. "We got your *coca*." He then cautiously reached into the false bottom of a seat, assuring me that he was getting the drugs, and only the drugs. I stood behind him, holding his right hand twisted with my left. He gently removed a kilogram of pure Colombian cocaine and handed it to me, saying, "This is for you."

"What's goin' on, Ves?" Box called out.

"I think you need to come over here, Box! Everything's fine! But you need to come here now! Tell Steven we need updates every minute. Or sooner if things change. I don't want the real Coast Guard to show up!"

Box boarded with Joey, Jeremiah and Rick. "What's wrong?" Box asked.

"This is what's wrong." I showed him the bag of cocaine.

"So? This is what we came for, right?"

"We came for several hundred pounds of the stuff, not a key." I shook the bag of cocaine in the man's face. "This is a fuckin' pay-off! These assholes have been paying off the Coast Guard. Shit! Why didn't our people know about this?" I hurled the bag into the ocean and then grabbed the man by the back of the neck. "Where's the shipment?"

He turned frantic, glancing toward his men. Not that they could do anything. We still had several guns pointed at them, and they were disarmed. "You can't do this! We have a deal!" the man protested.

"Not with us you don't," I replied. "Now, where's the real shipment?"

"We don't have any. Not on board."

"You ever heard the saying, 'If it ain't broke, don't fix it'? Well, there's gonna be a lot of fixin' going on around here if I don't see some snow real quick like." I signaled for Rick to toss me his shotgun. I pumped it. The man cringed. "Nice stereo. I'd hate to be you sailing all the way to Georgetown (in the Cayman Islands) without this," I said sarcastically and then blew it apart. No reaction.

I conferred with Joey and Box, just out of the drug trafficker's hearing. I asked Joey if it were possible to attach a timer to a charge of C-4 and set the timer off but not explode the plastique. He responded in the affirmative. In a loud, clear voice, Box then commanded the team to sink the vessel. Joey affixed the C-4 to the engine bay, in plain view of our captives. As the timer wound down to thirty seconds, the leader reconsidered. Visibly trembling, he muttered, "Sub. . . sub . . . submarine."

"Turn it off," Box directed Joey. "The cocaine," he demanded of the trafficker.

The man proceeded below deck, with Box and me trailing along. He handed me what appeared to be a video game joy stick and said tentatively,

"Remote. Thirty kilometers." He waved his arm in a sweeping gesture toward the stern of the ship.

"Steven!" I shouted. "Someone get Steven here ASAP! Debara! Tell Debara to do her best and work the SATCOM (satellite communications)!"

I settled the man down by placing my hands on his shoulders and repeating the words *It's okay* a few times. I then said to Box, "I think they've got some sort of submarine, and they control it with this dohicky here."

Steven entered. "What's up?"

I explained to him what had transpired. Meanwhile, Box called Rivas down for translation. After a short discussion with the drug trafficker, Steven explained what was going on. He said that they had towed a small submarine full of cocaine to this point, and released it as we were about to come upon them. The drop location was plotted on a map, and the sub was hovering just below the water's surface. They had intended to re-mote control it back to the vessel after our departure. We would later discover that Juan David Ochoa, eldest son of Fabio Ochoa, had pur-chased several of these Jacques Cousteau-type submarines for the express purpose of drug smuggling.

Steven guided the minisubmarine back to the boat, whereupon we emptied half the cargo onto our ship. Box then gave the man a sealed letter and instructed him to give it to Fabio Ochoa. Box told him that if Ochoa sent a representative to meet with us and with other drug lords or their representatives in Zurich, Switzerland, we would return the remain-der of his shipment to him. The man knew that he would be killed if he didn't return with the money or the shipment of cocaine, which assured us that he would give the letter to Don Fabio as an explanation for not having either.

We stowed the drugs in a specially designed fuel tank that allowed fuel to flow around a concealed compartment. Altogether we concealed more than 300 pounds of pure cocaine inside this trick tank, then transferred fuel from the other tank to insulate the cocaine from detection.

We cast all of our weapons into the ocean as we neared some Coast Guard patrol ships. With fishing poles dangling overboard, we motored back to Islamorada and did everything in reverse. All in all, it was a smooth operation. The same could not be said of the mission that followed, how-ever.

Chapter 7

The summer was nearing its end when we headed west for our next intercept. Box had received an intelligence report about a cocaine shipment originating in Cuba and the likely route it would take toward the U.S.

René Cruz ran the Cuban drug-smuggling operation for Fidel Castro, and it was he who masterminded the voyage of the *Lazy Lady II* some three thousand miles from the Caribbean to the Pacific Coast. This was the *Lazy Lady II*'s maiden voyage, and she lived up to her name by taking her good, sweet time about it. The craft, a new Hinckley Downeaster, had a greater drag coefficient than our Hatteras and was not designed for speed. The fuel requirements made a slower, less gas-gulping craft mandatory for traffickers shipping over such distances.

This was our inherent advantage, and we planned to meet it approximately three hundred miles north of the Tropic of Cancer in neutral waters. As with the prior intercept, the mission was to draw Cuba into Operation Pseudo Miranda by seizing half of the cocaine on board and sending the captain back home with an invitation to René Cruz to attend the organizational meeting in Zurich.

* * *

The team gathered in San Diego at the Hotel del Coronado, which has stood majestically for over a hundred years on the Pacific Ocean. The setting was serene. Everyone on the team arrived in pairs throughout the evening, gradually gathering on a large outdoor deck overlooking the beach. We relaxed and sipped frozen Margaritas, never getting quite as relaxed as we had in Florida, however. Box spoke somewhat openly in the midst of our very public surroundings about our impending mission. "Debara, the *Lazy Lady II* is a large sport-fishing vessel and should pose no threat to our team and shouldn't be able to escape you once you've got a visual. Intel shows four on board, as we expected. Again, nothing we can't handle. We show force like last time, and everything should go smooth. The key is communication. Steven? Where the fuck is Steven?"

"He's over there rapping with that chick," Jeremiah replied, directing our attention to a table at the opposite end of the deck.

"For God's sake, will someone drag his butt over here? Where the hell is his mind anyhow?" Box said, agitated.

"I think the answer's self-evident," Debara said, impressed with Steven's savoir-faire.

"I don't get it. I'll go to my grave never understanding women. Look at 'im. All he's missing are the pens in the shirt pocket and he's rubbing up against that," I said.

"Shit ain't right, man. You and I should be all over that," Rivas commented as he pointed to several other women, saying each time, "And that. And that. And that."

"I'll tell you one thing he *doesn't* have that you both have," Debara said leadingly.

"Well?" I asked her.

"He doesn't have an overinflated ego."

"Or good looks and a personality," Rivas added.

"Maybe he's well hung. Did ya ever consider that possibility?" Quinn asked.

"If that's all it took, Quinn, you'd be over there talking to her instead of Steven," Rivas retaliated in jest.

"Oh, boy. You're dead," I said, laughing. I ducked my head below the table.

"What's that supposed to mean? Huh, Jesus (pronouncing it JEE-zus)? Why don't we see what you've got down there." Quinn proceeded to flip Rivas to the deck, even though he resisted mightily. We were pulling her off of him when Steven returned to the table.

"Looks like I missed all the excitement."

"Glad you could join us. We're not taking you from anything more important, I hope," Box said sarcastically.

"No. I'm gonna get together with her later on."

"If we've interrupted you, please feel free," Box continued sarcastically, motioning in the direction of the beautiful women. Steven, now realizing Box was genuinely upset, pulled up a chair.

"Maybe I'm not running a tight enough ship," Box started to preach.

"Great," Joey interrupted. "Now his ship's getting tighter."

Box chuckled, changing gears a bit. "Who am I kidding? I never could keep a ship tight. If I could, I certainly wouldn't be sailing around with this character, now would I?" He pinched the back of my neck and finished by saying, "Let's just do our jobs the best way we know how. I don't have to tell you how important this is. Half the drugs." He now spoke solemnly, looking over the ocean. "Half the drugs. Gone. Who knows. Maybe thousands of kids don't grow up to become addicts and criminals. I mean, who knows. Maybe."

* * *

Everyone traveled to the rendezvous in rented vehicles, except Box and me of course. The atmosphere seemed much looser than it had the evening before. Box bellowed out Manfred Mann's version of the Bruce Springstein classic "Blinded by the Light," and I harmonized on the verses I could recall. Then we sang Golden Earring's "Radar Love," and by the time we finished singing we were pumped.

Each car in the convoy carried a hand-held radio in the event of a mechanical problem or, worse, an accident. No classified information was ever discussed on those bands, however. Throughout the trip, the only thing that could be heard over "the brick" was singing and perverse humor. I kept thinking that we were becoming a real team. I felt the other members of Pseudo Miranda would always be there for me through the laughter, the danger and the pain. These were certainly the good times.

Two large rubber boats took us to the Hatteras. Debara and Steven took the helm and guided us into the open sea. The water was rougher than it had been on the East Coast. About ten miles out, I found Christina leaning over the edge of the ship, puking her guts out.

"Morning sickness?" I asked.

She twisted her head slowly upwards, then dropped it suddenly overboard once again.

"I'm just kidding. You all right?"

She began to turn her head up once more, deciding instead to shake it from side to side.

"Right. Stupid question. Try looking straight out over the bow . . . or stern . . . or whatever. Just look straight out instead of down at the water. That's what Debara told me to do."

"I'm fine. You got sick too?"

"Hell, no! What kind of a wimp do you think I am? I'm playing. I'm just playing. You'll be fine. Just stay up here and look far out over the ocean until you feel better."

I lay down on deck and soon fell asleep. Over the next several hours, we would refuel at sea twice. I slumbered just below the surface of consciousness and was mostly cognizant of the events that happened around me. When I fully awakened, however, there was a rifle barrel pointed at my face. "Very funny, Joey. I hope that shit ain't loaded."

"We're closing in. Box said to wake your ass."

"You haven't puked on that gun yet, have you?"

"No, not yet."

"Thank God."

Everyone was busy preparing themselves and checking their weapons and protective clothing. Box asked Steven how long it would take to get there.

"What's our ETI, Steven?"

"Our what?"

"Estimated time of interception."

"Right . . . uhhh . . . Our ETI!" Steven said with a laugh, causing a bit of embarrassment for Box. "It's uh . . . It'll be about an hour. Sorry." Steven turned back to his equipment and chuckled some more.

"What are you all looking at? ETI! It's like ETA! What?!" Box shouted at us, half laughing.

The Hatteras slammed into high gear, and the chase was on. The hour passed quickly. "Slow it down! Tell her to throttle back!" Lourdes called out. "We forgot the signs! We've got to put the Coast Guard signs on!"

Debara got the word and trimmed the power. We hastily slapped the signs on the side of the boat and pushed forward. Nothing lost, we thought, as we neared our target. The Hatteras sprang from the wave crests like an airfoil, impacting the water heavily when it landed. We rapidly closed the distance between the boats. Almost everyone cheered Debara, although I remained mute, never one to underestimate the opposition. It came from playing high school football with a team that hardly ever won a game, and I learned to overestimate the strength of every opponent. I found my thoughts held captive by Debara's courage and determination. I was sure that I could never do what she was doing, and I was filled with pride for her.

"I'm gonna ease it in! They're not trying to go anywhere! Get ready!" Debara yelled over the noise of the engine.

Everyone immediately turned to Joey, expecting him to vomit on cue. "What? I can't prepare with you looking at me like that," Joey reacted.

Boxer sat on my right, and I reached out and grabbed Boxer's left arm. We watched emotionally as everyone reached out with their right arm, grasping the left arm of the person beside them. Joey vomited, making it complete.

Debara gave command to Rick as we closed in on the drug boat. It looked so much like the boat that Box and I had spent time on in Chicago that I almost forgot what I was doing there. Their engines purred as they tooled along. Four men stood on deck, appearing more bewildered than frightened. They had surely noticed our Coast Guard emblems and probably wondered why we were operating outside national waters. This was exactly what we had hoped.

I looked up at Rick, trying to interpret his expression and gauge our present status. I gripped my weapon—a Browning 2000 12-gauge shotgun—tightly. Strapped to my side was a Colt .45 automatic. Box stood up, making his presence known, just as he had in the previous interception. We were close. I could hear murmuring from the other ship's crew. Speaking in Spanish, Rick said over the intercom, "Halt your vessel! This is the United States Coast Guard! We want to board! Repeat! Halt your vessel!"

The *Lazy Lady II* followed Rick's orders and ceased forward progress. Rick continued, "Cut your engines!"

Box, standing now only a couple feet from where I was hidden from plain view, glanced down at me and smiled. Bap! Bap! Bap! Bap! Bap! Box collapsed at my feet.

"Machine gun fire!" I thought. A barrage of automatic weapons fire saturated the side of our metal-reinforced ship. Then silence.

"Now!" I screamed. Everyone spun up and toward the boat, and turned ten weapons on the *Lazy Lady II,* riddling it with an assortment of bullets and buckshot. The other crew erratically returned fire at close range, exposing themselves in the process. With singular presence of mind, we paused almost as one for a split second and meticulously took aim. Our return fire blanketed them with lead. One man tried to dash across the deck to better cover, but several of our weapons tracked their fire backward into his path, and he fell.

Everything became suddenly still. I looked across a smoke cloud hovering on the water by the side of the *Lazy Lady*. The smell was intoxicating, thick and oily. The motors were still idling, but the superstructure was splintered. We kept our weapons trained firmly on the wounded ship, not yet convinced that all was safe. We had already made the mistake of underestimating their resolve. I knelt down, dividing my attention between the ship and Box.

"How you doing, buddy?" I asked. I spoke loud because I could hardly hear my voice for the buzzing in my ears.

"I'm fine. It's just my shoulder," Box replied with a catch in his voice.

"Think we got 'em all?" I quipped. "Why don't you stand up again and check?"

Bap! Bap! Bap! Bap! Bap! Bap! . . . More fire.

"Joey! Joey!" I screamed at the top of my lungs. "Toss me a grenade!" He had one in his hand already, so I pointed to my own and signified what it was I wanted. I was unaware that he had already pulled the pin. "Throw me the grenade! Now!"

He threw it. Everything else seemed to freeze when, to my displeasure, I saw the pin separate from the grenade. In a singularly magnificent moment in my life, I stepped across Box, caught the grenade, twisted and threw it, all in one continuous motion, into the middle of the *Lazy Lady II*'s deck.

The result was not so magnificent, however. Not a crevice of protection existed within twenty feet of the explosion. Metal shrapnel from the grenade wreaked havoc, spraying wood and glass projectiles everywhere and butchering everything in their path. In the aftermath, a pillow of smoke swayed gently over the *Lazy Lady II,* and the carnage on the deck was screened from view. Our team rose tentatively from our hunkered-down positions, listening cautiously for the crackling sounds of gunfire coming from the devastated ship. We felt the oscillating, dull noise of the engines in our chests as we watched the craft wobble lifeless in front of us.

When we were convinced that all was calm, we boarded the ship. There were more people aboard than intelligence had estimated. Instead of four, there were eight. None of us were prepared for what we saw. Dismembered bodies arbitrarily strewn about. Blood still running from the sides of the deck and pooling toward the stern. Chunks of flesh stuck to the cabin walls, glued by blood. A torso, minus the head and legs, lay like a sad shield atop the body of another of our assailants.

"How frightened he must have been in his final moments," I thought.

"Over here!" Christina called out.

We gathered around Christina as she leaned over a bullet-ridden, middle-age man. "He's alive."

"So what," Joey said callously.

"So what? How can you say that? We're responsible for this. We've gotta do somethin'," Lourdes protested despondently.

"Yeah, I agree with Joey. So the fuck what. This guy wouldn't waste ten seconds worrying about you. He's shark bait if you ask me."

"I know CPR," Jeremiah volunteered eagerly.

"Well, Box?" Christina asked.

"Of course. Do what you can. But please hurry," Box answered. He knew, as I did, that it was an act of futility. But it would help the rest of the team keep their sanity, and that made it necessary. "Steven! Keep us abreast!"

"Yes, sir!"

"What's the holdup?" Debara hollered from the Hatteras. She had remained aboard in the event of a hasty departure.

"We're pumping air into a sieve," I murmured under my breath. "Shit. Would you look at that." I directed Boxer's attention to the Hatteras. As the smoke dissipated, Box looked in disbelief at the dimpled and mangled Coast Guard sign, which we had hung upside down and backwards. It was clear that we had screwed up royally, and eight people were dead as a result.

"He's opening his eyes," Lourdes shouted.

"Great. What are we gonna do if he lives? It's not like we can take him to a hospital or anything," Box said, still speaking quietly to me. He then pretended to be talking to a doctor. "Excuse me, Mr. Doctor, we're with the CIA, and we seemed to have caused this man serious injury when we intercepted his drug shipment as part of a clandestine operation. Here's our insurance card."

I dropped the safety off of my Colt and said, "Don't worry. He won't be leaving this boat."

Box gasped and turned his head away. "My God."

Rick came over to where we were standing and informed us that they had lost him. I put the safety back on and holstered the Colt. Box sighed openly, sending chills down my spine. He then turned back to me and asked what he should do next. I told him to sink the vessel.

"What about the drugs? And what do we do if these bodies wash ashore?"

"Screw the coke! As for the bodies . . ." I pondered the situation, then said, "Everyone! Listen up! Quinn, you and Jesus get with Joey and sink this tug in the most efficient manner possible. No big explosions, Joey! The rest of us will strap the bodies to the ship. Use the extra sheet metal screws kept below deck." The screws were long and sharp, and they were used to fasten the half-inch metal reinforcement to the sides of the Hatteras. "We'll have to use the butts of our handguns to hammer them down. Okay, let's get it done."

We gathered fragments of wood that had been torn loose by the grenade blast and laid them across the bodies, nailing them to the ship's decking. I continued to feel like I was going to vomit at any moment, but nothing happened. A lump filled my throat and pressure stiffened my neck and jaw. I nailed frantically, swearing each time I struck my hand with the butt of my gun. I completed the vulgar task and was making my way back to our boat when I heard Box say in a loud voice, "What the hell happened to you?"

Lourdes was crying hysterically and speaking incoherently when I arrived. "My God. What happened to you?" I asked in total confusion. Lourdes was spattered with blood. Her face had streaks of blood where she had apparently rubbed it away from her eyes.

"Are you hurt? Did you cut yourself or something?"

"In here!" Rick called.

I walked into the shredded cabin and saw what it was that had shaken Lourdes so badly. The wounded captive they had attempted to revive was nailed directly to the floor. Lourdes, in a state of shock, had done it by accident, not comprehending that she was supposed to lay the wood across the body and nail the wood to the deck. Everyone was sympathetic to Lourdes and did their best to comfort her. Rick led her off the ship and gave her a sedative from the first-aid kit.

Quinn, now in snorkel gear, popped up from below the waterline, where she and Jesus had been working. "Jesus is placing the last explosive charge below the engine bay. We'll have five minutes to get clear. Are we ready?"

"Yeah," I answered.

"Good. I'll give him the go-ahead."

We moved our ship away from the crippled vessel and waited for the explosion. A muffled, dull thump and then another could be felt as well as heard. Then the *Lazy Lady* slipped beneath the waves without fanfare, anticlimactically.

"We should say something. They were people, you know," Lourdes said. Tears streamed brightly down her cheeks. She repeated, "We should say something."

Christina bowed her head, glancing up to verify that we had done the same. With a cracking voice, she led us in the Lord's Prayer. We were of one voice, except the part where we asked for forgiveness; half said "trespasses" and half said "debts." After we finished, Joey commented sharply, "This doesn't mean I want forgiveness. We did what was right . . . what was necessary. They fired first; we just defended ourselves." No one spoke in rebuttal, not because we agreed with him, but rather because we were too mentally and emotionally exhausted for confrontation.

Box and I stood on deck, leaning against the rail as Debara throttled up the engines. "What's that in your hand?" Box asked.

It was the remote-control joy stick for the submarine I had removed from the *Lazy Lady II*. I held it up at eye level and said, "It's worth eight men dying for." I then dropped it over the side of the ship.

"I don't think that was such a good idea. Washington may have wanted that coke for somethin'," Box said without conviction.

"It's my ball, and Cuba can't play."

"Would you have done it?" Box asked, seemingly unable to free his mind of the thought of me almost shooting the man our team had so unselfishly attempted to revive.

"I guess we'll never know," I said, unwilling to face the philosophical dilemma his question raised.

The mood on board became somber. Only Debara and Steven spoke, and only as their work necessitated. A few hours into the voyage home, Box informed us that we would remain at sea for the evening and would sleep on board. Most of us piled into the cabin, sleeping anywhere we could find room. Box and I opted for the stars.

I hoped to find solace there but instead found myself as a frightened young man who wanted nothing more than to be a little boy again. For a moment, I could even hear my mom calling my brothers and me for dinner: "Dannnny! Bennnny! Kennnny! Time for dinner, boys!" If only for a brief moment, it gave me comfort. After a restless night, when I rose the next morning I returned to form, denying the importance of my fears and consternation.

The Hatteras's lead-pitted hull made it too risky to chance taking it through U.S.-patrolled waters, so Steven radioed for a swap. A similar craft headed out of Ensenada, Baja California, and met us halfway up the coast. The two-member crew received a technical briefing on our ship from Debara, and they made the exchange in a matter of minutes. Their attitude led me to believe that they were contract agents, doing what they were paid to do without question. We never even traded greetings.

By the time we got back to Imperial Beach, more than twenty-four hours had passed since we set out on the mission. Debara cut the engines when we came within a mile of the coast. As we waited for the rubber craft that would take us to shore, Box tried his best to ease our consciences.

"If they were willing to kill *us*, don't you think they would have killed anyone who got in their way? You have no right to hang your heads! You risked your asses out there. You didn't do it for yourselves. You did it for people you'll never even meet. People who would otherwise spit in your face. Now we have a job to do, damn it! Who wants to see this through to the end?"

"When's our next mission, home boy?" I answered with bravado in an effort to convince the others of my unwavering certitude. "Hey look, guys," I continued as I stepped to the fore and placed my hand on Boxer's shoulder. "We can mope around for the rest of our lives mourning the deaths of these people if we somehow feel it'll ease our guilt, but it won't change one simple fact." I walked to the side of the boat and pointed out to sea, saying, "Those people are killing a lot of our people with the junk they're hauling, and we're the only buffer in between! So if you want to feel pity for those bastards, go right ahead! But some day, when you're crying in you're corn puffs about how the neighborhood's gone to shit, just remember you had an opportunity to do something about it. But like so many apathetic, belly aching . . ."

"Okay, Gipper, enough already," Lourdes interrupted with a surprisingly flippant tone. "Count me in."

"If you promise not to finish the speech, I'm in too," Christina followed.

Everyone huddled around Lourdes and me, as Box looked on in relief.

"When the breaks are beatin' the boys, you gotta give it all you got and win just one for the Zipper," Lourdes noted, quoting a phrase from the movie *Airplane* that seemed applicable, and immediately led everyone in a hum-along of the Notre Dame fight song.

We were hugging one another when our escorts arrived. The transition back to land was made easier knowing that we were a fully functioning unit, tested under fire. The horror of that day would never fully leave us, and any innocence we may have brought with us was now gone forever.

Over the next couple weeks, we made two more interceptions off the coast of Florida, bringing Pablo Escobar and José Ocampo to the bargaining table in Zurich. The game had finally begun.

Chapter 8

The meeting in Zurich was scheduled for the end of August, but because the logistics were compartmentalized, I didn't know who would represent the various cartels or how they would get there. I did know, however, that 4PM would be staying at the Hotel Zurich and that the drug lords' representatives would assemble at the Europa.

To determine the authenticity of all the participants, they were made to surrender their organization's shipping code symbols for a prescribed time period—generally fourteen days. The symbols were colored bar codes that large traffickers used when they allowed smaller organizations to piggyback their loads on a given shipment. A commission of high-level officers within the group of cartels controlled the use of the symbols, and they handled the symbols with the same high level of security as nuclear launch codes.

I was asleep at my girlfriend Andy's side when Box called on the secure phone. I picked up the regular phone, saying, "Hello? Hello?" The phone continued to ring. "Oh, shit." Realizing that I'd answered the wrong phone, I crawled across the floor in search of the STU III. I found it.

"Hello?" I answered.

"Secure," Box said, wanting me to secure my end.

"Secure," I responded.

"That can't be. Are you sure it says *secure*?" Box questioned. "Because mine doesn't."

"No, it doesn't say that."

"You say 'secure' only when your phone reads *secure*," he instructed. "I thought I taught you how to do this! Did you turn the damn key?"

"Yeah. Nothing's happening."

"How 'bout the secure button? Did you press it?"

"Yes! The thing doesn't work."

"Who you talking to?" Andy asked, half asleep.

"You're not alone?" Box questioned.

"Like you *are*?" I said, quickly pointing out the hypocrisy of his position.

"That's different. I have a committed . . . Forget that! This isn't working. Hang up. I'll call you on your other phone."

"What! That's the dumbest thing I've ever heard. Hello? Box?" Now talking to myself, I muttered, "The dumb shit hung up on me." The other phone rang.

"Helloooo?"

"Does she know you have a Stew?"

"No. It's dark, she's drunk, and it's hidden beneath my dresser. Do you realize how ridiculous we must look? What's the difference between talking on a nonsecure phone and a secure phone that won't secure? And who the hell gives a rat's root what I say on the phone in the first place?"

"I just like to do things right. I'll see you in Paducah on Friday."

"It's a date."

* * *

I met Box at the Paducah Airport, where we boarded a T-39 aircraft bound for Andrews Air Force Base, Washington, DC. Accompanying us on the trip to Zurich were Christina, Joey and Debara. The five of us were the sole negotiators representing U.S. interests in this very unorthodox and politically sensitive meeting. This was to limit our exposure. In the remote chance that anyone found out about the mission, we had considerable plausible deniability, and if discovered, we were drug smugglers. An Air Force C-5 transport took us across the pond to Ramstein Air Force Base in Frankfurt, West Germany. More so than on previous missions, Box insisted that I not enter into any revealing conversations with the other passengers on board. I was surprised to see the number of people in civilian clothes. Box told me that military personnel and their families travel cheaply on such flights, although it frequently required waiting patiently for space to become available.

At Customs we went to the U.S. military checkpoint. Box flashed his identification and an official passport at the agent in charge and touched each of us to signify that we were accompanying him. On the way to the C-5 transport I wrested the ID and passport from his clutches. The identification was authentic CIA, and I was quite impressed. One of the last pages of the passport read:

THE BEARER IS ABROAD ON AN OFFICIAL ASSIGNMENT FOR
THE GOVERNMENT OF THE UNITED STATES OF AMERICA.

Box lunged at me halfheartedly several times in an effort to retrieve his prized possessions. "Fine," he said. "You've had your fun, now give 'em back. Come on. Before you lose the damn things!"

"Why don't I get a CIA ID?"

"Keep it down! You don't know who might be listening," Box, now worried, insisted.

"Yeah, we wouldn't want anyone thinking you're a real secret agent. Actually, maybe we would. It might give 'em a false sense of security."

"Funny. Very funny. You wanna know why they don't give you an ID? Because you'd be whipping it out every time you saw a pretty woman. Who would be safe?"

"Your wife?"

Box stared at me, resisting a smile. "Give me that," he said with a snicker, and grabbed the ID and passport from my hand.

As unthreatening as this conversation was, it made me realize that I'd be left flapping in the wind if this operation blew up in our faces. Box, on the other hand, was a card-carrying agent, so he was covered.

If anyone were to inquire, I was to say that my father was an active-duty colonel in the U.S. Army. With my hair long and unmilitarylike, people would expect my knowledge of military matters to be somewhat lacking. After about ten minutes in the air, I became bored. Invariably, this meant that I had to get to know the person sitting next to me. Box sat on my right, and I already knew him, so I turned to my left, where Joey happened to be sitting. His rather questionable sexual persuasion, and my need to know, prompted some rather probing and revealing questions.

"So, Joey. You gay?" I asked bluntly.

"What kind of question is that? What the hell business is it of yours, anyhow?"

"Oh, it's not a business question. I wanna know for personal reasons."

"You're gay?" Christina joined in with humor. She sat directly behind me and was listening in on our conversation.

"No. Mind your own business."

Joey answered, "Let's say, for argument's sake, that I am gay. What of it? Would you be bothered by that?"

"If you mean the Phil Donahue definition of *bothered,* no. But I have to admit, it's hard to respect a man when you envision him down on another guy. It's definitely unnatural. Not to mention gross."

"Okay. Try picturing Steven and Quinn getting it on and tell me that ain't gross?"

I shivered like I was having an epileptic seizure. "I think I'm gonna throw up."

"Why? What's wrong with Quinn?" Box came to her defense, oblivious to the possibility that anyone might find her physically unpleasant.

"Hey, man, I'm not judging you or anything. I'm the last guy that should do that. But I don't think there's anything wrong with passing judgment on the act itself," I reasoned.

"You can't judge the action either," Christina argued.

"Tell 'em, Seedy," Debara agreed.

"Yeah, God already passed judgment on homosexuality. I suppose you have the right to quote him, though," Christina finished.

"Tell her, Seedy," I said.

"Well, if you need to know the truth, I've tried it a few times, but I don't consider myself gay," Joey said candidly.

"If you ask me, you suck one dick, you're gay," Box said with absolute finality.

"Personally, I can't imagine looking down on a naked man and saying, 'I'm just gonna try this to see if I like it.' You rob a bank, you're a bank robber. You kill a person, you're a murderer. You suck another man, you're a . . . ," I reasoned, before being interrupted.

"A sucker. Look, you can't ride the back of a sheep and then ask yourself later if you're a Bestialiter," Box said frankly, creating his own prefix.

"Oh, sick! That's almost as gross as picturing Steven and Quinn having sex," I said.

"What the hell's wrong with Quinn?" Box asked genuinely once again.

"So what would you and Box have gay men do? It's not like they decided one day to become gay. It's natural for them to want men instead of women," Debara explained.

"I'm certain if you asked the guy riding the back of a sheep he'd tell you the same thing," I reasoned glibly.

"A sheep can't consent," Debara returned.

"The infamous 'consenting adults' defense. Sounds like the argument for legalizing drugs. You're not for that too, are you?" I said, hoping to entrap her.

"Please. Not the legalizing drugs argument again." Debara threw up her arms in frustration.

"If being gay means throwing a grenade to one of us with the pin removed, then stop it. If it means handling a weapon like you did in training, then by all means . . . Well, you know. Whatever it is you guys do. But until you decide what exactly it is that you are, I don't want you seeing me naked," Box said.

"Shit. If it means never seeing you naked again, I'll go down on the next man that walks by," I said, attempting to keep the conversation light.

The conversations were absurd throughout our trip but helped pass the time. I fell asleep four hours into the flight and remained that way until we made our descent into Ramstein. The base shared a runway with the international airport, making it convenient for our short excursion into Switzerland.

Getting through West German Customs was like driving into California with a trunk full of vegetables infested with fruit flies. You simply lied to the inspector and braved it out. We flashed our slick phony passports, with their fictitious names and ten-year expiration dates, and answered the Customs agents questions as innocently and convincingly as possible. I was only asked a single question: "What is the nature of your visit to Germany?" The answer was simple: I was abroad on a sightseeing tour with friends. The agent stamped my passport and I gallivanted past him.

Leaving Zurich International Airport, we were met by what I guessed was a U.S. military man in civilian clothing. In his early forties, he was tightly groomed and regimental. He recognized Box, which triggered images in my mind of clandestine meetings between Box and faceless agents throughout the world. He certainly knew Zurich. He gave us a grand tour of the city, starting with a short ride on the N1 to University Street, then crossing over the Limmat Quai (named for the River Limmat), where, just a few blocks to our left, in the theater district, was the Hotel Europa, temporary home of the drug lords' representatives. We continued on to the north end of Lake Zurich, where we turned onto the Bahnhostrasse, or shopping street. We then entered the main banking district and headed toward the Union Bank of Switzerland. The Union Bank is built underground, just below the main railway station, in a place called "Shopville." Box made a large cash withdrawal while the rest of us found relief in the public restrooms.

Our guide led us back up the Bahnhostrasse toward the Hotel Zurich. Although the temperature was a bit brisk, it certainly didn't deter the tourists from shopping. The thing I noticed immediately was the elegance and the cleanliness of the area. Most of the people strolling the street were window shoppers, not unlike the crowds who visited Rodeo Drive in Beverly Hills. After salivating over luxury items we could never afford, Box took us to a store that featured obscenely expensive suits, leathers and furs.

"Joey. Ves. You two pick suits of a conservative nature and get 'em fitted," Box said.

"How 'bout you?" Joey asked Box. I just stood there with a dumb look on my face.

"How 'bout us?" Debara followed quickly.

"Just these two," Box curtly reiterated. "I guarantee you that if we open Joey's suitcase right now, we'll get retina damage from the silk suits and patent leather shoes, and that's the wrong look for the folks we're dealing with."

"What's wrong with what I brought?" I said, somewhat embarrassed.

"Oh, please. Don't get me started. What is it this time, Big Daddy Cane or Scar Face?"

"Neither. And you're not gonna turn me into a Boxito." I added the "ito" to Boxer's name to sarcastically protest his treating me like a child. He understood the reference, having only weeks earlier been thoroughly briefed on Fabito ("Little Fabio") Ochoa.

"What's wrong with the way I dress?" Box felt the tables turning.

"I'm a now, eighties kinda guy. You're a then, seventies kinda guy. I'm flash. You're listless. I'm outgoing. You're . . . You're . . . catatonic. I'm funny. You're . . . You're not. I'm . . ."

Box stopped me. "I get it. I get it." He stared at me, and then through me. A few seconds passed, and then he said, "Why do you get to be all the good things? Catatonic? Where the hell did you come up with that?"

"Mark Rizzo," I conceded.

"The red head from Bellingham?"

"No, the Mafia Don from Philadelphia. Of course from Bellingham, you idiot."

"Remind me to have him audited," Box said straightfaced, fighting back a grin.

* * *

The Hotel Zurich, situated at the confluence of the Limmat and Sihl rivers, was rated five stars, of course, and was one of the most contemporary in all of Zurich. The facade was sheathed in glass, and I could see the wavy reflections of water and lights dancing off the windows. It was now evening, and more than twenty-four hours had passed since I left Paducah. At this point I was starving, having only eaten airline food and snacks for a day and a half. We ate at the hotel, which served fine Swiss cuisine. I had veal and mushrooms, smothered in a creamy white wine sauce.

The agency had reserved a conference room in the hotel for our meeting. Box would lay out the technical details of the proposed operation, and I would get involved if any disputes arose and attempt to resolve them in favor of U.S. interests. Christina would translate. We brought only one translator to avoid any attempts on the part of the cocaine traffickers to divide us on points of definition or meaning or any other issue. Joey would negotiate side matters with Mafia representatives, who would distribute many of the drugs allowed into the country. Debara's role could best be described as feminine persuasion. If her beauty, and not her mind, could be used to swing the pendulum in our favor when one of the drug lords teetered on the brink of indecision, then her presence was vital. This was not a game of political correctness.

At precisely 8:00 A.M. following morning, when we entered the meeting room, the place was already filled and everyone was helping themselves to breakfast from an abundant buffet. No one wore suits. If I hadn't known better, I would have thought it was the gathering of a bowling league. A number of them were American, and they weren't all men. Obviously, a pretty woman was considered a prudent addition by the drug entourage as well.

The room gradually quieted as our guests took notice of us standing in the doorway. As I gazed at our captive audience, I turned my head momentarily toward Box and said, "You must get this a lot when you enter a room," a comical allusion to the fact that there were no black people among our counterparts.

"I can handle it," Box asserted. He then glanced at me, saying, "You're in charge."

"What?" I blurted out.

"We can't take the chance that these people don't deal with black men. You're in charge. I'll advise you if it gets too sticky."

"I would consider now to be too sticky," I said anxiously, but Box had charged off across the room, weaving his way through the crowd. He stretched his arms overhead to make himself thinner and slip sideways past the final group. "Where the hell do you think you're goin'? Hey! Get back here! I'm in charge!"

"Come here! I want you to meet someone!" Box called out from across the room. As I approached, I was taken aback by the familiarity Box demonstrated toward the sophisticated looking, gray-haired gentleman he had summoned me to greet. He was the same height as Box, and quite svelte for a man of his age. As I stepped forward to shake his hand, Box said, "John Hull, this is Anthony Vesbucci. Ves, this guy and I go way back. He's here because both sides trust him. It's the *campesinos'* (*coca* farmers) way of ensuring we're who we say we are, also."

John Hull ran a small cocaine operation from a plantation out of northern Costa Rica. His plantation included a sizable runway—it would even accommodate large military aircraft—and the United States government, although fully cognizant of Hull's involvement in the cocaine trade, helped construct it because of the support he provided to the Nicaraguan Contras. Costa Rica's northern neighbor was evidently more threatening to our government than the insidious cocaine trade, and they utilized Hull's runway to fly in supplies for Contras and to insert Contra troops back into the field after they completed paramilitary training in the Costa Rican jungles. John Hull was a man who knew how to appease all camps. I would eventually learn that you couldn't sic the neighbor's dog on the enemy without getting bit as well.

"So, whatta ya think of our little get together here?" I asked.

"I'm not sure what to think yet. It all sounds a bit rogue to me. Of course, it mustn't be any more off-black [gray] than the little matter on my *coca* plantation. Huh boys?"

"I'm sorry. Did you say *coca* . . ." I started, but Box interrupted.

"Ahh. So! Ahh. We should probably get this thing rolling. If you'll excuse us, Mr. Hull."

As we made our way to the front of the room, Box explained himself. "Take a good look around you. These people are all connected to the drug trade in one form or another. Maybe you forgot that somewhere between the caviar and the crumpets . . ."

"They have crumpets?"

"No! I don't know. The point is, what the heck were you acting so shocked about back there. Of course he has a drug farm."

"Plantation," I corrected. "But you aren't friends with all the other farmers?"

"Well, someday you're gonna be explaining to some young agent why you're friends with Don Fabio Ochoa."

"I suppose. But I still want an explanation sometime."

"Fine. Get your mind on this now. It's time," advised Box.

* * *

Box distributed information folders to each of the representative groups and then made his way back to the front of the room, where he pulled down a large screen. Although I was supposed to be the one doing all this, I stood in place, awaiting some indication from Box as to what I was supposed to do. Box dimmed the lights in the room and turned on an overhead projector. The room became deafeningly silent.

"What are you waiting for?" Box whispered.

"A clue," I whispered back.

"Read the slide and wing it."

I knew that once I got the ball rolling, I could improvise my way through the briefing and the negotiations. I walked over and turned the lights back up. Box remained calm, but his face was drawn with concern. I wanted to get a quick gander at the folders Box had passed out, but I didn't want our guests to become alarmed at my lack of familiarity. I borrowed a folder from Luis Porto, the Peruvian drug baron, and brought it with me to the podium at the front of the room. After glancing at the contents, a matter of critical importance occurred to me. In addition to detailed information about aircraft modifications, IFF transponders, changes in codes, and intercept processes, the folder included several sheets of ordinary notebook paper and a cheap fountain pen.

"Ladies and gentlemen," I began, then read as much of the folder as I could while I spoke. "The contents of this folder are classified," I said, and Christina translated for our non–English-speaking guests, even though each group of representatives came prepared with its own translator and negotiator. "If you need to take notes, paper and a writing instrument have been provided. You will not be allowed to take any part of this document with you when you leave." Under normal circumstances, notes taken during a classified meeting would fall under the same classification as the meeting itself. However, in this instance we weren't concerned if the representatives lost their notes. We only worried about a trail of evidence leading back to the CIA. Everyone felt that handwritten notes could never be considered credible documentation for such an accusation.

"I want you to study the aircraft modification schedule included in your package. We would prefer you not to fly any aircraft into the U.S. from outside our borders at this point." The package did not address the question of where the planes would come from. I just assumed it would cut down on logistical problems.

"So, I would suggest a little capital investment at this point, if you don't already have a few aircraft in the United States." Everyone laughed, men first, except for us. I figured this meant that they already had lots of drug planes in our country. "I guess we won't have to worry about the section on 'Filing Flight Plans' then." They laughed once again.

"We'll equip your aircraft with transponders in Mena, Arkansas." I heard "Mena" repeated throughout the room accompanied by chuckling. "Stop me if I hit a subject you know nothing about," I said sarcastically. I was amazed at how smoothly it seemed to be going.

"Whatever aircraft you own right now and have in your own country, if you fly them to Mr. Hull's plantation in Costa Rica with your personnel, we will have a team of ours there to modify your planes." I committed John Hull to deeper involvement in the operation than he had before the meeting, although I wasn't quite sure why I felt it necessary to do so, other than the fact that we could more closely monitor his activities if we had CIA personnel on the ground there on a regular basis. Many heads turned toward Hull to see if he acknowledged the arrangement. Hull regarded me impassively, but gently pretended to tip the brim of a hat.

Each camp huddled in discussion as they carefully considered every nuance of the proposed deal. Altogether it covered sixty-two points. It was so detailed that when I read it I almost forgot what it was we were forming an alliance for.

When questions arose or an organization wanted to make changes, a representative would approach the table where we sat and request a parlay at their table. Invariably, it was the female who approached us. She would then escort us to her table, where I would negotiate with the English-speaking representative. If a question came up that involved the entire group and not just a single camp, then the woman from the camp raising the question would stand and wait for us to recognize her. Once we did, the English-speaking representative would ask the question in open forum. For the most part, everyone worked within the parameters of the extremely tight and condensed schedule, and the group reached consensus remarkably quickly and smoothly.

Luis Porto's and Roberto Suarez's organizations from Bolivia were elated with the final arrangement. They would produce most of the *coca* paste in South America, and would do so predominantly with their own crops. The climate, rainfall, and altitude of Peru and Bolivia produce the richest plant in the world, and for this reason, the Colombians were pleased to receive the paste from there. The fact that the Peruvians and Bolivians would no longer pose a competitive threat to their business also pleased the Colombians. For their part, the Porto and Suarez camps were happy not to have to fly drugs into America and face the possibility of arrest or extradition for drug trafficking.

Despite the prevailing mood of cooperation, there were still a few hurdles to surmount, but none was as difficult or acrimonious as the amount of drugs to be seized.

A short, somewhat pudgy Hispanic woman stood and cleared her throat. Her face was squeezably cute, but more like a puppy dog than a siren. She acted mild-mannered and polite, and I surmised from that she must be the sister of someone important.

"Yes, we recognize the distinguished emissaries from Puerto Triunfo," I said. Puerto Triunfo is some one hundred miles east of Medellin, Colombia, on the Magdalena River, and Pablo Escobar kept a palatial estate there.

A man with a southern accent rose to his feet, and with his hands bracing himself as he leaned over the table, he said in a cocky manner, "You expect us to just hand you half of our drugs? You must be crazy. Do you have any comprehension as to how much that is? We figure you're getting about two percent now, so we'll give you fifteen."

"If the fifty percent that we take is a large amount of money, then the fifty percent you get to keep is a lot also. Except now Mr. Escobar won't have to live looking over his shoulder all the time," I countered.

"We see what's gonna happen. Y'all take the fifty and tip the DEA off to another twenty-five or so more."

"If the DEA, or anyone else, intercepts a shipment coming through one of our safe corridors, then we will count that toward the fifty percent. But if you get caught running a shipment outside the guidelines of PM, you're on your own," I answered.

"We still think we're getting the short end of the stick. You'll have to do better, or count us out. And if we go, you can bet the others will too."

"Where you from?" Debara demanded.

"Excuse me? You don't speak to me unless I speak to you first. Do you understand me?" the southerner said pompously.

Debara climbed over our table, walked briskly across the room, and leaned over the man's table, getting in his face. Box jumped from his seat, but the grip I had on his suit coat restrained him. Debara said firmly, "I'll beat you like a red-headed step-daughter. Now sit!" She stepped back and continued, "It's simple, people! We can fill this room with organizations who would gladly hunt you down for a much smaller chunk of the market share. Now the way we see it, how Don Fabio goes, so goes everyone else. Not Escobar! So if anyone here is not pleased with our offer, leave now! But realize, we'll be giving everyone that stays the necessary information to destroy your boss's empire. If you doubt the Company's resolve, or its ability to wreak havoc on your lives, just take a close look at what we did in Vietnam. We'll work with you on all the logistical matters, but not the end result. Now, any more questions?"

"We're leaving. I won't have this *woman* speak to me in this manner," the southerner said, talking down his nose at Debara.

"Maybe you don't treat your women as equals in Colombia, but we sure as hell don't have them around as window dressing in the CIA. You want in on this? You have to make her happy first. We're not begging your participation in this! We're offering it. Now get your ass outta here, before I throw you out," I said in support of Debara, even though I wasn't convinced that she had made the right call.

"Fine! Good luck tryin' to make this work without us," he said threateningly. As he stood to leave, it was obvious that he had no support from his colleagues. The Colombian who accompanied him made a hasty appraisal of the situation and, to save face, said, "Sit!" sharply in English.

"Seedy, translate," I said anxiously.

"My American friend does not speak for the Godfather," the Colombian began.

"The Godfather?" I inadvertently blurted out.

"Yes," he responded, still being translated. "The numbers look real good to me. You must excuse my friend's ignorance. He doesn't know much about our culture. We respect our women." Now turning to face Debara, he continued, "Please excuse his rude behavior. You are a very strong and noble woman. Very intuitive. My apology."

He then said to me, "Come through with the weapons and reports, and we will make good on our bargain." He shook my hand, gripping my elbow with his free hand.

* * *

In this one meeting, we had accomplished all of our goals and the deal was set. Peru and Bolivia were virtually neutralized as cocaine traffickers, and Carlos Lehder would offset the Cuban drug trade. In effect, we had centralized the Colombian cocaine market and shrunk it in half. Not bad for four hours' work.

After bidding everyone good-bye, we stepped back from the events of the day to unwind. It was only then that I noticed Joey was missing. "Where the hell is Joey?" I inquired.

"He's off wining and dining his Cosa Nostra buddies," Box responded.

"Amazing. We're in Switzerland, saying 'Cosa Nostra' and 'CIA' like others say 'Moose Lodge' and 'PTL.' Somethin' doesn't seem quite right about that. Not sure what it is, but it doesn't sound quite right."

We went outside and strolled the neighborhood talking about things to come. The mood was light in the aftermath of the day's intense negotiations, and we all felt as if a burden had been lifted from our shoulders. We also shared a sense of unreality.

"I keep pinching myself," remarked Debara. "It's mind boggling what we've done here."

"Speaking of doing. Damn good job in there today. You brought us over the top, you know," I said.

"Not that I need your approval, but thanks."

"You know, one of these days that chip's gonna fall off your shoulder and break your foot," Box said.

"I'm sorry," Debara conceded. "You're right. I just don't want you to think I did all that to prove I was equal or something."

"What? You think men don't have to prove themselves? Not a day goes by that I don't feel I have to prove myself. Being female doesn't give you sole claim to that insecurity," I reacted.

Now speaking directly to me, she said, "Who do you have to prove yourself to?"

"You for one. Box. He won't ever feel comfortable around me."

"I'll settle for safe," Box said.

"That stuff about women not bein' window dressing. Were you serious?" Debara asked me.

"Hey, I don't particularly care about roles. I'd run naked through the Mormon Tabernacle if I thought it would help reduce the drug problem," I answered.

"That would just increase drug use," Christina joked.

"You know, with all our differences, we sure don't differ on this. I want Pseudo Miranda to work so bad . . . so damn bad," Debara said. Then she looked at me and asked, "What? Why are you smiling? What?" she repeated while biting her bottom lip.

"Nothing. It's just that whenever someone says 'Pseudo Miranda,' it blows my mind. I came up with that name, you know," I said.

"Oh, come on! Now you're gonna claim you named the operation too? Box?" Debara said, flabbergasted.

"Yeah, the shithead did," Box answered, then qualified his remark, saying, "He was screwing around at the time. 'Pseudo Miranda' just came out with all the other spew. It's a stupid name, I think."

"Where did you come up with it?" Christina asked.

"I thought *pseudo* was the ultimate in fake. People who use words like *pseudo* instead of *fake* are really phony themselves. So *pseudo* is the phoniest of fake words. I added *Miranda* because of the Supreme Court decision associated with constitutional protections against legal persecution. Also, Miranda himself was Latino, which I thought was appropriate," I explained.

"You are so full of shit! I was standing right next to you the whole time! He just blurted it out without thinking. He makes it sound like he was sitting in a think tank or something. Boy, I'll tell ya. You're gonna talk your way right into the presidency some day. Legal persecution. Give me a break," Box chided.

"Don't listen to him," I retorted. I leaned toward Christina and Debara and whispered, "He has this major jealousy thing goin' on. You have to feed his ego."

"You two crack me up," Debara said as she gazed at the Limmat River.

I silently regarded her and my other friends as they stared quietly at the running water. Their faces looked so young, and I knew they wouldn't remain so for very long. I studied their features, not wanting ever to forget their faces while they still had that glow. I came to value this moment of innocence more and more with the passage of time.

On the way back to the hotel, Debara asked Box if anyone had thought about the heroin problem. She was concerned that a decrease in the cocaine supply would somehow stimulate the demand for opiates.

"As we speak, Lance Motley is meeting with Khun Sa somewhere here in Zurich," Box said.

"Lance . . . ," I repeated, fishing my memory for his name.

". . . Motley," Box replied, filling in the blank with a tone of voice that implied I should know him.

". . . Is meeting with . . ."

"Khun Sa. Oh. Maybe I forgot to tell you about this. Yeah, well anyway, Lance Motley—who I can't stand, by the way—is sort of a soldier of fortune. He's been a hired gun in Southeast Asia since Vietnam. Khun Sa and he have had a business relationship for years. Hence his being hired for this operation."

"Who the hell is Khun Sa?" I asked.

"How the hell did you get chosen for this operation? You mean to tell me you don't know who Khun Sa is?" Box asked in disbelief.

"Why would a guy who grew up in Hopunk, Taxachusetts, and schooled in Possum Creek, Kentucky, know an Asian farmer from . . . where the hell's he from?"

"Asia," Box said without emotion.

"What part of Asia?" I asked impatiently.

"Burma," he said impatiently. He began to scratch his head. "Every time I begin to feel confident in your command of the situation something like this comes up," Box said, then he smiled and shook his head. We continued walking.

"So why do you hate this guy Motley?" Christina inquired.

"Sure as we're standing here," Box said, "he'll be making money hand over fist in the heroin trade. He has no particular allegiance to America. He's in it for the money. And he'd slit his mother's throat for a few more pounds of it. The problem is, the CIA needed someone who Khun Sa trusted."

"Why didn't they hire someone trusted by Ochoa or Escobar if that was so damn important?" asked Debara.

"Are you kidding? We'll never meet any of those people. We'll never even get close to them. No, I'm afraid this is as close as we get," Box stated.

It didn't matter. If we could get fifty percent of their drugs, that would be close enough for me. We met up with Joey for our trip home. He'd done nothing but party with his nameless Mafia buddies all day. Whenever I asked him about it, he would tell me that it was a Sicilian thing and that I wouldn't understand.

On the flight home we slept. I awoke periodically with that "I think I left the stove on" feeling. It didn't seem possible that we had accomplished all that we needed to in such a short period of time. I was sure that as we moved through the different phases of the operation, it would be necessary to continually modify it. If I only knew how much modifying was needed.

Chapter 9

When I returned to Murray, I wanted more than anything to meld back into the mainstream and enjoy an interlude of normal life before Box summoned me on the first mission under the new PM protocol. Unfortunately, I received some information that rocked me to my foundation: I got a D in Italian. So much for success in studying my "native tongue." It was becoming clear that my life was fragmented and discontinuous, rather like a series of snapshots in a photo album, with each page representing a profound change.

Box startled me one beautiful September afternoon as I sat on the green staircase of grassy hills overlooking the Murray State University baseball field, dreaming of what might have been, had I traveled a different path.

"What in the world are you doin' here?" I asked him somewhat nervously. "What if someone sees you?"

"What if? Who cares. As far as anyone's concerned, I'm a friend."

"Are you?" I retorted.

"What? A friend?" he replied, pausing for a response from me.

"Yeah, you are."

He said softly, "So why are you here? Why alone?"

"I was a pretty good pitcher, you know. My father taught me." I tossed some grass into the air. "Boy, could I throw a baseball."

"Ninety-something miles an hour, the way I hear it."

"How the hell did you . . . Oh, yeah. How stupid of me." I almost forgot who I was talking to. "I just don't ever wanna be a coulda been. No regrets. You know?"

"You'll always have regrets. Be content to look back and know you did your best. In fact, be content to be able to look back at all."

"You sound like you know something I don't."

"Oh, you know all right. You just chose to ignore the warning," Box declared. "Do you remember the shit in Tonopah about having a special burden to succeed? You remember that?"

"Yeah. So?"

"We knew about Pseudo Miranda. If we had failed in training . . . Well, you know what I'm gettin' at. They couldn't afford to have us running around with that information. It's damn lucky we made it through there, that's all."

"Come on, Box. Come on, man. No fuckin' way they'd kill us."

He didn't say anything in reply, but the somber way he regarded me spoke volumes.

"Son of a bitch."

I picked myself up from the grass and said, "You hungry?"

"Enough to eat a horned cow."

"Cows have horns. It just so happens that bulls do too. Which, I might add, segues nicely into where we're going for lunch."

"That means steak, right?"

"Sort of."

I took Box to my favorite restaurant, McDonalds. As we pulled into the parking lot, he shook his head in disappointment. "I should have known. What does this have to do with beef?"

"It doesn't. But a lot of cute college girls come here. And the food ain't bad either." We were about to enter the restaurant when I noticed two women on horseback. Even in Murray, this was a bit unusual. I tapped Box on the shoulder and asked him to follow me. After some friendly negotiating, we were ready to ride.

"Mount up," I said.

"Why?" he asked. "What in the world would possess you to get on that thing? We're in a parking lot, for God's sake."

Box spun around toward my Corvette. "They're taking your car by the way. Of course, you probably knew that. I'm sure it has something to with you sitting on the back of that damned thing."

"It's a horse, not a thing. Mount up. The girls said we could take 'em through the drive-through, but no further."

"The drive-through? We're going through the . . ." Box pointed to the drive-through, ". . . on these? Have you ever ridden before?" Box asked as he mounted the horse.

"No. I told her I had, but no, I never have. It's not like we have to break 'em or anything. I've watched 'Bonanza.' You steer 'em with these."

"Those are the reins. Even I know that."

I gave the horse a little nudge with my feet, and he miraculously began to move. "Oh my God, he's movin'! Look Box! I'm riding a horse! Yee ha!" The horse was only walking slowly, but I was overwhelmed by the novelty of it. Boxer's horse began to move at the same languid pace as my own, bringing creases of joy to his face.

"Giddy-up! Giddy-up! This is great!" he cried.

Even though our horses never moved faster than a walk, we were ecstatic they went in the direction we wanted them to. We pulled up the horses at the drive-through speaker and ordered our food like we imagined a Texan would have. I was first.

"Howdy, ma'am. I would be mighty pleased if you would be kind enough to get me some of them there fries you're a serving up at this here fine diner of yours. It'd be mighty hospitable of ya to fire me up a couple burgers on the griddle, too, and toss a hunk of cheese on 'em while you're at it."

The girl taking orders at the drive-through window could see us clearly, and responded, "Would ya like anything to drink with that, Little Joe?"

Box leaned over his mount and answered, "You're darn tootin' we want some beverage with our slop. But first, burn the moo outta a couple more burgers. And throw in one of those cute little apple fritters of yours. We'll be washin' our chow down with a couple of large Diet Cokes." Box leaned over and hugged his horse, kissing him on the neck.

"I need to get me a cowboy hat," he said ardently.

Under my breath, I said, "Two minutes on a horse, and he's John Wayne."

"What?"

"You should. You'd look good in a hat," I answered.

"I would, wouldn't I?"

* * *

I knew, of course, why Box had come. It was time for Operation Lighthouse, our first Pseudo Miranda mission. We were going to drive directly to Paducah Airport, and, with just the clothes on our backs, fly to southern Texas.

"What about my gun and stuff?"

"What about 'em?" Box answered.

"I don't have them. They're at home."

"Don't worry. Everything you need will be given to you in Mena, Arkansas, or Hondo, Texas."

"Well, which is it? Mena or Hondo?"

"I'm not sure."

"Oh, that's real comforting."

"Don't panic," Box said with a laugh. "It's just an in-country intercept. You won't even need a weapon. Only Joey will be armed. That way, if for some bizarre reason another policing force catches us, we won't have a lot of weapons to stash."

"Why have any weapons at all, then?"

"In case the people that catch us aren't the police."

"You mean we kill some poor bastard who has the terrible misfortune of happening upon us?"

"Where we're goin', no one's gonna just happen upon us."

"Fine. But in the future, let me know in advance when we're gonna be up all night so I can plan my sleep around it."

"Don't worry about that. We've got pills."

"Fantastic. You've got pills. I thought we were in the business of stemming drug use."

"These are prescription. You know . . . legal."

"Good. I'm sure my body'll know the difference."

*   *   *

We flew out of Paducah shortly before dusk, refueling in Mena before continuing on to Hondo. I would not get a good look at either airport at this juncture, due to the darkness that blanketed both airstrips. Inside a small aircraft hanger at Hondo, we met up with the other team members. Of the eleven agents who worked the pre–Pseudo Miranda interceptions, all were there except for Christina and Chavez. We suited up in camouflage fatigues and flak vests. Steven carried a miniature satellite dish and connecting phone, linked by several feet of cord. Joey was armed with a 30/30 hunting rifle but no grenades. We were each given a pair of ice hooks to make lifting and handling the cocaine easier.

A pair of Huey helicopters transported the nine of us to a location some eighty miles northeast of Laredo near the Nueces River. When we arrived, I was taken aback by the absolute darkness that enveloped us. The choppers departed, leaving me feeling abandoned. I wondered if anyone knew what we were supposed to do. I, for one, had no idea. I understood that our forces were to intercept an aircraft flying across the border and guide it over our position to release its cargo, but how it would happen was beyond me.

"Where the hell are we?" I asked.

Steven unstrapped a large, square flashlight and pointed it directly in front of him. "The ILS tower should be right . . . right . . . ," he repeated as he turned 180 degrees to his left. "Right there. There she is. We're fine. The aircraft should pass directly over the tower and drop its cargo."

His light shone on a twelve-foot pole with vertical and horizontal moving arms that made it appear like some android dropped by aliens in the middle of the wide Texas desert. I gazed at it in awe, wondering about those who had come before us to set it up and those who would follow us to tear it down. Did they know its purpose? Did they comprehend the importance of their endeavor? Only Steven was unimpressed with the high technology of the system and the genius of making it mobile.

"Where should we wait?" Box asked Steven.

"Heck, right here's fine," Steven said with assurance.

We huddled snugly between several yucca plants, careful not to sit on any mounds of fire ants. We sat facing the ILS tower and spoke of the universe and all its wonder. The talk started out poetic but became more scientific when I asked Steven, our navigator, which star was the North Star. Steven scanned the brightly lit sky while the rest of us waited expectantly.

"That's strange," he said.

"What's that?" Box asked.

"That constellation should be in the south," Steven replied. He seemed confused.

"Duh. Maybe that is the south, you moron," teased Quinn.

Steven spun around and breathed a sigh of relief when he spotted the star he was looking for. "There it is."

"So that's north, then?" I asked.

"Sure is," Steven responded.

"Then we're north of the ILS, correct?" I continued.

"Shit. You're a regular Magellan," Quinn prodded.

"The reason I'm asking . . . , " I said, looking back and forth, attempting to get straight in my head what course the drug airplane would follow. "Am I wrong, or are we in the direct path of the drop?"

Now everyone was doing what I had done, only now there were eight people mumbling aloud and twirling into one another.

"What is everyone so worried about? The plane's flying up from the south. You know, from Mexico. South. We're north. He just said it. We're north," Steven confirmed, although it didn't clarify the issue.

"Everyone calm down. Steven navigated for us on the high seas several times, and I'm quite sure he can handle the situation here. This is child's play," Lourdes assured us.

"Wait," I interjected. "Everyone please bear with me for a moment. I know I may be panicking here a little, but—for me, please—one more time about that Mexico being in the south stuff, see, because the way I understand this . . . the target plane is in the south now, but it's flying north, right? And we're north of that ILS thing. So doesn't it stand to reason that it'll fly directly over our heads?" I felt a bit embarrassed raising the question since, after all, we were there carrying out a complicated and dangerous clandestine operation for the U.S. government, but none of us could readily answer this most basic question.

Box became impatient. "Steven. Look at me! What side of an ILS tracking beam does an aircraft land on?"

"This side," Debara said, sounding discouraged.

"Fine. Now where should we be sitting?" Box said, annoyed. Steven was reluctant to answer, baffled somewhat by his confusion with directions.

"On the other side of the pole," I said, as if stating the obvious.

"Let's do something, for God's sake!" Jeremiah declared.

"Yeah, let's go. He's right, we should be over there," Debara said, taking control.

We moved with little immediacy, feeling more stupid than afraid. Steven moped along, pointing his flashlight in front of us as we zig-zagged our way around the prickly plants and ant mounds to the other side of the

ILS pole. Jesus made a few rattlesnake sound effects to keep our blood pumping.

Then something split the evening sky with a loud Sssssssshhhhhewww!

"What the hell was that?" Jesus said loudly.

"The chase plane. Take cover!" Debara warned.

We scattered in all directions, not knowing which way would be the safest. I sprinted off to the right, only to stop sharply as a yucca thorn pierced my thigh. I pulled my leg back, cringing in pain, yet resisting a shriek. Steven became the brunt of profane condemnation as everyone had a similar encounter in the Texas landscape. The shouting ceased abruptly when we heard the drone of a twin-engine, propeller-driven aircraft. It sounded close.

"What the hell do we do now?" Quinn called out.

"Listen for the percussion of duffel bags of cocaine hitting the ground. If they get louder, run for your life!" Box advised.

"Which way?" Joey screamed in panic.

"Any way!" Debara yelled back.

Because the plane flew at extremely low altitude, the 200-pound, cocaine-filled duffel bags seemed to hit the ground the instant the craft passed overhead, preventing us from anticipating the drop pattern.

"Fuuuuck!" Joey screamed as a string of bags landed directly behind him. He sprinted to the side and passed within three feet of where I was standing. Although I couldn't see him clearly, I knew it was him. Then the thumps impacted loudly all around me. I stood perfectly still, waiting for the storm to pass. A breath, then a thump, another breath, another thump. Every time I took a breath I expected another thump. I heard what sounded like a vehicle skidding on dirt as a duffel bag plummeted from the sky and landed no more than ten feet in front of me. The dust it kicked up flowed over my body. I stood motionless. The plane sputtered away, the pilot not knowing what havoc he had just caused. When I could no longer hear the engines, I let my head drop forward and exhaled my pent-up breath.

Box conducted a roll call. As each person responded to his or her name, Steven shined his light at him or her to determine each one's condition. When Box called my name and I replied, the light followed a tightly spaced line of brown duffel bags to where I stood cloaked in dust. The beam of light dimmed as it met the cloud of dust particles, causing them to sparkle and flicker as they fell to the earth. Everyone slowly came into view as they gathered along the line of duffel bags and the dust settled. Box stepped in front of me, blocking the light and creating a seraphic silhouette.

"You okay?" he asked.

"Yeah," I said, not able to express the depth of my fear. The *Lazy Lady II* incident had certainly frightened me, but not to the degree that this had. I could define the enemy at sea, and they didn't attack capriciously or anonymously in the dark. Here, in the middle of the desert, there was only faith and luck. I was never very lucky, and I didn't feel that God owed me any favors.

"Well, we'd best grab this shit before our limo returns," Box said, referring to the helicopters that would soon return to take us and the cocaine to Mena. To collect the heavy bags, we formed teams of three. The middle person gaffed a bag in the center with each of his hooks, while the other two gaffed the ends. But first we had to gather up as much of the spilled cocaine as possible and resecure the ends of the duffel bags.

"Uh-oh. Holy shit," Steven said anxiously. "I'm losing feeling on the side of my face. I think I'm having a stroke!"

"Did you rub your eyes and mouth?" Quinn asked.

"What? Yeah, I think so."

"It's the coke, you moron," Quinn said, shaking her head. "You have coke on your hands."

In all, there were eight duffel bags full of pure cocaine. We piled them at the point of our arrival. The chase aircraft by now had reported back to Hondo, alerting them that the drug craft had rendezvoused with the ILS tower. Steven struggled to radio our friends in Hondo but didn't have much success.

"Carry it over there," Steven directed Jeremiah, referring to the miniature satellite dish and pointing to his left. He listened for a signal. "Hold it higher! Higher!"

Jeremiah stood on his tiptoes, aiming the dish into the vast nothingness. "Do you even have a clue what the fuck you're doin'?"

"Wait!" Steven shouted. "Holy cow. I think I've got 'em," he said softly, as if completely surprised. "Hold it steady now!" Steven then began to speak into the mike. "The CIDE (pronounced *city*) comes alive at four P.M. Over." Steven was identifying himself as the 4PM component of Central Intelligence Drug Enforcement (CIDE). Because our radio was antiquated, it could only accommodate one-way transmissions, and Steven had to say "over" whenever he completed a sentence. By saying "over," the other party in Hondo knew it was their turn to speak. If Hondo replied, "Miranda is alive and well," we knew that the operation was terminated and we were on our own.

In this instance, however, our controller in Hondo came back with, "Make it five and you've got a date," telling us that all was well. Steven then informed him that we were ready for an immediate evacuation from the drop zone.

When the choppers arrived, we scurried to load the cargo and then crammed in alongside it. The flight to Hondo was quick. We remained silent, due to fatigue and the noise of the rotor blades. Arriving in Hondo, the choppers departed hastily with the cocaine, leaving us to wait patiently in a dark hangar.

"Well, that went well," I commented, wearing a smirk of relief.

"No thanks to Steven 'I got my head up my ass' Hall. What the hell's wrong with you? How can a guy that tracks satellites not know north from south? Would ya please tell me that?" Box complained.

"I have this directional problem. If you asked me to point to a particular satellite, I could tell you where it is, and whether it's in the north, the south, or wherever. I just have problems with things that move from one point to another. Like when the weatherman says there's a southwest wind. Does that mean the wind is blowing into the southwest or from the southwest? For some reason north always seems to mean what's in front of me, and south behind me. I don't know. I have the same problem with right and left. I don't know. I'm sorry I let everyone down," Steven apologized.

"It's common sense, for cryin' out loud. You simply . . . ," Quinn started.

"It didn't seem too common this evening," I disagreed.

"No, it sure didn't!" Debara laughed. "Could you imagine what it would have been like if Facey (Bill Casey) had to be told that the operation was scrubbed because the team was squashed by falling duffel bags?" Debara lowered her voice and said, "I'm sorry, Director Casey, but, even though the unit was highly trained in guerrilla warfare tactics, we failed to teach them to find north and south."

"Quinn, you're a pilot. If anyone should have known better, it was you," Jeremiah stated.

"If I had a compass. Or if I paid attention to our flight coordinates. I just assumed the 'Old Man and the Sea' there knew what he was doin'. I didn't even pay attention until it was too late. Shit. It all happened so fast," Quinn said defensively.

"Forget it. No one's hurt. We'll learn from this," Box said with composure. "From now on, Quinn, you'll handle navigation for us on all interceptions. Bring a compass. If any of you are debriefed on your way back home from this mission, everything went smoothly. Dig?"

"Yeah, we dig your jive, turkey," Lourdes joked, not fully understanding the slang.

"Shhh. Quiet! That's it. Our rides are here. Let's rock and roll," Box ordered.

We ran onto the rough tarmac yelling farewells like relatives departing from a holiday get-together. As we split up and boarded three separate aircraft, bound for different locations, I turned to watch my friends leave. Debara turned in the hatchway of her aircraft and directed a revealing smile toward me. I smiled back, hoping more than anything that she understood. Box, looking over my shoulder, yanked me into the plane. The door closed and we were on our way.

"You and I need to talk when we get back," Box said in a businesslike manner.

"Let's talk now."

"It can wait."

"If it's about Debara, don't worry. I've got a girlfriend waiting for me in Kentucky."

"Well, it's sort of about Debara. I mean the way you two look at each other. Man! But about that girlfriend in Kentucky. Uh . . . shit, how do I say this?"

"She's cheating?"

"Yeah, I'm afraid so."

"With who?"

"Steve. The guy who sat in front of you in your Italian class."

I laughed in relief. "No way! She's always joking about him. Calling him a geek and shit."

"Well, it looks like she's screwing a geek."

"Jeez, Box, don't mete it out to me slowly, in manageable portions or anything. Is this how you tell a friend his girlfriend is being unfaithful?"

"Hey, I'm sorry. But you need to realize this job takes precedence over relationships. Now that you know about her, you can't trust her with anything. She's a security risk."

"Great. Andy's a national security problem. This sucks, you know."

"I know."

"The agency could have gotten this wrong, don't you think? I mean, they're fallible too."

"They've got pictures."

"They've got pictures? They've got fuckin' pictures. I don't believe this. Is nothing sacred? Have you seen these pictures?"

"Do you really want to know the answer to that?"

I shook my head in disbelief. "This really blows."

"I know."

"Is that all you're gonna say, I know?" Box shrugged, befuddled, so I continued. "I wanna see naked pictures of your wife."

"Excuse me. Is that what this is about? Do you think I took the pictures into the bathroom or somethin'? Look. I glanced at them just long enough to know what it was she was doin', and with who."

"So what was it she was doin'?"

"I'm not answering that. You're just gonna drive yourself crazy. The only thing that's important is that she cheated."

"Wait till I see her. And him. He's supposed to be a friend. I'm gonna rip his fuckin' head off."

"Oh, no! You can't tell them you know anything about this. When you see her, just tell her you've found someone else or something."

"I'll do my best."

"No, damn it! You'll do it. Period!"

"Is this how you'd handle it if your wife cheated on you?"

"Look. I'm sorry for sounding so cold. I just don't want you getting in trouble. Don't learn the hard way about this. People like you and me, we have to protect our identities with our lives because our lives truly depend on it." Box leaned toward me. "I know you love her. I know this won't be easy. But you have to keep your eye on the ball. She's your past. We're your future. I hate to say your country needs you, but they do. She's small town. She could never deal with what you've become, and I think you know that. Anyhow, she doesn't hold a candle to Debara."

I giggled. "Great. You sound like my mom. When my dog Gypsy died, she brought a puppy home the next day to replace her."

"Did it work?"

"Well, yeah. But . . ."

"But what? Think of Debara as a little puppy."

"I'll expect to see her on my kitchen floor when I wake up tomorrow then."

"Consider it done," Box said, leaning his head back in his seat and closing his eyes.

* * *

Morning broke while we were still in the air over Arkansas. Box awakened and began to brief me on the next mission. He told me that we would be flying into Colombia and that we would be raiding a cocaine laboratory deep inside the country. I was concerned about geographical problems that might arise, especially in light of the comical incident that had just occurred in the territorial United States and terrain that we were supposed to be familiar with. Box told me that a CIA friend of his—namely, Bob Terpening, who worked in Langley—was an expert in these matters. Box said that he was so good, in fact, that the CIA waited outside his classroom one day, just before he graduated from college in Oregon, and offered him a job. The story sounded all too familiar. Terpening was so valuable to the CIA that although he told the recruiters he would be on vacation in Mexico all summer and would be unavailable to take the position, they waited for him to return and called him the day after he got back.

Terpening allegedly prevented the U.S. military from committing a grievous error during the Vietnam conflict. The story was that we were planning to attack the Vietnamese from a certain island, but Terpening informed military intelligence that even though they had photographs of the island, it simply did not exist. The way the story went, the Vietnamese created a fake island to lure the Marines into an ambush. Box's account of this incident eased my mind quite a bit. I repeated this man's name to myself over and over, wanting to remember it in case anything went wrong. I didn't know exactly what I would—or could—do, but it seemed like a name worth remembering.

Back in Murray, I scrambled to get my affairs in order. Box told me that after we completed our mission in Colombia, I would be leaving Kentucky forever. I needed to travel light, so I arranged to have all my furniture picked up by a used furniture store. I gave my landlord two weeks notice, then I waited restlessly for the mission to begin.

I went out with Andy a few times, taking her to church on Sunday in hopes that it would prick her conscience. I figured that if she confessed her transgressions to me, it would demonstrate that her infidelity was a one-time affair. I also felt scared about the future, and I longed to have someone I could turn to who wasn't part of the operation. I suppose I hung on for all the wrong reasons. I needed her but no longer wanted her. I didn't tell her what I knew. I just didn't want to hear her say she no longer loved me.

*　*　*

Eleven of us would enter Colombia, but not all would return.

Chapter 10

I was awakened at 3:10 A.M. by the Motorola STU III secure phone hidden under my bed. The sound was penetrating even though I was still partially intoxicated. My reaction was Pavlovian. I dived from the mattress, struck my head on an end table and landed on the unforgiving hardwood floor, muttering woozily, "I'm going to regret that in the morning."

"You okay?" asked Dana, a Little Sister of the fraternity, as she leaned over the edge of the bed, clutching the sheet to her bare breasts. She was at ATO with me for a one-night stand.

"Define *okay*," I mumbled. "Yeah, I'm fine." I picked up the phone and slithered under the bed for privacy. I turned the side key.

"Secure," Boxer said at the other end. The phone displayed the verification SECURE.

"Secure."

"The city comes alive at four P.M.," Box said, informing me that the Pseudo Miranda team was to embark on our newest operation.

Dana, from above, asked, "Who the fuck is calling so late?"

"Please shut the hell up," I told her. "It's my mom."

Said Boxer, "Good ComSec, Ace." *Comsec* stood for communication security.

"Oh, yeah," I replied. "Miranda is alive and well."

"Politico," Boxer responded, using the code word that signalled the conclusion of our exchange. "Paducah Airport, five P.M. tomorrow, Vosotros. Repeat and sever."

"Paducah, five P.M., Vosotros. That's it."

"Tomorrow!"

"I thought you said 'sever'!"

I hung up and crawled back into bed. But I left space between Dana and me, both physically and mentally. I could no longer be as selfish and irresponsible as in the past, and it bothered me. I lay there motionless, thinking of my recent days in college and then to the challenges that lay ahead.

"Who's Miranda?" Dana asked petulantly. "The chick who's so lively."

"You mean my cousin?"

Dana got out of bed and started dressing. "I'm leaving," she said, skipping on one foot while attempting to lace a shoe.

"What the hell's wrong with you?"

"Do you really expect me to believe your mother called you long distance at three in the morning to talk about your Hispanic cousin? Who do you think you're talking to?"

"Rates go down this time of night."

"Bye, asshole."

"Wait! I'm just kidding!"

But Dana left. And that was, in reality, exactly what I wanted her to do.

As I drove to Paducah the following afternoon in my 1982 Corvette, I realized clearly, for the first time, that I had been trying to simultaneously go in diametrically opposite directions. The events of the night before demonstrated the futility, if not the self-deception, of trying to reconcile my past and present life.

* * *

I parked in the Puducah Airport lot in late afternoon. I met Box on the far side of the ramp, and we boarded a Titan 404 airplane parked in a remote corner of the airfield, from which we took off immediately, bound for Mena and Operation Vosotros.

Vosotros, meaning "you" in Spanish, was the fitting counterpoint to the Colombian drug lords' alliance, called *Nosotros,* meaning "us." As in Operation Lighthouse, the code name for missions involving interception of Colombian aircraft flying into the U.S., Vosotros was a component of Pseudo Miranda and therefore mutually beneficial to both sides. Unlike

Lighthouse, however, Vosotros operations were conducted outside U.S. borders, making them far more precarious.

When Boxer and I landed in Mena, we met up with Jeremiah, Lourdes, Rick and Christina.

"Remember, Booch," Lourdes warned me condescendingly, "don't speak to anyone."

"But, ma'am!" I protested sarcastically. We all were outside on the airstrip, standing beside the C-130 Hercules military transport that would take us into Colombia. The weather was mild and breezy, with the temperature in the seventies.

"Loosen up, girl," Rick said to Lourdes.

I strolled over to a small tin building painted green. The roof sprouted numerous antennas, which were searching, I decided, for signals from all points of the globe. Just behind a cluster of similar small structures stood satellite dishes of various sizes. I entered the green building, startling a man working inside. He was so thin you could see his skeleton through his clothes. He wore glasses and a button-down white shirt. His pants were oversized, baggy and pleated.

"Close the damn door!" he exploded. "This room has to maintain a steady temperature of 72 degrees." I ignored his reaction to my intrusion and matter-of-factly tried to convey to him a sense of my authority.

I said, "Quite an operation you've got here. You've been handling all our communiqués." I read the name of a piece of equipment off its base to buy time and to avoid getting an ugly reprimand if he activated an intruder alarm. "So this is the KG-84 cryptographic machine I've heard so much about."

I continued to talk as I moved around the room, searching for a logical transition out the door. Then on the wall I saw a Safe Driver's Program Award that the man had obviously received. I walked over to him, shook his hand and said, "Mr. Brown, Equatorial Communications is damned proud to have you represent us in such a distinguished fashion. Mr. Casey himself has made laudable comments about you. I just want you to know that you make us all look good. So . . . give me some fodder for my next meeting with Claire George."

"Who?"

"Don't kid with me. You know darn well who the director of operations is."

He obviously wanted to avoid acknowledging Claire George because he said proudly, "I've kept the C-200s at a 99 percent in-commission rate."

"I'm in personnel. All these pieces of numbered equipment get confusing. So please refresh me so I can speak well on your behalf. The, uh, C-200, why is 99 percent good with that particular piece of equipment?"

"I see what you mean. That is, I know that it already has a high reliability . . ."

"We both know that," I said, inventing my way. "But what would you like me to say in respect to why such a high in-commission rate is invaluable?"

"I suppose," he replied, "it's because so much of the message traffic originates from, or is destined for, distant places."

"That goes without saying. I thought you might have something unusual to offer, something my staff hasn't considered yet."

With that, I politely left. I regarded the other team members urgently waving me back toward our aircraft but took my time, focused more on what I'd just learned than on what lay ahead. I hadn't recognized the power and scope of the C-200 step-up and step-down equipment in receiving satellite transmissions, decoding them, processing them, then transmitting responses or new communications throughout the world.

In the case of Pseudo Miranda, the C-200s transmitted weekly changes in the Identify Friend or Foe codes used by aircraft transponders and ground transponders so 4PM units and the Medellin drug cartel could identify each another and avoid unnecessary confrontations in the air and on the ground. Although I was unaware of it at the time, I later learned that the Nicaraguan Contras also used most of this sophisticated satellite communication network.

* * *

The complex at Nella airstrip outside Mena, Arkansas, as I came to learn, was the hub of CIA operations in Central and South America, which included the state-of-the-art communications system I had just stumbled on; the clandestine airstrip itself; facilities there and at the Inter-Mountain Regional Airport in Mena for refurbishing and retrofitting aircraft, especially with IFF transponders and other communication and navigational gear; a barracks and training program for Contra pilots during the Nicaraguan civil war; air transport of weapons to the Contras; and shipments of cocaine and money into the U.S. through Operation Lighthouse and similar programs. In short, it comprised a vast array of activities taking form as what Oliver North later referred to as Casey's dream of an "off-the-shelf, totally self-sustaining, stand-alone entity that could perform certain activities on behalf of the United States."

The location of the airstrip in the midst of a pine-smothered mountain range and bordered on the southeast and northwest by vast reserves of federal forest land made it an ideal site for these purposes. Its remote inaccessibility due west of Little Rock near the Oklahoma border meant that just about anyone could operate with impunity—drug traffickers, the military, foreign nationals, and weapons dealers. A host of unrelated CIA missions were performed out of this obscure locale in utter anonymity.

Operation Pseudo Miranda sent cartel aircraft to Mena for retrofitting communications systems and installing IFF transponders. Mena also coordinated the security and dissemination of codes and passwords for all Pseudo Miranda participants.

Our 4PM team utilized the airfield as a place for gathering discreetly before missions or for changing airplanes and as the destination for interdicted cocaine. While on the ground, we were supposed to limit travel and speak with no one. Except for a refractory few, most adhered to the guidelines religiously. I was, naturally, one of the few who did not.

*   *   *

"Are you crazy?" was how Jeremiah welcomed me back. "What kind of rogue behavior was that? It's contrary to team!"

"Rogue behavior is inherently contrary to team. Why don't you loosen up? I only went in there to take a piss."

"Don't give me that shit, unless you expect me to believe you pissed on a circuit board."

"Why don't you come along next time, and I'll let you shake it for me."

"Come on, guys," Christina said. "Get serious."

"Listen here," said Box, coming up to us. "Now. All your equipment is on board, labeled by member number. Go check it out. Everyone but you, Anthony," he said to me. "I need to speak to you first."

He then informed me that, following his advice, Bill Casey and George Lauder, who was essentially a public relations man for Casey, had placed me in charge of all field operations except logistical support decisions.

This did not include the preplanning stage because they accurately assessed that I performed best when shooting from the hip. Box was to remain my handler, and he would continue to play a major role in Pseudo Miranda planning.

We then boarded the plane, and Box related what he'd told me to everyone else. He would do the same when we met up with the rest of the team at Howard Air Force Base in Panama. For the most part, no one seemed surprised. But it was my guess that they might secretly be concerned, given my penchant for throwing caution to a hurricane.

The ride on the C-130 Hercules, apparently named by a nonvisionary, was so bumpy it was like whitewater rafting in a rowboat. By the time we reached Howard, everyone was beat.

Waiting for us on the tarmac were Debara, Steven, Quinn and Joey. They had taken a more direct route from Homestead Air Force Base in southern Florida. I concluded that the Air Force Office of Special Investigation had considerable knowledge about Pseudo Miranda, considering the critical reconnaissance support supplied to us from a high-level operation code-named Olympic Victor after the OV-10 reconnaissance aircraft they flew.

But they couldn't help us on this deployment. We were stuck in Panama without a plane, even though the Zurich agreements provided for Panama-based aircraft to be available around the clock and flown by Medellin cartel pilots. Apparently none were ready for our use. This was an obvious ploy to provide some of the larger laboratories in the Llanos jungle time to disperse some of their product.

The CIA anticipated this kind of activity, however. From the outset, Director Casey planned to send a great number of decoy missions into Colombia, making it utterly infeasible to shut down production every time a Pseudo Miranda team crossed the border. This strike, however, was the real McCoy. Our target was what was then considered a large lab, producing two metric tons of cocaine a month, and the coordinates had already been handed down.

* * *

The team managed to find an antiquated C-123 transport—vintage Air America. The blowfish shape of the aircraft only proved that with enough thrust you can get a brick to fly. We had a few laughs over that, then the word arrived that the team was cleared to Panama City. We attempted to prepare ourselves mentally for the challenge that lay ahead. Intense silence replaced the boisterousness of a moment earlier. All of us worried whether or not we were prepared and whether or not we would react properly to the almost certain pitfalls we would encounter.

None of us, however, could have anticipated the magnitude of the crisis that lay ahead.

Chapter 11

The trip across the Panama Canal to International Airport was quick. The pilot, an American, seemed very proficient and knew exactly where he was going. After we landed, he taxied off the runway toward an unmarked hangar and stopped our craft close to a CH-60 helicopter parked on the tarmac in front of it. We transferred our equipment swiftly. The helicopter taxied almost as soon as we were aboard and took off immediately.

The helicopter was flown by a Spanish-speaking pilot and owned by Pablo Escobar. Escobar's tail flashing—the sequence of colors on the rudder—identified that chopper as his to others in the Pseudo Miranda operation. The flashings of all cartel families, including Escobar's, Ochoa's and Ocampo's, were changed periodically for security reasons. At that moment, the flashing on our helicopter was green and white and surprinted with the number 777.

At about 11:30 A.M., in the mountains of northern Colombia due east of Barranquilla, the chopper landed for servicing. Members of our team, armed to the teeth against ambush, and acting tense but determined, disembarked as soon as the rotors wound down. I hoped that the intelligence we received on all non-4PM labs was accurate, although I didn't hold our Washington support personnel in high regard.

Then, out of the surrounding jungle came countless gun-carrying individuals riding American-made pickup trucks and Japanese motorized dirt bikes. It looked like a bandit attack, although my gut instinct told me

it really wasn't. I am not sure what my eyes picked up that told me everything was all right, but I immediately ordered our team to get back in the
helicopter.

They hesitated, as though waiting for Box's approval. Box, sensing the
potential for a breakdown in the command structure, immediately supported my order, even though doing so went against all of his previous
training. Everyone returned and lay down on the floor of the helicopter,
carefully peering out the windows.

All of that happened in seconds.

Box said to me, panic in his voice, "I hope you know what the hell
you're doing." We had been warned about the Revolutionary Armed Forces
of Colombia (FARC), an organization that had been killing and kidnap-
ping rich Colombian landowners and battling the government. If it was
the FARC, however, they would have ambushed us from cover rather
than come out in the open. I noticed something else, too.

"Look over there," I said, pointing at a truck.

"What about it?" Christina asked nervously.

"Yeah," said Boxer, "what about it?"

"I wasn't sure at first," I said, "but that's a fuel truck. The people on
board aren't panicking. My guess is they belong to Escobar."

Jeremiah responded angrily, "How do you know the FARC hasn't killed
the driver and stolen the vehicle?"

"Our pilot was cleared to land here with the preset IFF code. So unless
the fucking FARC knows about Pseudo Miranda and exactly where we
were going to put down, we should be okay. Anyhow, I see something
else now. Look over there in the trees. See those sniper pods? Anyone
attacking this airstrip, including the FARC, would have first knocked them
out. But the trees don't look as though they've taken any gunfire lately."

"All right then," Christina said. Joey added with sarcastic relief, "Maybe
the fact that the pilot is talking and laughing with that gray-haired guy in
the Jeep might also be a good sign."

"Oh, yeah," I agreed quickly, leaning my head back and blowing a
large sigh of relief. "That, too."

"So you weren't absolutely sure of anything, were you?" Box said.

"The only thing I've been absolutely sure of is our inability to play
Audey Murphy in the middle of the Colombian jungle."

"Good call, Ace."

* * *

It turned out that the airstrip was owned and operated by Don Fabio Ochoa. The people who'd appeared to be bandits were, in fact, exactly that—the notorious Cocaine Cowboys. These were the Medellin drug cartel's enforcers. They acquired their name from a purported ability to shoot enemies with exacting precision from vehicles speeding at 70 miles an hour or more. My decision not to confront them had obviously been a wise one.

* * *

The Colombian pilot, reentering the cockpit, seemed oblivious to what had happened—the breakdown in communication and the danger of something much more deadly. Fearful of this happening again, I snapped myself up off the floor and headed out of the helo, calling for Lourdes to follow me to translate. She spoke Spanish, as did Rivas, Rick, Christina and Debara. I did not.

Outside, I headed toward the front of the helicopter, where I was met by the older bandit who'd been talking with the pilot. He was a stout, pudgy man in his middle forties with a gray-and-black beard grown over the several previous days. He took my arm firmly and attempted to guide me back aboard. I resisted, saying, "Lourdes, get your ass up here. Tell this guy I need someone in authority! Translate."

She did. The bearded man responded in Spanish by telling her that he was the commander of this group. He identified himself as Colonel Borda. His uniform was ill-fitting and rumpled with some of the pockets turned inside out. I decided that here was a decidedly uncivilized man who found fulfillment as the leader of a band of dangerous nobodies.

I said, as Lourdes translated, "Colonel Borda, my name is Anthony Vesbucci. I'm the United States government's appointed leader of this group. I need to request that one of my translators ride up front in the cockpit of this helicopter in order to render continual communication with the rest of us in the back. My reasoning is simple . . ."

"You're Vesbucci, of the CIA," Borda suddenly bellowed in English. "Your group is Miranda team!" It was surprising to find out he could speak English, but welcome.

"Sir, I need this request granted or . . ."

"You get in plane. Everything go smooth."

I could smell an aggravating combination of raw beef and licorice-flavored aguardiente on his breath. And I definitely did not appreciate his lack of respect for my leadership position. On the other hand, I didn't forget that Colonel Borda and company were toting automatic weapons, namely MAC-10s.

I said, "Interrupt me one more time, Colonel, and this group you call the Miranda team is going to turn the area into a thousand-hole golf course. I don't particularly give a shit what your rationale is for not wanting my translator in the cockpit. But that's precisely where she's going. Whether you realize it or not, we came within milliseconds of cutting your men in half. Capiche?" I added, somehow believing that the Italian word might assist his understanding.

There came a formidable pause. Then, with a face-saving grin, he pulled a bottle from a pocket of his rumpled jacket. "Have some Scotch! Then we go wherever you like."

"Do you mean you're coming with us?" I asked with surprise.

"I'm your guide," he said matter-of-factly.

Chapter 12

The flight to the Llanos region was magnificent. Colombia, from the air, is as rich and flowing and green as any country in the hemisphere. In order to avoid Colombian radar, the helicopter skimmed the terrain, giving us a close-up view of the diverse landscape.

When we reached the Magdalena River, the chopper altered course slightly and followed the river on a southeasterly track toward Puerto Triunfo, approximately one hundred miles east of Medellin. The terrain below started changing as we descended in altitude. Patchy jungles with pastures and squares of farmland began to crop up. Small bodies of water mirrored the belly of the helicopter as we swooped down from the hillsides. We all napped intermittently, but no one got enough sleep.

Finally the CH-60 slowed as we approached an unlikely airfield in the midst of the jungle and came to a sudden hover. As the craft touched down, we saw another entourage of welcoming bandits swarming toward us from the tree line. But this time Lourdes, translating a message from the pilot, reassured the rest of us that all was well. We had reached the staging point established when the missions, including ours, were planned. Quinn was our team navigation expert, and she confirmed that we had been transported to the appropriate location.

The group of bandits swarming around the chopper worked for Fabio Ochoa. They were known as *Muerte a Secuestradores*, or Death to Kidnappers, and had been organized after Ochoa's youngest sister was kidnapped by M-19, the April 19th Movement, a revolutionary group of the socialist variety. Fabio's men helped us unload the helicopter and set up our tents and gas generators in a tidy campsite on the south side of the clearing. Four tents were pitched: three for us, one for Colonel Borda.

The fatigued PM team went straight to bed, but the colonel had been drinking steadily and wanted me to join him. I believe he also had a great desire to distract me, get me drunk, and deprive me of sleep in order to keep our team from seizing a lot of cocaine. I wanted the others to get their rest, however, so I gave up on mine and followed the pudgy, scraggly bearded man to his tent, where he raised his bottle in invitation.

I said, "No, thank you."

Borda exited the tent and began to rant and rave, demonstrating that he would prevent the other team members from sleeping if I continued to refuse him. I signalled my acquiescence with a shrug and droop of my shoulders and wearily said to him, "Okay, okay."

"You drink now?" he asked with a touch of surprise, slapping an arm around my shoulders. He held the bottle to my mouth and said, "Bazookas!" That's what they said when you smoked coca paste and it blew your mind.

I took a gulp.

He did the same and handed the bottle back to me, shouting, "Bazooka brains!"

I was momentarily taken in by his sloppy charm. I took another drink and then shouted back at him, "Cannonball!" But I was beginning to realize that there was no way I was going to keep this intoxicated bandit from achieving his objective.

That was precisely when Box, who'd obviously trailed us, suddenly stepped into the tent, saying, "Buenas noches, Colonel."

Box then planted an overhand right on Borda's jaw, sending him into sudden unconsciousness. He turned to me, grinning. "Let's get some shut-eye." Then he added, in his wild-and-crazy impersonation of Steve Martin, "You done gooood today."

* * *

As dawn gilded the treetops of the surrounding jungle, most of the team was still asleep, but I had gotten up at first light and walked to the top of a small hill, where I sat down to enjoy the view of the valley below.

Moments later I was surprised when Debara joined me, asking, "Am I bothering you?"

"Not at all." My guard was often up with Debara, but not at this moment, and she sensed it. "Take a look," I said, gesturing in the direction of the valley below at the rolling fields, the streams, the camels, giraffes, kangaroos, buffalos, llamas, elephants, hippos and ostriches, all imported by Escobar under the pretext of acquiring them for zoos throughout Colombia.

Debara sat down at my side, breathing heavily. "Wow!" she exclaimed.

"Those animals are found only in places like Africa and India . . . at least that's what I thought. They're beautiful, aren't they?"

"From here they seem so majestic. Down there it's nothing more than survival of the fittest."

"Like up here."

"But . . ." She seemed reluctant to let go of the serenity we'd momentarily found, saying, "It's still nice to fantasize that we could be a part of a simple world again . . . at least in a vicarious sort of way."

I nodded. But I was simultaneously aware of the vulnerability of our tranquil hilltop. Surrounding the base of the hill was what could only be called a moat. On our side of the moat stood an enormous metal fence crackling with electrical current. The hill was only accessible by a gated bridge over the moat or by air. An airstrip was built on top of the hill. Three sides of the strip were bordered by immensely thick jungle, which made defense of the area relatively simple, while the fourth side had been cleared of trees for arriving and departing aircraft. Aircraft had to come in and leave in the same direction. Occasionally, when the bridge gate was opened for personnel and vehicles, some of the more domesticated animals would meander through. Because of that, the hill was speckled with these docile beasts.

"I hope I'm ready for all of this," I said to Debara. "You know, when the whole thing began back in Maryland, and even during that sadistic training in Nevada, I somehow never recognized the reality of what we're going to do. If I fail, you could all be Dixie cups." I paused, thinking about it.

"What do you mean, 'Dixie Cups'?"

"You know, disposable, throw-away."

"Oh."

"I just don't want people thinking we were drug dealers. I want my life to mean something. I want all of our lives to mean something. I don't know." I found myself sighing, shrugging. "I probably sound like the millions of dreamers who came before me."

"You sound human. Finally." She paused, then added, "I didn't intend that to be mean."

"I know." I felt a hand tightening into a fist. "It's just that I'm more successful when I'm showing people another exterior—when I'm extroverted, spontaneous."

"Hey, when we're working, you need to be that way. But you've got to have some avenue of release from that, somewhere, sometime. I bet you can be real personable when it's necessary. And selfless. Well, I take that last comment back. I mean that maybe much of what we're doing is selfless."

We stood up and started back in the direction of our encampment when, from somewhere ahead of us, there came the ominous staccato sound of machine gun fire.

I dove for the ground, pulling Debara with me.

I reached for my weapon, an automatic Colt .45, telling Debara to stay where she was. No Colt .45. "Damn!"

I bounded to my feet and ran toward my tent. No one else was in sight. Inside, I grabbed my handgun along with its holster and belt, which carried additional clips and grenades as well. As I came out, both Box and Borda stepped from their tents. Several voices screamed loudly nearby. We scrambled in that direction. The tents were pretty spread out. As we came around the front of the forward tent, I saw Joey sitting dejectedly at the opening with his M-60 in his lap. Strewn in front of him was what once was a living creature, now an unrecognizable heap of meat and hide and bones and blood-soaked fur.

"I killed a horse!" Joey wailed. "A hoooorse!"

"Shit," said Quinn, "you murdered a llama, you idiot!"

We gathered around the carnage. Box, interlacing his fingers behind his head, said to me, "Your problem, Ace."

I turned to Colonel Borda. "Is llama edible?"

"Absolutely!" Borda responded with a jolly chuckle.

I turned back to Box. "Not a problem."

Chapter 13

Operation Vosotros rules only allowed the Pseudo Miranda team three days to hit a cocaine laboratory. The reason for this was simple: There were many labs under the control of the different cartels, but only the 4PM team knew which location we were going to hit, not the coke lords, so this was still in essence a game. For the Medellín cartel to allow us more time to find a laboratory would virtually ensure our success on every mission, and the cartel would never agree to that.

So Colonel Borda continued his attempts to distract and deter us from finding the target lab. We were authorized to confiscate 50 percent of any cocaine produced during a specified period of time, but we weren't guaranteed it, and there was no doubt that Borda would be richly rewarded by the cartel if we ran out of time and blew our mission.

I quickly grew tired of his games and quietly informed the team that we would proceed immediately with the mission, but I decided to orchestrate the operation differently than planned and to throw in a twist. Instead of flying directly from Escobar's base to the lab as we had intended, we would set out on a decoy mission to Leticia, a small, dilapidated shanty town on the Amazon River. From there, our team could theoretically launch a strike on any one of several locations, which would keep Borda off balance.

We flew the helicopter south by southeast, crossing the most dense jungles imaginable. All of us wore his or her game face. On every first-time mission, some ridiculous mistake invariably happens, and with the llama incident behind us, everyone seemed relieved.

After a while, the mighty Amazon came into view in the distance. There was a lot of mud in the water, which turned the river milky gray as it carved its way across the continent. Shouting over the noise of the rotor blades, Box said, "The Sicilian Mafia often looked for refuge on that river."

"It's like traveling with the fucking National Geographic!" Quinn exclaimed. Then, as though realizing how rude her remark sounded, she said, "I mean this is very educational. Really!"

Box only smiled, signalling that her natural enthusiasm was okay. Quinn smiled back. The rough edges were softening.

"Did you two have a moment there?" I asked genially.

Then, to everyone except Colonel Borda, Lourdes and the pilot, who couldn't hear me from where they sat up front, I said, "We'll stay in groups of at least three when we land. Exactly an hour from touchdown we'll return to this helicopter and head to the target zone." Team members understood that they would simply head in different directions and look busy during that hour as part of the twist in this decoy mission.

I looked forward at Borda, adding, "It'll be my job to shed the colonel. We're close to striking the primary target. Let's be careful!"

* * *

When we disembarked from the CH-60 on the outskirts of Leticia, we were swarmed by little children. They had learned that it was customary for the Colombian elite, especially the drug barons, to offer gifts and food to the poor when they visited. Our helicopter was a signal to them.

Colonel Borda reached under his seat, where normally the windscreen protective cover was stored, and pulled out a large canvas bag. It was filled with coins. He began giving them to the children surrounding the helicopter by the handful.

Jeremiah, his strong jaw usually set and his dark face grim, suddenly got caught up in the excitement created by this generosity. He ripped the bag from Borda's hands and began showering the kids with cash. His face relaxed so that he appeared years younger. He continually glanced at the rest of the team, grinning at our laughter, unable to control his childlike jubilation. The colonel, however, was not amused. He'd made it clear that he intended to reserve a portion of that money for his sexual pleasure with the local girls.

But Jeremiah emptied the bag, then stepped back beside Borda, eyes full of tears. It wasn't just the excitement, he explained. "My father would have loved to have done that if he could have afforded it. Do you have more money for these children, Colonel?"

Borda smacked a palm against his forehead and muttered several expletives. But I decided that he was still intent upon that sensual interlude even if it meant spending his own money.

Debara bent down to hug one of the cutest of the dirty little boys, saying to Jeremiah, "You've got yourself some new friends."

"Now that I'm out of money?"

"It's your personality they love, Jeremiah," I said, "not your cash."

"Thanks, Kabooch."

Then, to dupe Colonel Borda into thinking he had plenty of time for his whoring, I said to the others, "Remember, everyone be back here at noon tomorrow."

Borda took off quickly. Several of the team did the same, but leisurely. Box and I closed in on the pilot with Rick, who spoke Spanish, to engage him in useless but diverting conversation.

Exactly an hour later, everyone except Colonel Borda reassembled beside the helicopter. I asked the pilot to get in. He refused, so I put my gun to his skull and walked him in.

The chopper took off with Colonel Borda's seat empty. Destination: the jungle region south of Tranquilandia.

*   *   *

The CH-60 landed about 2,500 feet from the cocaine laboratory, a small hill that jutted out considerably, its surface covered with fernlike bushes. The helicopter's IFF transponder had already identified us as Pseudo Miranda so as to avoid confusion and the inevitable conflict if we were mistaken for a rival organization. We got off and proceeded on foot from the north toward the lab. Three hundred feet from the target, I signalled everyone to get down.

Crouching, surrounded by the team, I gave instructions. I wanted a frontal assault in the shape of a half-moon. On either end would be our best personnel, Jeremiah and Rick. In the center would be Joey, armed with his M-60 tree killer. Behind Joey, wearing his ever-present fishing hat, would come the quiet-spoken Steven. He needed to trail because he was the SATCOM, responsible for satellite communications. If a serious problem were to occur, he would radio the States for help. Or if the problem appeared to be fatal, he would deliver the news of our impending demise. Box and I took second point, just inside of Rick and Jeremiah, with Debara, Lourdes, Quinn and Christina paired on either side of Joey.

I signalled the go-ahead with a flick of my Colt .45. We started forward again.

I felt the tension building inside me. And I remembered the conversation with Debara on the crest of that hill earlier in the day . . . or was that a lifetime ago? Right now was the reality I'd been worrying about. If I failed . . .

I glanced at Debara and found her looking back at me as we moved. The expression in her lovely green eyes told me that she was reading my mind. I knew instantly that I would have to be more than simply a man aware—and all too clearly—that right here, right now we could all get our asses shot off.

Then I was thinking of football—specifically, the kickoff. Defensive players tended to leave their lanes and move in the direction of the ball carrier. The same was true of us moving through the jungle toward that cocaine laboratory. It was becoming hard to see straight because of the trees. Maintaining proper spread was nearly impossible.

But we proceeded to the edge of the lab clearing. I saw that Jeremiah was about to break through the tree line into the open. Before he did, I waved everybody down again and checked our line of battle. I repositioned Joey so that he and Rick and Box formed a straight rank.

Then I scrutinized the laboratory, which was positioned in a corner of the clearing. Constructed primarily of wood, it had long, horizontal timbers for ceiling beams running across the top, and these were covered with thin metal sheets and then some sort of grassy vegetation. The roof was long and narrow, with a very shallow slope. The sides were open and revealed the poles that supported the building. The entire structure was approximately 100 feet long and 50 feet wide.

With the tension continuing to build, I was most concerned with one thought: where were the *campesinos*? The *campesinos* were the poor local farmers who ran the labs and cared for the crops. They weren't paramilitary. They weren't capable of slipping away undetected as the Viet Cong had done in another era and in another part of the world.

In a whisper I ordered everyone to move ahead slowly.

When we reached the lab, we found it abandoned, and a feeling of relief settled over all of us. With that came a sense of security. We lowered our weapons to our sides. This lab had been producing up to four tons of pure cocaine a month. The assembly line started with the cocaine paste acquired from Peru and Bolivia as part of the Pseudo Miranda setup, which they purified to crystalline form. The crystal was then dissolved in sulfuric acid and filtered to remove many of the impurities. Ammonium hydroxide was then added, and another filtering process followed. The base that this process created was made into a powder by combining hydrochloric acid with the most important ingredient of all—ether. In my opinion, ether should be controlled on a worldwide basis as though it were uranium.

Surprisingly, the *campesinos* had left quite a lot of purified cocaine—there were approximately 500 kilos of it. I instructed the team to gather it up and place it in the center of the clearing for destruction.

Box said, "According to Pseudo Miranda guidelines, we're not supposed to harm any of the facilities."

"Too bad," I told him. "As a matter of fact, I'm thinking maybe we should demo this whole piece of shit."

As I finished saying that, all hell broke loose. There was a flash and an intense, penetrating heat and a blast of high pressure. I was close enough to be knocked unconscious by the concussion. The next thing I realized, Christina was shaking me violently. I started pushing myself up groggily, looking for the enemy.

A 6-inch mortar round had landed at Jeremiah's feet, where it exploded.

"Don't get up!" pleaded Christina, still flat on the ground.

But I was on my feet now, running toward the dismembered remains of Jeremiah. Looking at what was left of him was like looking at that llama back at the camp.

I twisted around, shouting, "Joey, over here! I want some plastique! The rest of you, back to the chopper!"

Box came running in my direction with Joey, who handed me enough C-4 explosive to blow up half the hillside. Joey then hurried to the southern edge of the clearing and began thrashing the area with his machine gun. Rick assumed command position of the rest of the team and led them back in the direction of the helicopter. Joey followed.

Box and I gathered up Jeremiah. No matter the sticky blood that covered us. No matter that this had not only been a human being but also our friend. There wouldn't be time, I knew, to give Jeremiah a traditional burial. We placed the torn-up body in a vat of acid as another mortar round sailed into the clearing. This time, however, it exploded harmlessly.

I took a grenade from my belt and methodically wrapped it with the plastique.

"We've got to get out of here!" Box shouted. "Come on!"

I yanked the pin from the grenade and dropped it into the acid. "Run! Now!"

We sprinted back into the jungle, firing blindly behind us because now there was a barrage of gunfire from the clearing. It stopped as we hurried over grassy ground glistening with dew and shadowed by a thick canopy of tree limbs and leafy branches. We paused then, listening, certain that no one was pursuing us.

"What happened?" Box asked in disbelief.

I shook my head. "Who are those bastards?"

"All I know is that we're picking up the proverbial prison soap," Box responded. This was his euphemism for getting fucked.

There was no answer at that moment to the question of who our attackers might be. All we could surmise was that the Medellin cartel had double-crossed us.

It was very quiet, but I knew that the sulfuric acid was eating away the plastique, which held the handle of the grenade. When the handle sprang free the timing mechanism would be activated.

I heard the grenade explode. I'd forgotten the enormous volume of ether stored at the facility we'd just escaped, but a huge chain reaction began, and the lab became Mount St. Helens erupting. A huge fireball engulfed the area and the lab was blown away. Debris was strewn at least a mile by the blast. The thick jungle was all that protected Box and me from serious injury.

Bullets suddenly began to fly at us again, although from a new direction as our attackers circled to cut us off. We plunged on. Moving almost blindly now, our skin lacerated by the unforgiving brush, we finally made our way back to the small hill where the helicopter had landed.

It was gone.

Chapter 14

A desperate numbness enveloped us; we were paralyzed by indecision. We twisted and paced as bullets whizzed through the leaves and punched the tree trunks around us. Then a light flickering through narrow slits in the canopy caught Box's eye. He tugged on my shoulder, pointing to the sky. We saw the chopper's rotor blade intermittently as it passed between us and the sunlight, and then we could hear its distinct, pulsating signature.

The pilot, desperately searching for an opening in the jungle large enough to accommodate the helicopter, hovered about twenty feet above the treetops and twenty yards from our position. We charged toward the helicopter, but it moved away abruptly.

We watched helplessly as the other team members, leaning out the side door, motioned us to follow. We darted after them. We ran for a long, long time. Without so much as a breath left in us, we staggered to a halt. Resting with our hands on our knees, we faced each other and wondered aloud if our friends were trying to kill us with exhaustion.

Just as we were about to throw our hands up in frustration, Box noticed the helicopter descending. With a grin and a deep gasp, we bolted for the point it would touch down. We moved with what we felt was the final ounce of our energy, expecting to make the rendezvous and be whisked away. No such salvation. There wasn't enough clearance through the trees.

We slid to a halt below the hovering helicopter and signaled them to drop the cable to hoist us up through the canopy. Turning sideways so we could view both the helicopter and our pursuers when they came into sight, Box and I waited for the cable to descend. We stared dumbfounded when it stopped eight feet short of the ground. We would have to jump. We would also have to climb all the way up to the chopper because it didn't have a winch to haul us up.

"Go ahead, Box! You first! I'll cover!"

"Bullshit! You get your ass up there. You won't need to wait for me!"

"Listen, just get your ass . . ."

"I can't climb! Never could! My daddy said it would come back to haunt me. And here it is just as big as shit."

"Good luck, Box," I said, clutching his arm.

"You too," he said solemnly. "Now get your butt outta here."

I leaped as high as I could, hoping to grab the cable, climb quickly, and make room for Box to follow immediately. I barely snagged the end of the cable and, swinging back and forth, struggled to climb higher, using only my arms.

Intermittent gunfire peppered the jungle once again. I removed my Colt .45 automatic with my right hand while holding on to the cable with my left, and attempted to cover Box. This proved to be an exercise in futility, however, due to the piddling size of the weapon and the effect of riding a pendulum. Nevertheless, it was a moot point. Joey provided our assailants with a condensed lesson in deforestation as he shredded the jungle with his .50-caliber tree killer.

Box lunged at the cable three or four times, leaping more forward than upward. He couldn't grab it. I feverishly attempted to coach him.

"Don't run at it! Stand below me! Jump straight up!" I screamed.

"What?"

"Straight up!" I signaled, pointing my thumb upwards. "Straight up!"

"No shit, asshole! What the hell do ya think I'm doin'? Help me, damn it!"

"Stand below me!" I pointed downward. "Below me! Below me!"

"Oh, right. Okay. Yeah, I think I get it," Box said, calming down a bit.

He figured out what it was I was attempting to tell him and pointed at the bottom of the cable. Box stood directly below me, getting into a crouch. He sprang toward the cable with all the intensity of a lava lamp.

"You're a dead man!" I hollered with a nervous laugh.

"This is funny? Help me!" Box pleaded.

"What am I supposed to do? Jump! Hurry!"

Box tucked into a ball, with his head between his knees. He exploded into a twelve-inch vertical leap and finally made it. He held onto the cable for dear life with one hand and clenched my calf with the other, digging his jagged fingernails into my skin as he climbed. My grip slipped momentarily, but Box felt for the cable and got a firm grip. Just in time. The pilot began his ascent. Unfortunately, the helicopter's angle of climb was low, and as it flew forward the cable dragged through the jungle canopy, needlessly hauling our already battered bodies into the jagged treetops.

There was no feasible place to set the chopper down, so we remained dangling precariously until the pilot finally found a clearing some fifteen miles from the place he picked us up. By this time, Box and I were physically exhausted and in danger of losing our grip. With no gentle way of lowering us to the ground, the pilot did his best to soften the landing, but we nevertheless bounced off the rain-soaked earth. I crawled toward Box, who was lying face down in the mud. Placing my hand on his neck, I was able to feel the rhythm of his heart. This was enough to tell me he was all right. Not that it would have mattered if I needed more proof; I was too tired to speak. Rick and Steven carried us into the helicopter for what I hoped would be an uneventful trip home.

No one spoke a syllable as Box and I, saturated in blood and earth, lay on the floor of the chopper staring blankly upward, with our heads resting in the laps of Quinn and Debara, respectively.

In keeping with the exciting adversity of the previous forty-eight hours, the helicopter pilot executed another unexpected nose-in approach. Lourdes radioed back to Rick that the Colombian Special Operations Group (GOES) had transmitted the detection of an unauthorized aircraft in the area—4PM. The GOES unit was traveling in a De Havilland DCH-6 Twin Otter, capable of the kind of speed that would make it futile for us to try to outrun them. By this time we had returned to Tranquilandia. The CH-60 slowed to a crawl, as if the pilot were searching for something. There weren't any airstrips or buildings or even people for that matter— in the area. The pilot's actions were a mystery. In the middle of this wide-open emptiness he initiated a landing approach.

"Lourdes, what the hell is going on up there?" Rick demanded over the intercom system.

"What's going on?" I echoed, fearful that the worst wasn't over yet.

"I'm not sure. The Colombian government is on our tail. But for some ungodly reason we're setting down in the middle of nowhere," Rick explained.

I grabbed the intercom from Rick's hand and was about to demand answers when the helicopter touched down. The pilot rushed to the rear of the cabin, leaving the engines running, and adamantly demanded that we all get off immediately. We were so astonished by his suggestion that we deplane in the middle of nowhere that we remained frozen in our seats. Then, as if to demonstrate it could always get weirder, Bob Crane's Colombian counterpart appeared from nowhere. He was tall and awkward and armed with an M-16. You may recall from the TV series "Hogan's Heroes" the fake rock that functioned as an access to an underground tunnel network. In this case, the rock was a fake tree. The man hastened us off the aircraft by snapping the barrel of his gun against our shins. Box and I needed assistance getting to our feet and gaining our balance. As the Colombian herded us through the tree door and underground, we were painfully aware of our isolation and loss of control.

Once inside, we descended a long, narrow staircase and stood anxiously at the bottom waiting for the Colombian. The closing of the lid brought absolute darkness. We spoke to identify ourselves if we brushed up against each other. Finally, a dim light went on, illuminating the barren cubicle we now occupied. The staircase was cast in iron and dropped straight down through the middle of the floor. Three sides of the cubicle were made of eight-inch-thick reinforced concrete, typically associated with bomb shelters. One wall, however, reminded me of a military SCUPS (Self-Contained Universal Personnel System), an underground facility the U.S. military used to protect soldiers from chemical attack. In the center of the wall was a six-foot-wide, bulletproof window that protected the facility's lone guard. He controlled access to a series of three rooms that served as a sequential staging area with an electromagnetic switch that opened each door. The first door opened on his right, and he could monitor anyone he admitted through a window on that room and the other two rooms and control their progress through the staging area.

In the first room, we had to disrobe and shower. Everyone bathed together. There was no time for modesty, so we simply gendered off, standing back to back, and did what was necessary. In the next room we donned antistatic clothing. Essentially this consisted of a white cotton jumpsuit and black rubber boots that tied around the leg at the top. The final room was a compartment that removed any latent static with what can only be described as a gigantic magnetic eraser. The guard instructed us to remain perfectly still, then left. The walls began to converge from two opposing sides and came within a foot of us before stopping. They emitted a monotone buzz, completing the process, and then retracted. As frightening as it was when the walls closed in, no one let on that he feared for his life. In part, this was probably the result of the fatiguing and shocking experience that we had just undergone. We all felt numb.

We were herded to the large steel door of an unmarked area and made to wait. Still, none of us had yet uttered a word. Could it be that the thorough cleansing and preparation was merely a trick to ease our fears the way the Nazis told the Jews that they were going to the showers, only to be herded off to their demise? What we didn't know was that our safety was so important to the cartel that they had risked giving us access to this secret underground facility.

The door finally opened, revealing a pristine cocaine manufacturing plant. Huge rooms with rubberized floors and counterbalanced explosion doors were filled with *campesinos* wearing the same antistatic gear as we did. Each cavernous room was designed to seal itself in the event of an explosion. The doors, counterbalanced with huge, rubber-coated cylindrical weights, would slam closed in a millisecond if a threat were detected, instantaneously sealing in the occupants to face any fire or explosion on their own, but preventing the spread of fire to the rest of the facility. Each phase of the cocaine production process occupied a separate room, diminishing the possibility of accident. We stepped from room to room, careful not to trip over the twelve-inch-high threshold below each door, agog at the size and sophistication of the operation, until we came to the last chamber, where the finished cocaine was stockpiled. Stacked floor to ceiling, the stockpile by my conservative calculation was about twenty tons. Intelligence considered this beyond the capabilities of a single lab. Little did they know.

The cartel's operational plan for protecting these subterranean laboratories was to destroy the primary access cavity. In the unlikely event that the GOES unit had detected the camouflaged entrance, it was necessary to bring us further inside the location. Adding insult to injury, they made us wait in the cocaine storage room because it was the least likely room to be damaged in an explosion.

The storage room also doubled as a spacious bunker. It was designed to accommodate up to twenty people for six months or more. Cocaine wrapped in thick, green polyethylene was piled against the entire length of a hundred-foot wall, blocking abundantly stocked shelves from view. Pull-out beds were only visible by the seams they left in the walls when they were closed. These beds tilted out from the wall and stacked one over the other, like the shelves of a refrigerator. Fully functional bathrooms were located at opposite ends of the bunker. For recreation there was table tennis and pocket billiards; the tables were disassembled and stacked in the corners of the room.

*   *   *

The team regained focus through an unlikely mechanism: blame. With time on our hands, everyone had ample opportunity to dissect the day's events and express an opinion. Remarkably, Box and I were the only ones not to shift responsibility away from ourselves. The simple reason lay in the unspoken CIA credo "You can delegate authority, but you can never delegate responsibility." This most certainly figured in. However, the fact that the mission would most likely have gone wrong irrespective of who was in command pointed to a deep problem.

"Why the hell didn't we stick to the original plan?" questioned Quinn.

"Yeah, why did we change our plan?" asked Lourdes.

I sat up, and then, feeling it really didn't matter, sat back in my seat without saying a word. Putting my left hand to my forehead, with my eyes closed, I sat expressionless as the attack persisted.

"A loose cannon, isn't that what he called you? That shit may work with your college frat buddies, but it doesn't fly with us. Look at you. Why don't you say anything? If you had anything to say you'd have said it. There must be nothing to say," Rick asserted as he hung over me.

Opening my eyes, I gazed at Chavez, wondering why he was doing this to me, and then turned my attention to the arm rest.

"Why was the lab empty? Where were the *campesinos*? I don't get it. I don't get any of it," Christina said in frustration.

"They know the answers!" Rick replied, glaring at Box and me. "You can just bet that. I'm sure there were plenty of explanations in those intelligence briefings Box has been attending. I can only assume he shared that information with Vesbucci too."

Box glanced at me, not knowing how to react, or even if he should react. I stared emptily through him, gradually lowering my eyes to the floor. Box had never seen me act this way. He folded his arms and stared down Rick in a manner that was anything but empty. Still not speaking, Box seemed to be calculating his response.

"I can't believe it. There were intelligence reports on all this and we weren't told? You let us just walk in there without warning us or coming up with a plan or something? I don't believe this," Lourdes rambled.

"It sure sounds like you do," Debara rebutted sarcastically.

"Sounds like I do what?"

"Sounds like you've already made up your mind. Damn Rick goes off on a tangent about some presumed intelligence reports, and you've got them withholding critical information against their own self-interest. My God, girl, you're gullible."

"Whose side are you on?" Rick inquired.

"Four PM's side, you asshole!"

"It's time you face reality, girl. These two bozos almost got us all killed!"

"They did? Who the hell came within a cunt hair of starting a war with the Cocaine Cowboys!?" Debara retaliated, using the word *cunt*, which she despised. "So, enlighten me. What exactly would you have done?"

"Certainly not what Vesbucci did! That's for damn sure," Rick responded.

"Could you be a bit more specific?" Debara pressed.

"I'd need to see the intelligence reports first, then . . ."

Box cut him off, spluttering, "There weren't any such reports, you idiot! You hold the intelligence community in much too high regard. Stop reading that damn Tom Clancy shit. In the real world we rely on quick thinking. That's why Vesbucci's in charge. If he hadn't reacted the way he did, you'd be strung up by the balls with piano wire. And lest I forget," Box said, striding over to Rick, where, standing toe to toe with his index finger shaking tensely in Rick's face, he continued, "if you ever talk to me that way again I'll, I'll . . . You don't wanna know."

Lourdes looked erratically about the room, realizing she'd sided wrongly. "Look, I'm sorry. I guess I'm a little worn from this whole affair."

"Can I say something?" Steven interjected, waving his hand in the air. "First of all, the finger pointing is just stupid. Nothing's gained from it. None of us would have wanted, or for that matter been able, to do a better job. So let's drop it. Unless you're forgotten, we just lost a very good agent. And for some of us, a very good friend." Steven's mouth began to quiver with emotion. He bent his head and folded his arms, and then he rocked back and forth. Whenever Steven had anything to offer, he received everybody's undivided attention. It only now occurred to everyone why Box and I were unable to defend ourselves. After all, defending one's leadership ability pales in comparison to the significance of a man's death.

One of the Colombians informed us that we would have to remain in the bunker for the evening. We dedicated the down time to saying what could be said about Jeremiah, based on our limited shared history, and what he meant to us. I didn't contribute any thoughts, even when probed. I felt consumed with remorse. In my mind I reconstructed the day's events endlessly, hoping to find no alternative to what I did. After the others had fallen asleep, Box crawled over to the side of my bed to tell me that I had done it right. He also noticed tears rolling off of my cheeks. Box simply said, "Tomorrow's a new day," and slipped back to his own bed. I never acknowledged his presence, or even moved, but his kindness did matter to me. I seldom let my guard down because it made me vulnerable. Nevertheless, I knew, as Debara did, that it was a necessary part of being strong—admitting to yourself that you're not. I also knew that tomorrow I would be able to put back on the facade that made me successful.

The following morning a guard entered the room around eight and instructed us to bathe, but he was too late. We had already showered and were waiting to depart. The guard left and returned promptly with the dirty fatigues we'd removed when we entered the facility. They had been washed and degaussed, and we changed back into them and made ready to leave. In the outer concrete cubicle, the guard had placed our weapons below the cast iron staircase. He simply pointed up, signifying that we should depart. The hatch was already open. A bright, flickering light shone in, and, although making the transition from fluorescent lighting to the blinding natural light was difficult, breathing fresh air again made it easier. The land was as we'd left it. The reality that the world had continued on in spite of our own tribulations was a harsh reality check.

Chapter 16

Colonel Borda wasted little time giving us an "I told you so" speech. Rick promptly interrupted, grabbing him by the shirt collar, and threatened to throw him into the rotor blade of the idling CH-60 helicopter if he continued. This was apparently a manifestation of Rick's desire to improve team solidarity and a way for him to put yesterday's dispute behind him. We boarded the chopper and headed for Puerto Triunfo, specifically, a *finca* called Hacienda Napoles.

Shortly before reaching Puerto Triunfo proper, Debara remarked on the numerous small lakes and the number of exotic animals wandering about. It seemed all too familiar. Without knowing that we were in fact on Pablo Escobar's doorstep, I expressed a nagging concern: "We're flying in Escobar's plane. With Escobar's pilot. Over Escobar's notorious stomping ground. It can only mean one thing. Trouble."

"Why trouble?" Box said hesitantly, leaning toward me.

"We blew up his lab. Remember?"

"What's this *we* shit? You got a frog in your pocket?" Box chuckled. Suddenly everyone began to laugh uncontrollably, giving their own renditions of the lab going "Boom!"

As everyone continued to joke, Lourdes radioed, "What's going on back there?"

"Nothing . . . ," Rick began to say, but Quinn suddenly relieved him of the intercom.

"Nothing, you gullible geek!" she said with a laugh.

I snatched the mike from Quinn and, giving her a smirk, told Lourdes, "Everything is just fine. In fact, it's perfect. Quinn was just having fun with you. . . . Quinn, Lourdes says she's gonna kick your dyke ass when we land," I joked, hoping to get a rise out of Lourdes.

"Don't tell her that. Does she think I really said that? Holy cow. She's gonna kill me!" Lourdes replied in a panic-stricken voice.

Knowing full well that I was kidding around, Quinn took the mike back from me and said, "You'd best run when we get off this chopper."

Lourdes didn't say anything after that, and the helicopter began its descent. I neglected to inform Lourdes that Quinn and I weren't really serious. We landed in a field bordered by tiny lakes and the Magdalena River. As soon as we touched down, Lourdes flung open the hatch and began to run. Fleeing what she anticipated to be an ugly scene with Quinn, she ran in the direction of one of the small lakes. Colonel Borda lit out after her, attempting to stop her. The sight of this pathetic out-of-shape man trying to keep up with the gazelle-like Lourdes had us all laughing. The colonel turned back toward the team, short of breath, and wailed the word *caribe* several times. When no one reacted, except to wonder among ourselves what *caribe* meant, Colonel Borda screamed out the word *fish* in English. At just that time Rick said, "I believe *caribe* means *cannibal*."

"Oh, my God. Piranha!" Box, Debara and I yelled simultaneously.

Feeling as if she were to blame, Quinn ran frantically after Lourdes hollering, "Piranha! Piranha!"

The problem, of course, was that Quinn was the reason for Lourdes running in the first place. When Lourdes saw Quinn running toward her, she jumped into the water and began to swim across the small lake, M-16 and all. Joey's gun, which was still slung over his shoulder, was handy, so I fired off several rounds to get Lourdes' attention. Unfortunately, the gunfire stampeded all the animals in the vicinity, and the sound of hooves and trampling impeded communication. Lourdes began to tread water, realizing that she wasn't going to make it across.

I said, "Me alone!" and proceeded to run past Quinn to the shore of the lake. I didn't want to panic Lourdes, fearing that she would generate too much turbulence hurrying back to shore if I told her about the piranha in the lake.

"Hey, don't tell me that getting shot at doesn't frighten you, but the thought of fighting Quinn does? Come on in now." I didn't want to tell her that we had been kidding her, fearing she would start a long, bantering dialogue with me before coming ashore.

"I just wanted to show her I could wear her out. Then I'd pounce on her," she said in a feisty, childish tone.

"Well, you won. Quinn realized she couldn't catch up and quit a ways back. Now come on in."

Lourdes swam to shore without making a ripple. As she crawled onto the rocky bank, everyone sighed in relief.

"What's wrong?" inquired Lourdes.

I just gave her a big hug. Lourdes pushed back gently and asked again, "What is it? What's wrong?"

This entire area, covering no more than a few square miles, was cartel property belonging to Pablo Escobar, and was kind of a buffer zone or staging area around his home. There were lakes erratically strewn about the rolling hillsides. Many of the lakes and streams throughout the property swarmed with piranha, which Escobar's lieutenants had placed there for the express purpose of deterring infiltrators. Even friendly *campesinos* would send a farm animal into a lake or stream before crossing themselves, just to be safe.

It so happens that the lake Lourdes was swimming in was not laden with piranha, but that was sheer luck because the many connecting streams had an abundance. As Lourdes and I returned to the group, Quinn came up to us, nervous and sweating profusely, and hugged Lourdes to her, saying, "God, I'm so sorry, Lourdes. That was so stupid of me."

"Will someone please tell me what's going on!?" Lourdes demanded.

"Can't we just show how much we care without you being so suspicious?" I replied.

"Now I'm really worried."

"Its really nothing. There . . . uh . . . there may have been some . . . uh . . . some . . . piranha in there. Really very slight chance. Hardly worth mentioning," Quinn stammered.

"Ooow," Lourdes complained. She twisted her pelvis, exposing her torn fatigue trousers. "I thought I felt something nip at me when I climbed out of there." Her pants were shredded and strips of her flesh dangled like rashers of bacon. It appeared much worse than it actually was, but nonetheless she bore the pain well. Before we moved on, Steve treated and bandaged Lourdes' wounds.

We switched from the CH-60 to two smaller Bell helicopters. The flight into Los Napoles was a pleasant jaunt. Flying north along the Magdalena, we passed over numerous cars and buses crossing into the unrestricted portion of Escobar's property. The camels, giraffes, kangaroos, buffalo, llamas, elephants, hippos and ostriches that we had seen earlier at Escobar's camp site were plentiful here too. The only creatures we didn't see were the carnivores: the jaguars, lynx, cougars and leopards. This wild menagerie was Escobar's treat to the average folk of Colombia.

The choppers landed a short distance from Escobar's palatial house. As we exited the craft, we were escorted by armed guards to the rear of the *finca*, past a large swimming pool with a jacuzzi at either end. The most conspicuous amenity of all was a marble statue of Aphrodite, the Greek goddess of love, that adorned one side of the pool. Gazebos sheltered several vintage automobiles of the 1930s and 1940s reminiscent of gangster movies. Thompson submachine guns served as taps for beer barrels, and Colt .45s replaced the usual kind of handles on the sliding glass doors.

Upon entering the house (if an edifice capable of comfortably accommodating one hundred twenty people can be called a house), it became all too apparent that the acquisition of wealth for wealth's sake was the primary motivation for these drug lords. Incongruent luxury furniture filled every room, and art works were piled on tables and the walls like big game trophies mounted by a hunter. If the decor had a common theme, it was probably Victorian, only because the style conveyed traditional elegance and wealth to the Colombians. Following our escort down two flights of stairs into a vast game room, we were told to relax and get comfortable. Meanwhile, a guard was posted outside the door. So much for comfortable.

"Steven, will that thing transmit a signal from here?" I inquired, pointing at the miniature satellite dish attached to his bulky radio.

"No way. Why?" Steven replied.

"Oh, I just wanted to send a message back to headquarters that we wouldn't be able to meet our rendezvous. It's no big deal. Don't worry about it." I was considerably worried though. I didn't want anyone in Langley to overreact and exacerbate the problem.

"Anyone for a game of pool?" I asked nonchalantly.

"Sure," Joey enthusiastically agreed. His voice was full of relief. The fact that I wanted to shoot a little stick sent a message that we weren't in any danger. The enthusiasm caught on, and everyone began to have fun. Rick found a juke box and played the only artist on it, a Spanish singer named Roberto Carlos. Quinn raided the bar—one of four in the game room—and began to serve Black Label scotch to everyone. Debara and Steven slid the slot machines close to the tables, and, with a little jury rigging, we were pulling one-armed bandits for free.

After drinking a shot, I pulled Box aside very subtly so as not to draw attention and told him that I'd had enough waiting. Unbeknownst to him, I'd removed a vintage, nonfunctional German Luger from a display above the bar. Standing behind him, I placed my hands on his shoulders and controlled the gun by inserting my thumb through the trigger guard and pressing it firmly against his spine. Box could not feel the gun as it dangled a millimeter away from his back. The guard would be able to see my naked fingers on Box's shoulders but not the Luger. I told Box to follow my lead as I pushed him to the door. The guard was standing just outside.

"What the hell are you gonna do now?" Box wanted to know.

"I'm not taking this crap any more. These idiots are gonna learn that we're in control here, and we won't be imprisoned or prevented from doing our job. Not to mention being killed. Now open the damn door," I whispered harshly.

"I notice you doing all the talking, but it's my ass up front."

"Next time you come up with a plan, you get to live . . . I mean trail behind."

"What?"

"I'm just kidding. Now keep your voice down and get going."

I told Box to pretend to be drunk, but not too belligerent. Relying on human nature I expected the guard to stop the lead person by pointing his gun at Box's belly. I would counter by putting my gun to the guard's head. Initially it went like clockwork. Then the guard unexpectedly spun Box around and placed him in a headlock, pointing his MAC-10 at Boxer's temple.

"For God's sake, Box! You're not supposed to let him spin you around like that," I said, criticizing him in an almost playful manner. "Damn! I wish I knew some Spanish."

"That's it? That's your plan? You have to know Spanish to make this plan work?" Box grumbled in a raspy voice. "Rick's right! You are an idiot!"

Placing my gun firmly to the guard's head, with my eyes affixed on his, I began to count, "*Uno. Dos. Tres. Cuatro.*" The guard immediately relinquished his weapon and slunk away. The likely explanation is that he wasn't authorized to kill any of 4PM. Consequently, he wasn't prepared to risk his life on a shallow bluff. The counting in Spanish probably made him quite nervous because he was aware of but couldn't understand all the other things that were said leading up to it.

"I thought you said you didn't know any Spanish?"

"I don't. But I know a little Italian. It's basically the same thing."

"Umm . . . that stuff about . . . you know . . . about you being an idiot and all. I was just concerned, that's all."

"Is that what you call it? Concerned? I think you'd best check your shorts and come up with another adjective."

I led Boxer up to the main level, where a meeting was in progress. To avoid detection, we skirted that room and entered an enormous study decorated in traditional fashion. In the darkness we moved about as quietly as we could, not trying to retrace our steps or to escape, but wandering through the house looking into various rooms. I did not have a specific intent except to send a message to the highest level that Pseudo Miranda would fold if the type of treatment meted out by the cartel continued. Box was toting the MAC-10, and I carried the useless Luger. Although a maze of escape tunnels ran beneath the *finca*, and countless surveillance cameras covered the perimeter of the immediate property, the dwelling itself was equipped with motion detectors and monitors only at the windows and doors. Once inside, you could move about freely without fear of detection. At least that's what we thought.

Sliding down the hall past an Italian marble fountain built into an alcove in the wall, I busted into another meeting with the Luger outstretched in my hand, snapping it firmly in all directions. Box trailed after me, covering the entire room.

"Now what do we do?" Box said, looking over his shoulder at me. "It's that Spanish problem again, isn't it? Why the hell didn't you just bring Chavez?"

"By the time I came up with this idea, he was already drunk!" I argued.

"What plan, with the possible exception of shooting everybody, would not require a translator?!"

"This one," I replied sarcastically. "Who in this room doesn't seem to fit the drug trafficker image?" I asked.

My eyes immediately fell on the only white boy in the room. I grabbed the man by the back of his collar and demanded that he tell me what was going on. He was a businessman pure and simple. His soft, pale skin, manicured nails and Mariani suit from Beverly Hills epitomized the true villains of America's drug-infested streets. Whimpering, he said he didn't know anything. Before I could ascertain the truth of the matter, armed soldiers of the M-19 flooded in. A lot of them. It was none other than Pablo Escobar himself who had alerted them. He had his own screen for viewing the main meeting room from his bedroom suite. Many times the three family patriarchs, Escobar, Ochoa, and Ocampo, didn't participate in gatherings involving sensitive issues such as money laundering and left the details to their representatives, who would zealously carry out the will of the family. Nevertheless, they wanted to keep an eye on things.

Pablo Escobar had received his own brand of intelligence reports about our escapades of the day before. He was about to summon Box and me to his office when we came to him instead. The M-19 disarmed us, and soon after Escobar came down the curving staircase into the cathedral ceilinged meeting area, stopping along the way to talk with one of his lieutenants and ensure that the situation had been defused.

Escobar was a sophisticated-looking man of unusually tall stature for a Colombian. His wavy black hair, parted on the side, as well as the well-groomed mustache said a lot about the way he saw himself and the way he wanted others to see him. His attire and his posture were casual, as if he wanted others to think of him as unpretentious. Speaking in short sentences, and allowing breaks for translation, Escobar politely asked Box and me (who he called "friends from the American government") to join him at the pool for drinks.

By this time, the M-19 had resecured the other members of our team, who had made it as far as the staircase after they had discovered we were missing. With Escobar's permission, I briefly went back to the lower level to let everyone know that we were fine. Upon returning poolside, I discovered Box laughing with Escobar.

I wasted little time in destroying the mood, saying, "Who the hell do you think you are attacking us like that? The rules were established in Zurich, and you agreed to those rules! If you want things to return to the way they were a few months ago, I can make that happen!" I pounded my open hand on an antique automobile while being simultaneously translated.

"We were not the ones who ambushed you," Escobar asserted in an aristocratic manner. "The Cali group is retaliating for our assault against them. The same assault that your government funded to produce the Pseudo Miranda program. I am terribly sympathetic to your loss. Believe me when I tell you that. Pseudo Miranda serves our interests as much as it does yours. We will strive to preserve it as much as you."

"Where were your *campesinos* when we entered the lab?"

"I think he just answered that," Box reminded me in hopes that I would not agitate the man any further.

"No! He answered the "who" part of my question, but he has yet to tell me how his people were able to slip away before the onslaught."

"We have a network of former *cocaleros* (*coca* farmers) spread throughout the jungle, whose sole job is to report unusual activity to our laboratories," Escobar explained, sensing my next question.

"Aren't your labs equipped with IFF? Don't bother to answer. Just tell me why the hell they didn't recode to warn us!"

"Would you trust us if we did that? No, you wouldn't! You would assume that we were chasing you away from a large seizure!"

Escobar was absolutely correct in his assessment. His forthrightness also helped open up a much-needed dialogue and led to agreements that would preclude a repetition of the disaster that befell us in the Llanos jungle.

Nevertheless, one problem remained unresolved—at least in my mind. I had no intention of departing without reciprocity; that is, although I recognized that we could never be fully compensated for the loss of Jeremiah, we expected equal treatment. I politely asked Escobar to follow me back into the house. Walking directly into the meeting room, I pointed to the American.

"I want him to accompany us—right now—on our next intervention."

"What? Are you nuts?" Box whispered to me. "Let's not push our luck with this guy." Box smiled and looked at Escobar.

I ignored Boxer's plea and pushed Escobar for an answer: "So when do we depart?"

Without so much as an objection, Escobar acknowledged the need for reciprocity, saying to me, "Do what you need to do." He motioned to Colonel Borda and told him, "Give him what he needs." He then offered me his handshake, the two-handed type. "I'm glad we had an opportunity to meet one another. Don't take this too far."

"An ambiguous warning at best," I thought.

"Okay, Colonel. Get my team. We're back in business!" I enthusiastically proclaimed. "Let's go, you geeky motherfucker!" I said with a laugh and grabbed the American in a headlock. "How many people did you kill today, asshole?" I demanded with disdain.

"I don't know what you're talking about! I haven't killed anyone. You've got the wrong guy. I swear!"

"Wrong-oh, buck-oh. I've just the right guy."

People like this accountant represented all that was so nasty about the drug trade. Protesting that they only fulfilled a market demand and never bore any responsibility for the consequences, most of the beneficiaries were wealthy, and a good number of the users were middle class or below and were caught in a web of addiction and criminality. At the same time, the users all had "blood in their mouths" from the innocent people who died in an effort to prevent coke from getting to their table. I thought how ironic our struggle was when good men and women were slain attempting to prevent ignorant people from hurting themselves.

*   *   *

The team formed up minutes later at the helicopter pads behind the house. Accompanied by Colonel Borda and the accountant, I instructed Quinn to sit with the lead pilot and direct him to the mission's secondary target. Lourdes and Chavez separated in order to have a translator aboard each of the two Bell helicopters we were flying. The new target was in the northern Andes, due east of Barranquilla, not far from one of Fabio Ochoa's many homes.

The flight was long and required refueling the aircraft along the way. I passed much of this time psychologically torturing the accountant. At one point I tied a string around the frightened man's scrotum and asked him if he'd ever seen the movie *Scarface*. The thought of being pushed out of the aircraft with his testicles tied to the door put him into a hysterical fit. I tried to remain cold even though it made me feel lower than the man I was attempting to frighten out the business. I withdrew the threat and instead began to ask some rather innocuous questions:

"So where the hell do you work?"

"What's the difference? You're gonna kill me anyway!" he sobbed.

"Why don't we just shoot him and get it over with?" Joey suggested, placing his gun barrel in the accountant's face. He continued to sob.

"Great. Now you've got him bawling again!" I said in frustration. "Hey! I'm sorry! Look at me! I'm sorry. Really. Take some deep breaths. That's it. In and out. In and out. Feeling better?"

"Yeah. I'm okay."

"So. Who are you laundering money for?"

"Bank of Boston in Miami."

"That's my bank! Kill this son of a bitch! I'm just kidding. Put the gun down, Joey!"

As we approached the target site, I radioed ahead to the lead chopper and told Quinn to pull up three hundred feet away from the lab in plain view. Once the IFF showed "Green" and cleared us, she did as I instructed.

"Follow our lead," I advised.

Banking the helicopter to one side, my group fired over the heads of the *campesinos,* scattering them. I then had Joey fire on the lab. Without hesitation, Joey riddled the structure. Boxer's group followed suit, demolishing the lab with several ensuing explosions. When the firing stopped, my chopper whizzed over the top of the burning lab, and we dropped grenades the length of the structure. Box trailed behind us, doing the same. Everyone cheered, and at least one person in each chopper said, "That's for you, Jeremiah!"

I radioed once again to Quinn, this time to have her direct us home. By the time the helicopters touched down in Panama City, more than five days had elapsed since we began the mission. Our feelings were mixed. We felt exuberant on the one hand for destroying the two largest labs the Air Force's Strategic Air Command (SAC) had identified and for uncovering an underground network of labs that far surpassed the production capabilities of most conventional labs, and we felt remorse, of course, for our fallen comrade.

Back at Howard Air Force Base, it was time to say good-bye, if only for a short while. Our common understanding of the fragility of our existence in this perilous occupation created a solid bond that would have otherwise taken years to develop. Good-byes really could mean forever.

Everyone returned home by the same route they had taken to get to Howard, except of course for the accountant, who stayed aboard the Colombian aircraft in Panama City. During the last leg of our trip through Mena, Box and I prepared for our debriefing in Paducah. Our conclusion: We had to show force and resolution south of the border, and we had to limit our visits to only hunt "Big Game."

*　*　*

When I arrived back in Murray, I immediately became Ken Bucchi again, except for a part of me. One part had changed forever.

Chapter 17

Almost as soon as I returned to Murray, I departed for Massachusetts and home to Bellingham. The day I left, Andy was with me all day, helping me pack away all my memories. I had the U-Haul attached to the rear of my Corvette, and I was ready to roll. It was odd knowing what I did of her infidelity and not disclosing it to her. I deliberately hid my feelings, deciding it was a good test of my ability to keep my life secret. Nevertheless, when it came time to leave, a supressed emotion welled up untempered, and I took Andy in my arms and began to cry. I wept for the loss of innocence and security that college represented and the loss of a woman I knew I would never hold again.

As I drove across country, I reflected fondly on all the women I'd loved and let slip away. I remember thinking, even at this early stage in my life, that the possibility of having a wife and kids was gone forever. I realized that I was ready to sacrifice much of myself for Operation Pseudo Miranda. What I didn't realize was that I could never be entirely that altruistic.

Over the next few months, I performed many domestic missions across the South—from Arizona to Mississippi—intercepting tons of cocaine in the middle of the night as duffel bags continued to fall from the sky. These excursions typically lasted no more than forty-eight hours, from beginning to end. With few exceptions, Box drove me to Andrews Air Force Base in Washington, DC, from which I flew to a number of bases throughout the South and which in turn became the nexus for regional operations. These bases included, among others, Davis-Monthan in Arizona, Holloman in New Mexico, Kelley in Texas, and Columbus in Mississippi. Whenever we had to travel in and around Arkansas, we went through Mena Airport.

For at least an hour each day, I would make myself available for approach by a courier from CIA higher-ups. This simply involved going somewhere that provided anonymity for myself and any courier delivering the latest instructions. Box was rarely that the courier, so I needed to be able to exchange encrypted messages. To do so, Box had given me the key to a briefcase and a schematic featuring random holes in a laminated piece of paper before I departed Murray for Massachusetts.

Whenever a courier wanted to exchange coded messages with me, I would inconspicuously follow him or her to the briefcase, which the courier would have earlier stashed. If I was unable to accompany the courier at a given time, I would respond to the coded message inappropriately by saying the wrong words. When I did follow, the courier would hand me a briefcase that my key opened. Inside was a coded sheet with a new key and a new schematic. I would immediately remove the new key and replace it with one I used to open the briefcase. I would then overlay my schematic at a predesignated position on the coded sheet. The sheet would include instructions for our next mission and the overlay position of the next message. After memorizing the message, I would switch my schematic with the new one enclosed in the briefcase and burn the message in a small metal box that was provided in the briefcase, placing the box of ashes back in the case. If burning the message proved impractical, I would tear the message up and take it with me. Throughout this process, the courier would stand watch and alert me to any danger.

Initially this cloak-and-dagger activity was exciting, and it made me feel that I was a part of something very important. After a while, though, it became cumbersome. I found myself having to lie to friends and family about my whereabouts and my unusual behavior. The more it happened, the more incredible the lies became. I felt compromised and pathetic lying to the people I most cared for over matters that they probably would have considered unimportant, not knowing what the lies were actually about. I discovered that it made it easier to have only one lie that covered everything and that reasonably explained my short absences. I created a fictitious lover in Holliston, Massachusetts, who I would visit sometimes for a day or so. If I anticipated a mission to take longer, I would say that I was going back to Kentucky to visit friends and look for a job.

One courier delivered a message instructing me to take a written entrance examination for the CIA. The message gave no explanation, and I was unable to contact anyone to ask the purpose of my taking such a test at this juncture in my career with the CIA, so I did what I was told. My friend Mark Rizzo took me into Boston to the Government Building, where the exam was given. I told him that I had always wanted to work for the CIA, but that my chances of passing this test were probably remote.

He said, "Why would you think that anyone working for the CIA had any more ability than you?"

"If it were a test of skill—dealing with people and such—I think I'd fare pretty well. But this written examination crap? I don't know."

"What do you have to lose? You shouldn't worry about the geek portions of the test anyway. I don't think you want a desk job with them, do you?"

"No. But I bet that's all they're testing for."

Mark seemed to sense that I knew more than I was saying, but he was never one to press further than it appeared I wanted to be probed. "Why do you say that? Did I miss something?"

"You never miss a thing. Just remember I took this test, okay?"

The examination lasted several hours. The room was filled with candidates sporting Coke bottle eye wear and pocket protectors. I paid no attention to the instructions the proctors gave us and exerted little effort on the test. The only thing I remember about it was a section that asked you to create sentences from a fictitious language. I recall making a sincere effort on this section because the uniqueness of it intrigued me. Intrigue didn't provide me with enough intelligence to figure it out, however. The fact is, I was already working for the Company, so this test wasn't very important anyhow.

I later came to find out that my disinterest in taking the exam was in keeping with the CIA's intended use. If any team member were discovered directly involved with Operation Pseudo Miranda and claimed an affiliation with the CIA, the Company would deny that they had ever employed that individual by pointing out that the alleged employee had taken but failed the entrance exam and was never hired.

* * *

It was late January or early February, 1985, when Box caught up with me in Framingham, Massachusetts, at a huge nightclub called The Other Side. I had gone there with a friend named Chris, and was forced to tell him that I'd met a girl and that I was going home with her. He was accustomed to me departing abruptly, leaving him stranded, but he never became comfortable with it. In fact, this was the last time he went out with me when I drove.

I found myself at Andrews Air Force Base shortly after dawn. Box had no idea where it was we were going, or why.

"Don't you find this a bit strange?" I asked.

"More than a bit. I'll tell ya, I don't like this at all. I mean, look at you. You look like Don Johnson. What can you do dressed like that?"

"You know, that was a great TV show. Did you see "Miami Vice"? The premiere?"

"It was stupid. Guy drives around in a Daytona Ferrari. First bust he makes, the whole city knows he's a cop."

"You ever heard of suspending disbelief? Anyhow, it's great escapism. The last scene was the best and worst I'd ever seen on TV. The reflection of the city off the black, hand-rubbed paint job of the Ferrari as it cruised down the lit street with "In the Air Tonight" playing in the background was incredible."

"What was the worst?"

"The part where Sonny calls his wife and asks her, 'Was it real?' "

"Oh, yeah! That was stupid!"

"Oh. So you watched to the end."

"Well, yeah. You know. I was with my wife, and I told her that there was this guy . . ."

"Me? You were comparing me to Sonny?"

"Yeah, and . . ."

". . . And if you take away ten years and the melodrama, you have a white guy that dresses good."

"I guess so." Box chuckled. "Maybe it's just the fact that one's white and one's black." He smiled gently. "We're kind of clichéd, aren't we?"

"Our whole team is clichéd. Let's see. We've got both men and women, black and white, Hispanic and Asian . . ."

"Asian?" He looked puzzled.

"Yeah, Ming."

"Oh, yeah."

"We've got the heterosexuals and homosexuals."

"Have we actually confirmed that? Oh! And let's not forget Indian!" Box pointed out.

"Noted."

"I suddenly have this strange impulse to call my wife and ask her if it was real."

"Well, I don't think this T-39 is equipped with a phone, so it'll have to wait."

*   *   *

We flew to Wright-Patterson Air Force Base, located near Dayton, Ohio, refueled, and headed south. We made stops in Paducah and Mena to top off the tanks and transfer passengers as we headed on a journey into the unknown. At Mena, everyone else got off, and Boxer and I traveled on alone. When our path took us more south than east, Box became concerned.

"I had an argument with . . ."

"Your wife?"

"Mmmm."

"So? You'll make up. We'll be back in no time."

"This has never happened before. I always know what we're doin' and where we're goin'. . . . Always."

"I'm sure everything's fine." In truth, I wasn't at all sure, but I figured I'd better get used to this scenario because it was probably going to be the theme of my existence thereafter. After all, it wasn't as if I could do anything about it. Looking out over the puffy clouds, I realized that my life was no longer my own. I'd surrendered it back in Chicago.

We touched down once again, this time in southern Texas. When the T-39 came to rest on the Chase Naval Air Station runway, we were leisurely transferred to a small Huey helicopter. We didn't know it at the time, but we were waiting for clearance to proceed to a large ranch in Beeville, Texas.

"So what do you think this is all about?" I inquired of Box.

"Beats the shit outta me."

I yawned deeply, even though I'd slept along the way. "This job's gonna give me an ulcer."

"I wouldn't worry about that. Ulcers take time to develop."

"That's real comforting. Thanks. Thanks a lot."

"I'm just kidding."

"Why is it your sense of humor only flares when we're in deep doo-doo?"

"Who needs humor when everything's fine?"

*　*　*

We landed in a large field dotted with trees. When we exited the chopper, a short, gray-haired man in a hunting hat approached. His face sagged, but his demeanor did not. He aggressively interrogated us on the operation. "I want answers, gentlemen, and I want 'em now. Are you, or are you not, assisting smugglers bring cocaine and heroin into our country? Has this country been supplying weapons to the Colombian drug barons? How involved are we in the illicit drug trade? Gentlemen! He only authorized not making arrests. That's it! If we have to violate their constitutional guarantees, then so be it. Then we won't make arrests. But we don't help them for God's sake!"

As he spoke, Box tapped my leg lightly and glanced off to my left. I turned my head slowly, stopping when my eyes fell on a group of hunters. My focus rested on the tall gentleman in the middle. I couldn't believe what I was seeing. The man, dressed in hunting fatigues and toting a shotgun, stared patiently back at me. I blocked out everything that others were saying to me. I began to understand why we were brought here. "I'm talking to you!" the gentleman in front of me exclaimed.

"Yeah, I can hear ya. Hey look, buddy. I don't have the foggiest idea what you're talking about. We're not helping anyone traffic drugs. We're just putting them outta business by taking away their protection against illegal searches and seizures. All right? Now I don't know who the fuck you are, and I don't wanna know. So if you don't mind, I'd like to get home because you're givin' me a splittin' headache."

"You get this administration in trouble, you're gonna have more than a splittin' headache."

"Well, they better send someone more intimidating than yourself."

"Hoo! Oh, shit. Ah! Mr. George. Ahh, he ahh. He's just tired. I'm sure he doesn't even know who he's talking to. Do ya, Anthony?" Box said, somewhat startled.

"Why? Who is this?" I asked, feeling a bit ignorant.

"Never mind who I am."

He stepped closer to me. "You remind me of myself when I was your age. You like automobiles, don't you?"

"Not all of 'em."

"Fast ones. I know, I know," he said smiling, and then became more serious. "Learn when it's appropriate to shift down. I'm a tough corner at a hundred and twenty. You can't run it flat out for very long doing what we do for a living. Believe me. Learn that before it's too late."

I didn't respond, even though an endless supply of corny retorts ran through my mind.

Box refused to discuss the meeting during the entire flight to Washington, DC. He finally loosened up as we drove back to Massachusetts. "Who did that look like to you?"

"I have no idea. You're the one who called him Mr. George. For all I know, he's Mr. Ed's talking mule cousin."

"No, you idiot. That was Claire George. I'm talking about the guy standing about thirty feet from us."

"Claire George?"

"Please tell me you've at least heard of him?"

"Could we skip the ritual name calling and just tell me who the hell he is."

"Your boss. Director of Operations. Stop me if any of this sounds familiar. Oh, please. You're serious? How the hell did you ever get this job?"

"He's not my boss. My boss would know what the hell was goin' on. In fact, my boss is obviously above him. This operation, and everything we're doing in it, came right from Casey's mouth, and I was there to hear it! So don't give me that crap about him being my boss! If he's such a big fuck, why doesn't he ask Casey himself? Better yet! Why doesn't Bush ask him. He works for him for cryin' out loud!"

"So it was George Bush," Box said somberly.

"Yeah. Who the hell did you think it was?"

Box let out a large breath. "I think we just witnessed the escalation of Pseudo Miranda to level two: establish deniability."

"I don't get it. Why not have this conversation with Casey and let him deceive them?"

"Because that would put it too close to the presidency."

"That doesn't make sense. Come on, Box. That doesn't make any sense at all."

"I know it doesn't! All I know is that things just got a lot more convoluted and probably more dangerous. We have to tread a lot more cautiously from now on."

"Whenever you do that you get hurt. Box, I'm telling ya. Keep it together or get the hell out. You're gonna become a liability if you don't remain aggressive. Nothing's changed. Everyone's just getting their ducks in line. It's probably a good sign. It probably indicates that they've decided they're in it for the long haul." I paused to pat Box on the back as he drove. "I know what you need."

"Yeah, I do too. And I'm goin' home to get some."

"No, not that."

"What?"

"Cow tipping."

"Oh no! I'd rather take my chances with the Colombians than tip another side of beef with you. It's too cold, anyhow. There aren't any cows around this time of the year, are there?"

"No. But I'll keep your interest in mind the next time we're in Texas."

"You do that, Bucchi."

*　*　*

Back in Bellingham, I made a more conscious effort to build my cover. This meeting hadn't frightened me like it had Box, but it seemed prudent to bury my true identity deeper than it already was. I put together a resumé and began to peddle it around, while simultaneously doing what was necessary not to get hired.

One of my couriers brought a message informing me that I was to apply for a slot in the Air Force's Officer Training program. The sender didn't say why this was necessary, but I assumed it had something to do with supporting my cover story by making it appear I was an airman, especially when abroad. Not knowing the exact reasoning behind it, I took it upon myself to apply to the Army's Officer Candidate School also.

After submitting the applications, I received instructions to ready myself for another *Vosotros* operation. I felt more prepared to cross the border this time, having learned so much from our initial mission. This deployment would teach me, however, that there was no such thing as enough preparation when performing an intervention.

Chapter 18

I next met up with Box at Randolph Air Force Base, near San Antonio. I flew in on another T-39 from Paducah. After we landed, the pilot taxied to a hangar on one of the side runways referred to as Hangar 17. As I exited the plane, Box met me with the most incredible audacity. "Where the hell have you been? What the hell kept ya?"

"I had a compressor stall on the number two engine, which slowed me down a bit," I answered sarcastically. "What do you mean, what took me so long? What the hell do I have to do with the timing of anything? I did my part. I was at the airport on time."

"Just get in the plane, please."

"You know, it really pisses me off when you don't apologize for criticizing me by mistake." I then turned around to look out over the number of large transport planes on the ramp.

"So. Which one is ours?" I wanted to know.

"That one," Box said, pointing to a pint-size transport that looked like the kind they used to fly in vintage Tarzan movies.

"We're goin' in that? You're kidding me, right? Because there's no way we're gonna make it in that . . . that . . . What the hell is that anyway?"

"It's a C-47."

"God. Don't the names of these aircraft like follow—well, you know—sequentially?"

"Whatta ya mean?"

"You know. C-123, C-130, C-135, C-141, et cetera."

"Yeah. I guess that would make this pretty old, huh?" Box said, nervousness creeping into his voice.

"World War II, probably."

We eyed the aircraft somewhat distressed about making the impending journey in such a relic. The plane had been performing CIA missions in the Caribbean for some time now, disguised as an island transport, but that still wasn't very reassuring. That this aircraft was still in service was surely an aberration. When we boarded the plane, we found it outfitted with one row of seats on one side, and two rows on the other. The seats were modified with race car harnesses, which restrained both shoulders with wide nylon straps. It didn't make me feel any more secure knowing that the technicians found it necessary to add such a safety feature. It was probably easier to add harnesses than to fix some major flight control problem.

Before we took off I thought of how I would one day cherish the memory of Boxer's petty disagreements with me, knowing as I did that pettiness was a luxury enjoyed by those with no great hardship in their lives. His persistent trifling would become a constant reminder that all was fairly normal—a security blanket of sorts.

We flew for hours due south, stopping periodically for servicing at small airfields along the way. At one pit stop in southern Honduras near Toncontin, at an American air base situated in the midst of a jungle, I began to notice a trend: wherever there were encircling mountain ranges covered in trees, there was likely a CIA staging area nearby. The U.S. Army had trained transplanted Nicaraguan Contras here, only to send them back across the border to die. I wanted no part of anything I saw there. It turned my stomach to watch paramilitary training on TV shows like "60 Minutes." I hated, and still hate, the mentality of the soldier who kills for its own sake. Killing, under the most profound of circumstances, can become a necessity, but should never, under any circumstances, become enjoyable. Those who train people to kill, excluding recognized government military officers, have lost their sense of humanity. I realize that much of what I did may seem hypocritical in light of this philosophy, but killing, in my case, was an ugly necessity in the war on drugs.

Day gave way to night, then we finally approached Howard Air Force Base in Panama. The runway lights were the first thing I'd seen all day that told me I hadn't left the twentieth century entirely. Our aircraft followed a pickup truck with "Follow Me" written in yellow lights above the vehicle's rear window and parked on the Hot Pad, a place normally reserved for aircraft carrying dangerous materials or explosives. The pilot informed us that he'd received instructions to remain there until the rest of our people arrived and were shuttled over to us. I looked out the window while we waited. Parked adjacent to us were a couple of C-130 transports. "Damn. I never thought I'd be happy to see one of those pigs again," I said, relieved.

"I don't know what the hell you're so happy about! I'm piloting you all the way into Colombia!" the pilot said in a manner that you might tell someone to have another drink while they puked their guts out. He was a chubby man with pulled-back hair that concealed a balding crown. His clothes were loose and had a Hispanic flavor to them. His second chin was like an udder, ballooning and smooth. He chose not to give his name, but that was the only thing he chose to withhold. He certainly had no misgivings about telling us how great a pilot he was.

"Shit! Don't worry about this bucket of bolts! I've flown bigger pieces of shit into tighter spots than this."

"Look, buddy. We're not looking to have you fly us into anywhere tight. If indeed we have to fly with you to Colombia in this death trap, it's only to a nice runway owned by one of the PM players," I said rationally.

"The PM players? Did someone let the cat outta the bag?" he taunted me. I didn't consider the fact that he was just a pilot and had little idea of the purpose of our mission into Colombia.

"Look. You do what you do best, and fly the plane. Ask any more questions, and I'll do what I do best," I responded in frustration. I was more upset at myself than him.

"Oh. Now don't go getting your ovaries in an uproar. I just like to know as much as possible about a mission, that's all. You may not believe this, but I'm a good person to have on your side. I've pulled a lot of people's asses outta the fire in my time."

"Yeah. Of course, what you're not telling us is that you probably put their asses in the fire in the first place," Box amended.

I said softly to Box, "Let's be careful. Don't forget, there's a lot of fires in Colombia he could put our butts into."

"You carry on for ten minutes, and I say one thing—and you're blaming me?"

"Remember Zurich. We can't take the chance that this guy hates black people."

"Funny. Very funny."

*   *   *

A van arrived carrying our comrades Debara, Christina, Lourdes, Joey, Rick, Quinn and Steven. Jesus was recovering from an allergic reaction to a large-scale attack by fire ants, which he suffered during another interception. As humorous as this sounds, he was out of commission for weeks as a result.

"Hey, good looking," Debara said cheerfully.

"Hi!" Box, the pilot and I responded simultaneously. I could understand Box mistakenly responding to the reference of good looks, but the pilot was another matter. His cockiness far surpassed any realistic expectations he could possibly have had for himself.

"Gee. Three good-looking men. What's a girl to do?" Debara said flirtatiously.

"Puke?" Quinn answered.

"You know, my mom says that the most sincere compliments given to women come from women. So, Joey. Who's the best-looking man here?" I said in jest.

"Quinn," Joey said, dead pan.

"Boy, you're pushing it with me," Quinn reacted, only slightly serious.

"I can see this is gonna be a fun trip," the pilot said, jokingly castigating our outward appearance of friction. In reality, we were becoming comfortable with one another and able to speak our minds without worrying about adverse reactions.

*   *   *

Ten hours after I set out on the mission, we finally reached Panama City, and landed at the international airport in Tocumen, where we awaited word that one of Manuel Noriega's aircraft was ready to take off for Colombia. Because it had a scheduled flight plan, we would fly with it in close proximity so the images of the two planes would blur into one on any radar screen and our presence would be "shadowed."

The basic plan was to fly to a small airfield in Aracuara, Colombia, some 900 miles away, detouring along the way to drop into a small airstrip located near the Magdalena River, south of Medellin, in the Andes Mountains. We flew between, not over, the mountains of the Andes range. The aircraft's limited flight envelope restricted the altitude we could achieve. At certain points, our wing tips came within meters of the mountains' walls. My confidence in our pilot's competence grew with each near miss. This "seat of the pants" flying through the mountains made it infinitely more difficult to detect us on radar, explaining why it was not necessary to provide us with an airplane capable of flying at higher altitude.

Time passed quickly, despite the white-knuckle piloting, but when our altitude dropped suddenly to treetop level, we became keenly aware of our rather precarious position.

"What the hell's goin' on up there?" Box worried aloud.

"Nothing! Just looking for a sign," the pilot shouted nonchalantly.

"A sign?" I said in a puzzled manner. "Like from God?"

"Like from the road, I think," Quinn murmured.

"What! This crazy mother's gonna get us killed!" Box shouted.

"Someone with good vision and good Spanish, get your ass up here pronto!" the pilot demanded.

"Is this guy serious?" I asked. "Quinn, get up there and help him."

"I don't speak very good Spanish."

"You're a pilot. If he really needs to read street signs, speaking the language is the least of our problems. Now hurry."

Quinn rushed to the cockpit, expecting the worst. When she saw that most of the gauges were inoperative and that we were dangerously low on fuel, she called out in horror, "Oh, my God!"

"What?" the pilot reacted.

"What do mean, 'what'? Look at this mess! We're gonna ditch! We're gonna ditch!" Quinn responded hysterically.

"We've got plenty of fuel. That gauge only measures the preconfigured tanks. We added a wing bladder and a fuselage tank to expand the flight envelope. Of course, if we don't get our bearings soon, we will run outta fuel."

"Does this thing have a fuel transfer set-up?" Quinn asked rationally.

"A what?"

"Fuel transfer? You know, from the wings to the fuselage, and then to the engines. It's quite possible that your wings have already drained. The wing tanks are normally set up to pump first, then the fuselage. If that's what happened, we're low on fuel," Quinn explained. It was all technical mumbo-jumbo to me, but I did understand that part about being low on fuel.

"Is she right?" I asked, leaning into the cockpit.

"There's one way to find out. I could turn off the fuel pump, bank the aircraft, and let it gravity feed for a bit. See if one of the engines fails."

"Oh, that's a great plan," I said. "Where are we? Oh wait, you don't know that either, do you?"

"You catch on quick," the pilot bantered. "All I know is that I flew the course I was supposed to, passing over the Cordillera Central, and I never saw the strip."

"The Corri-what? What the hell is he talking about?" I asked Quinn. "Give it to me in English."

"The Andes. We flew over them. No fuckin' runway where they said there'd be one."

"You know, the Andes are a pretty big mountain range. Maybe you missed it! Did you ever think of that! That you mighta missed it?"

"Yeah, dipshit. I thought of it. You wanna fly around at nine thousand feet looking for a runway in the sky? We run out of fuel up there, you can put your head between your legs and kiss your ass good-bye!"

"All right, I get your point. But now whatta we do?"

"Pray," he said, twisting around to face forward and sliding back into his seat.

"Okay. Quinn, get in back with everyone else."

"I thought I was needed up here."

"Just go back and tell everyone to prepare for a rough landing."

"What are you going to do?"

"I don't know. Pray, I guess."

*   *   *

Unbeknownst to us, the pilot had flown much further south than he had intended. The landscape became much greener, and the mountains shallower. We had descended into the rain forest, and that was not on anyone's agenda. Suddenly, a squawk on the radio asked us to identify ourselves. Unknown to us at the time was that the signal originated from Puerto Leguizamo, on the Putumayo River.

"So where's it coming from?" I asked.

"Don't know. But at least it's a safe landing."

"No, it's not. We can't be discovered." My speech quickened. "Drop down even further."

"What? Are you fuckin' crazy? Look how low we are!" he shouted. His hands were shaking in front of him.

I ignored his concerns. "Wait. First find out where they're calling from, so we can get our bearings."

The pilot radioed back and was told that the signal came from Puerto Leguizamo on the Putumayo River. Moments later, we lost contact. "Great! That's just fuckin' great! Now what the hell do we do?"

"You're the badass. Put us down somewhere safe, and my SATCOM man will call for help."

"That was help!"

"No! That would have been the end of the whole operation! As long as I have a breath in me, that ain't gonna happen! Now put the fuckin' plane on the ground and shut up!"

"You got it, Hoss."

We flew along, praying that our IFF transponder would locate a PM installation, whether it be an airstrip or a lab—just somewhere safe. Neither of us wanted to consider the alternative. The chances of landing in a remote field and being extracted safely were slim at best. We altered courses several times, continually recalculating our location. Then a loud bang rocked the aircraft. "What the hell was that?" I asked gingerly.

"That, my friend, was the number one engine." Then there came another loud bang. "And that was the number two." The pilot kept his cool, however, and miraculously flew over a ravine with some terrain that looked negotiable as an improvised runway. Our comparative altitude increased, as the plane crested a small mountain peak.

"You can start kissing that ass right about now," he declared. "One of our mains is stuck," referring to the main landing gear. If one hangs up, you have to pull up the other one to prevent a cartwheel landing.

"Here we go!" he screeched, and we dropped into the ravine, bouncing and sliding our way across the target field. Bushes and debris blasted the front of the aircraft like artillery shells. I was tossed and jerked for what seemed a lifetime, waiting for an explosion, or worse, to flip. We plowed over vegetation with speed and force, caroming off obstructions like a pinball until we began to decelerate. We came to an abrupt stop when the right wing engaged a small, brush-covered hill.

I slumped forward, exhausted and relieved. My hands were quivering uncontrollably. I tried to unfasten my seat belt, but I couldn't get my hands to cooperate. I looked to my left and stared at the blood trickling from the pilot's head. He was unconscious and in need of help, but I couldn't summon enough strength to assist him. I closed my eyes, thinking that I'd regain my energy if I rested for a minute or two. I felt very sleepy. I didn't know that I had a concussion and that the grogginess would not immediately dissipate. I also didn't know that falling asleep was counterproductive, and possibly deadly. The hot, humid air rolling in through the shattered windscreen encouraged my lethargy. I started to fade, feeling no pain, when I imagined I saw a black panther perched on the nose of the aircraft. I gaped at this mystical sight, drifting in and out of consciousness, before slipping away completely.

The next thing I remember was my heels being dragged over the metal floor of the aircraft. Rick was pulling me from the mangled wreckage of the C-47.

"The pilot," I said with a tired voice.

"He's fine. Just relax," Rick comforted.

"How's he doin'?" Box asked.

"Seems okay. Let's get 'im some water," Rick advised.

I attempted to gather my wits and strength and stand up, but stumbled, falling to the ground on all fours. I asked, "Is everyone all right?"

"We're fine. You and the pilot are the only ones who got hurt," Debara said to ease my mind. She rubbed the back of my head with her hand as she knelt beside me. Ducking her head under mine, she looked up at me and continued, "You had us all scared."

"I saw a black panther."

"What?" she said curiously.

"A black panther. He watched over me." I'm not sure why I worded it this way, but I did.

"He saw a black panther," Debara announced to everyone.

"Where?" Box inquired, doubtful.

"On the nose of the plane," I said to Debara.

She raised her head above mine once again and said, "He says he saw it on . . . on the aircraft."

"He's delirious. Panther," Box said, leaning down to feel the knot on my forehead. "Wooo! You got some schnozzle there!"

Box turned away and walked toward the aircraft. It looked as though it had been there for years, enveloped by plant growth, its tail severed. Just then it began to rain, steady but light.

"I suggest we take cover in the hulk of the C-47 and crash for the evening," Box said. "Well, maybe *crash* is not the best word."

Debara assisted me to my feet and walked me to the plane. "I did see a panther," I said.

"I believe you. I do," Debara responded.

"It could have been a guardian of sorts, you know," Christina suggested.

"You mean like an angel. Right?" said Lourdes.

"Yeah," Christina asserted. "Of course, you could just be hallucinating from that bump on your head."

"Way to stick to your guns, Christina," Joey teased.

Everyone carried their bumps and bruises into the aircraft and turned in for the evening.

*   *   *

Shortly before sunrise, I awakened with an uneasy feeling. While everyone slept, I stepped outside the plane, not knowing what drew me there. A gray haze cascaded from the mountain top. I walked a hundred feet or so across the hillside to the perimeter of the jungle. I felt drawn into it. At first, it seemed nothing more than curiosity. I had never experienced a forest so dense. The sunlight, as it rose on the rest of the region, barely touched the earth in this jungle. The vegetation was comparatively thin at ground level, making it easy to explore. The deeper I drove into the forest, the more I wondered how far I would go before turning back. I could no longer see the clearing where we'd crashed our plane. I paused, debating whether I should return, when I heard a faint moan, or it could have been the purr of a cat.

"The black panther," I thought. The forest was alive with the sounds of birds and monkeys, but this sound was distinctive. It called to me. Chills ran up my spine as I turned toward the source of the sound. I searched tentatively for the panther. I drew my gun and pushed back some leafy branches. I was seized with a sudden fear, causing me to step backward in retreat. I stopped and crouched, spinning in a slow circle with my Colt .45 leveled and ready for action. I paused, drawn to a line of elephant-leafed plants. I knew that whatever my intuition had picked up was behind that wall of leaves. I had sensed something, that's for sure, but what? Was this cat so mysterious to me that I feared confronting it? I was confident in my ability to shoot it before it laid a paw on me, so it couldn't be that. But what if it were more than just an ordinary cat? What if it were symbolic of a fear, or worse, of God? I didn't feel I was ready to meet God that morning.

Pulling back the leaves, I was frightened out of my gourd, yet couldn't resist doing it. I moved with caution, placing my weapon in the hair-trigger mode. I breathed deeply twice, calming my heart as much as possible as I pushed through the big, bright green leaves. I expected to be immediately startled by what I found on the other side, but there was nothing. I looked around expectantly. My eyes, scanning the jungle, froze on a curious object only partially visible through the undergrowth: a human hand bound to the branch of a tree. The closer I came to this bewildering sight, the more my throat filled with pressure. "Oh, my God. Oh, my living God. Oh, God, help me. Oh, please help. Oh, my God. What's happened here?" I whispered aloud.

A woman, stripped naked, was tied to one of two adjoining trees with safety wire, her throat slit from ear to ear, with her eyes plucked out and stuffed in her mouth. A man tied to the base of the other tree was skinned from his nipples to the top of his forehead. His skin was tacked to the tree behind him. In his lap was a baby—dead—having been stabbed through the chest. I sat down on a log directly in front of them. I was twisted inside, hurting beyond comprehension for their agony and wanting to vomit at the same time. The man's eyes seemed to stare at me, so I rotated on the log to face away from him.

Then I heard the sound that had drawn me here. It was directly behind me. I knew now what it was, but I didn't want to believe it.

"Hmmm."

"No. Oh, please, God, no," I pleaded as I turned timidly back toward the family. I stared at the man, knowing it was he who called to me. My eyes filled with tears and I told him how sorry I was.

"Oh, God, what do I do?" I asked aloud.

He moaned one more time.

"I know," I told him. "Your family, they're at peace," I said, attempting to ease his mind.

Tears, now flooding my eyes, blurred my vision. I wiped them away reluctantly, since they screened some of the horror. I moved close to him, easing my gun to the back of his head. "Our Father, who art in heaven . . . ," I prayed, slowly and succinctly, contemplating what I was about to do, hoping that he would die naturally. He didn't.

"Unnhh!" he moaned one last time.

"God, please forgive me."

I shot him through the temple. His blood spattered over me. I slumped to the ground, blood dripping from my face, and felt numb, but I somehow knew I would get through it. I reasoned that the panther and the feeling of being drawn into the forest were somehow connected and that I was supposed to be in this place at this time. I wiped my forehead, streaking the blood across my face like Indian war paint.

"Ves! Anthony!" I heard ringing out across the forest. The 4PM team should never have broken discipline and revealed their presence, but they were driven by circumstances and desperation, and their concern was touching. Although I heard their cries clearly, I was unable to respond. I tried to summon the energy, breathing deeply, but I couldn't find the will to even say "I'm here!" Everything paled in significance compared to what I had just participated in, and I simply remained quiet, listening as the voices closed in on me.

Chapter 19

I discerned Joey's voice just beyond the veiling leaves as he called out, "Tony!" Then, in a more fragile voice, he said, "Come on, Booch. Where are you, man?"

"Here. Over here," I finally answered.

Joey plowed through the rubbery leaves, stopping abruptly when he saw the bodies in all their horror. He knew me well enough to piece together the chain of events leading to my being covered in blood. "We gotta get outta here, Tony. Whoever did this may have heard the gunshot. Come on. Let's get away from this insanity."

"We've gotta bury 'em. My God, Joey. Look at 'em. For God's sake, who would do this? Who could? We gotta bury 'em," I demanded in a mournful tone.

Joey, now concerned about the danger of making so much noise and drawing unwanted attention to ourselves, canvassed the immediate area for possible interlopers. Not discovering anyone, he yelled to the rest of the group, "Over here!"

"This way! It came from over here!" yelled Lourdes. She emerged through the undergrowth and called out once again, "Here! He's here!" She approached us with a smile but froze in terror when she spied the bloody corpses. "What happened?" she asked, weeping. "Joey? What happened?"

"What the hell's it look like happened! Some people were fucked up by some sick mothers, and Tony put one of 'em out of his misery."

"Is that what happened, Ves?"

"Would you shut the hell up!" Joey yelled, stopping her from interrogating me. "Do you think he did it!"

"Of course not!" she shouted back, now bawling.

"Then shut the fuck up! Nothing else matters!"

"We gotta bury 'em," I said in an even tone of voice.

Joey calmed down, then leaned toward Lourdes. "He wants to bury them."

"With what?" Lourdes asked.

"Good question. But look at him. He ain't leavin' until we plant them."

One by one, everyone came on the scene, including the pilot. Joey gathered them together and explained the situation. I glanced up periodically to find each of them intermittently looking over their shoulders at me. I felt like a freak in a circus show.

"All right," Box began, speaking rapidly, "Rick, Steven, Quinn, you (the pilot) and myself will grab some dirt. Use your knives or anything sharp to help you dig quickly. Lourdes, Debara, muster up some rocks if you can—as many as you can. We'll have to make the graves shallow. Bury the child with its mother. Joey and Christina, move around. Look for anything that doesn't fit."

Joey cleared his throat and motioned Box in my direction. Box nodded and then came to my side. "We're gonna give them a proper burial. You just relax and let us take care of this, okay?"

"No, I wanna help," I said firmly.

"If you think you're up to it. You can help find some rocks."

"I'll help dig the father's grave."

"Okay. I'll help you."

We worked at a bee's pace, ripping and gouging the earth. The more I dwelled on the cruelty of these murders the more violently I thrust my knife into the dirt. I vented my anger in my labor. Box kept pace. This was his way of reassuring me that I wasn't going mad. I couldn't bear to watch as Joey detached the man's skin from the tree and laid it back in place. I continued to look away as Box and Rick laid the bodies in the ground. They had covered their faces with dirt before I turned around to assist in the burial. We placed several rocks on top of them, and Christina marked the graves with crossed branches, layering a modicum of humanity over the barbaric butchery. As Christina said a prayer, I asked the Lord if I'd made the right decision. I also asked Him to allow this family to look down on the earth one last time to see that someone cared.

We huddled tightly beside the graves, holding onto one another for strength and reassurance. We were becoming segregated from the rest of the world by circumstances, but I liked it. The tougher things got, the closer we were drawn. Even the pilot, who now seemed like one of us, threw his arms around those standing beside him. We waited for a moment, staring down at the mounded dirt, when I heard it.

"Huh." I smiled.

"What?" Box asked.

"The music," I said, assuming he must have heard it too.

"What music?" he continued.

"That beautiful music. The trumpets . . . the brass. Oh, how soothing." I closed my eyes and swayed back and forth, not considering the absurdity of hearing orchestral music in the thick of the jungle.

"I hear it," Lourdes said convincingly, and she began to mimic my swaying motion. Box followed suit, probably deciding that I had gone crazy. His clumsy dancing started me laughing, although I continued to dance. We were all dancing now, and laughing, and it released us from that place. It was uplifting. Something divine had happened, and no one was questioning it. We departed as if something good had happened there.

*   *   *

When we got back to the plane, we gathered up all the food and water we could carry and hiked out. At the edge of the forest, I looked back at the wreck, wondering if it had really killed us and we just didn't know it yet.

The pilot led us due north, telling us that we would soon come upon the Macaya River. There, he said, we would find help in the form of the drug smugglers we were originally searched for. We feared using the radio because, if we were in Peru, an extraction would take such an inordinate amount of time we risked capture. Quinn confirmed the connection between this river and a secondary target she was given back at Howard Air Force Base. She could not, however, assure us that we were where he said we were.

"What makes you think we're near this river?" Debara asked.

"Yeah. We could just as easily have crossed into Peru last night, you know," Quinn followed up.

"The radio transmission. If we were in Peru, they would have asked us more than just to identify ourselves," he said, attempting to convince himself as much as us.

"I hope you're right," Box added.

"But . . . ?" the pilot started.

"But? But what?" I asked.

"The eyes."

"What eyes?" Box pressed.

"The ones in—you know—her mouth," he said with caution.

"That meant somethin', didn't it?" Joey asked anxiously.

"Yeah." He gasped. "It means she talked about something she saw. Something she wasn't supposed to talk about. It means betrayal."

"So how does that mean we're in Peru?" Box asked.

"It's used by the Shining Path," I answered.

"And they're in Peru, I bet," Joey injected.

"Now the question is, how far into Peru?" said Debara.

"Well, let's not give up hope that this form of torture is common to the Colombians, too." Lourdes attempted to build our confidence.

"Yeah. It's comforting to know that we might be tortured by capitalist Colombian drug traffickers as opposed to socialist Peruvians. And even if we're not, it's nice to know that some poor, unsuspecting Colombian family will be," I retorted, sarcastically pointing out her mistake in reasoning.

"That's not fair. You know what I meant."

"I know. I was just playing," I said, sharing a chuckle with my friends.

* * *

We walked for about five hours, never running across the Shining Path. As we came to the bank of a river, we hunkered down and considered our options. The worst scenario was that this was the Putumayo River; the best scenario was that this was the Macaya. In either case, we would have to cross it. At this point, the river ran much too rapidly to cross safely, so we decided to follow the bank in search of a safer crossing. We had gone about a mile when we discovered a section of the river where the current seemed manageable. However, it was still much too deep to wade across. We had to decide whether or not we should leave behind everything except the weapons and swim across.

"We shouldn't have any need for water, what with all this rain," I said.

"And food seems quite plentiful around here. Joey could shoot a monkey or something, if we get desperate. So that's not a problem. I, for one, will feel a lot better over there."

"I'm not such a good swimmer," Box said, not arguing with my suggestion but rather hoping to receive some sort of solace.

"Why does that not surprise me," I commented.

"My father said it would cause me problems, and here it is, just as . . ."

"Big as shit. I know. You know, your father was a very wise man. You could have saved us a lot of headaches had you just not been such a pussy when you were a kid," I razzed him.

"Hey, you won't have to wait for me," Box snapped back.

"Where have I heard that before?" I taunted him.

"We're gonna cross? Is that what we've decided?" Christina asked.

"Yeah. So let's go," Debara said, cutting to the chase.

The pilot waddled in front of us, still wheezing from the hike. "If we're gonna do this, there's a couple things you need to know. First, swim with the current, on an angle to the opposite shore."

Quinn interrupted him. "Great. Mark Spitz with glands."

He shook his head and continued, "The other thing to remember is not to thrash around in the water. You never know when you'll run into a school of piranha."

"No problem. We'll send you first, and they'll be too stuffed to bother with the rest of us," Quinn said harshly.

"Say, what's your problem, bitch? I don't need this attitude of yours."

I separated the two, throwing my arm around the pilot and walking him to the edge of the water. "I wouldn't press my luck with her. She can do more damage than some flesh-eating fish, believe me."

The pilot waded into the murky water first, and I entered directly behind him. I was astonished at the pilot's grace as he sidestroked his way across the river, never rippling the surface of the water with his feet. He had rhythmic short kicks and extended arm strokes that moved voluminous amounts of water. I was never much of a swimmer, though. No matter how I attempted to emulate his stroke, I couldn't maintain my calm, and ended up kicking and pawing at the water in panic whenever I lost buoyancy.

As I approached the opposite shore, I developed what can only be called an anxiety attack. I kicked and tore at the water with short choppy

strokes, then swallowed a mouthful of water and sank below the surface.
I was only twenty feet from the shore. I surfaced, coughing and spluttering. I thought I should be able to touch bottom, but it seemed out of
reach. The pilot offered his help, saying, "Just stand up. You can do it."

I reached for the river bottom with my toes and was relieved to find
that, when fully extended, I could stick my nose above the water. I had
lost track of the others and had absolutely no idea how they were faring.
I inhaled a couple of refreshing breaths of air, when Steven suddenly
flopped on top of me, pressing me underwater once again. Soon there
were nine of us churning there in six feet of water. With some effort, we
managed to get to the river bank.

Except for Lourdes and the pilot, everyone was completely exhausted.
We lay sprawled out on the bank, struggling to stabilize our breathing.
We soon regained our energy, however, and continued north. With what
we thought to be Peru and the Shining Path behind us, we felt like a
burden had been lifted, and our fears evaporated.

Traversing the mountains was grueling, and soon we were consumed
with fatigue. "Does anyone have a clue where the hell we are?" I asked,
sapped of all my strength.

"If that river was the border back there, then we're somewhere in the
Amazonas region," Quinn stated. "It's a big area, with few breaks in the
jungle. The chances of us going on unnoticed aren't very good, though.
We need to do something, and soon. I'm not sure what, but we can't stay
out here indefinitely. There are poisonous snakes, carnivorous animals,
and let's not forget the *campesinos*. They don't carry IFF. They're not going to know who we are."

"Well, we're not goin' to be extracted here. The forest is just too
thick," I replied. "Let's sleep here tonight and attempt to find a clearing
tomorrow."

We were without blankets, so we nestled under the thickest canopy we
could find and readied ourselves for slumber. "You know, this kinda reminds me of when I was a little kid and my dad would take me, my
brothers and a bunch of the neighborhood kids camping in the woods
near Beaver Pond. Of course, there you could see the stars and light a fire
without fear of being killed. How circumstances change."

"At least you've had some experience with this," Joey said. "I grew up
on concrete. The old man always talked about the great camping trip, but

it never happened. I don't know. It wasn't his fault. He worked hard, right on through his dreams."

"Well, someday maybe you can take him on that trip," Lourdes consoled.

"I don't think so," Joey muttered despondently. I knew what came next. Joey continued, "He shot himself last winter on his way to work."

"Son of a bitch," Box said under his breath.

"God, I'm so sorry. I didn't . . . ," Lourdes stammered, struggling to find the right words. "Camping is overrated anyhow."

"Yeah, so are fathers," Joey mumbled.

"Is your mom still alive?" I asked Joey.

"Yeah," he answered slowly.

"Good. 'Cause I don't want to start a sweet mother story and find out she's dead too."

"I think my father saw himself as a failure and a burden to us. I just wished I could have told him—convinced him—that he was a hero to me. He gave up all his dreams so we could someday have a shot at our own."

Joey paused. "And here I am in the Colombian jungle with pilots that can't navigate, a satellite expert that can't tell left from right, a guy that can't climb, swim, and lord knows what else, a dyke in denial, Mary Magdelene, and a guy that thinks he has all the answers to the world's problems. Boy, would my old man be proud. Yeah, boy!" Joey smiled.

"I'll let the dyke comment pass this one time," Quinn joked.

"Who's the guy that's supposed to know everything?" I toyed.

"He didn't say 'knew everything'; he said that he *thought* he knew everything," Debara clarified.

"Oh, Box," I stated.

The mood became relaxed, as if we were on an ordinary camping trip.

Debara made her way to my side while the others gabbed away. They soon fell asleep, but Debara and I chatted quietly for a couple hours. We never once considered tomorrow. Chatting turned to intimacy in the tropical night air. I knew immediately that this was not something I would regret come daybreak. Unlike so many females I knew in college, Debara was a woman, emotionally and mentally. She understood herself and held no unrealistic expectations of me. We came to each other honestly, without masks. I held her close to me for the longest time, clinging to a moment that I wished would last forever.

My internal alarm clock awakened me before the others. I started to slip away from Debara, but she woke up, too. "Where you going?" she whispered.

"It wouldn't be good if the others saw us like this."

"I'm sure they heard us kissing and panting last night."

"Probably, but . . ."

"I know. Come here and give me a kiss good morning," she sweetly asked.

I did, and it felt right. I had fallen in love with her during the past few months and didn't even suspect it was happening. "I'll see you in the morning."

"Not as well as you saw me last night," she playfully responded.

"Sshhh! You kook."

*   *   *

The following day it rained. A steady flow of water could be heard pelting the thick jungle canopy. Some water dripped through and splattered our heads, but we were mostly sheltered by the natural umbrella of the forest. Ironically, in this drenching weather, we desperately sought an open field. If Steven's equipment had even the slimmest chance of contacting the CIA in Mena, we needed to make our way out of this jungle or find a sizable clearing. To compound our plight, the clearing had to be virtually obstruction free and on flat ground or an elevation, not in a ravine.

After a few hours of trudging our way through the hilly jungle, I expressed my discontent. "This isn't working, Steven! Isn't there any other way of making this thing work?"

"I've gotta bounce the signal off a satellite. That just isn't possible from in here," Steven replied reasonably.

"What if we held the dish up above the treetops?" I questioned.

"If the tree was on a peak, sure. But how the hell are we gonna do that? Even if you could climb one of these trees, the cord won't reach the top," Steven reasoned.

"It would if you climbed up a ways yourself," I said, realizing that this was our only hope.

"There's no way I can climb . . . " Steven began to object, but I cut him off.

"Okay! Let's find a tree on a peak. The next hill looks promising. When we get there, I'll climb to the top of the tallest tree. It'll be up to the rest of you to persuade Steven up the tree behind me."

"The radio isn't that hard to figure out. Maybe someone else can do it," Steven suggested.

"Good try, but we need this to work the first time. I don't want someone halfway up a tree trying to figure this thing out. No, you've gotta go."

"Okay, I'll do my best."

"No, we don't want your best," Box insisted. "We want your ass up that tree."

"You can do it, Steven. You swam that river, didn't ya?" Lourdes said supportively.

"I wasn't terrified of swimming."

"Good lord! Who else is afraid of heights? I want a show of hands," I demanded. No hands were raised. "That figures. The only two who have needed to climb something in a crisis have had phobias."

* * *

At the crest of the hill, I turned to watch the rest of the team come up behind me. I was proud of our determination, yet uneasy with our obvious collective lack of experience. Box, who was pulling up the rear, glanced up at me, grinning tensely as sweat poured off his brow. He dropped his head back down and continued up the hill. "You're almost there! Just a few more yards!" I yelled encouragingly.

Turning back around, I was startled to see a boy, maybe nine years old, standing directly in front of me. Fear crossed his face as his eyes swept from me to the group struggling toward us and back to me. I sensed that he wanted to run but feared exposing his back to us. He carried a small handgun. He held it raised, but hanging loosely, not pointed. I could have killed him with little effort.

"Halt," I called to the others, who were unaware of our visitor. "Halt," I said in a soothing voice. "Everybody halt. No talking, no talking. We've got a small friend right in front of us. Mind you, an armed small friend. Just relax. I'm going to attempt to disarm him."

Box couldn't believe it. He said, "Are you outta your fuckin' mind? Look where we're at, for God's sake. This is not your average little boy."

I softly said to the boy, "It's okay." I lowered my weapon to the ground. "Spanish," I thought.

"Whoever's nearest me with good Spanish, please tell this kid I'm unarmed and don't wish to cause him any harm. "I was now in a crouched position, having just placed my weapon on the damp ground. Lourdes began to speak, distracting him a bit, as I stood up again.

But the kid shot me anyway. I heard nothing initially. I just felt my arm being smashed backwards. It was like being hit with a baseball bat. Pressure filled my arm, but no real pain. I wasn't sure if indeed it was my arm that had been hit. Before I could consider the extent of my injury, I heard a barrage of gunfire.

"No! No! No! I'm fine! Stop shooting! Stop shooting!" I screamed, hugging the ground as the bullets wailed over my head. The shooting soon terminated. I closed my eyes, not wanting to see the body. Box leaned over and grabbed me by my injured arm.

"What?" I shouted. "What? Do you think you used enough firepower! Would you like my gun? Maybe there's an ounce of flesh left we can still shoot!"

"We shot over his head," Box said solemnly. "We just chased him away." He turned my wrist, exposing my forearm. "I thought you were dead. I really thought . . ."

As I sat up, I saw Debara crying in the arms of Christina. Many things raced through my mind. I knew that she loved me and that she must have thought, as everyone probably thought, that the little boy had killed me. I also knew I could never bear to watch her get hurt, and, as a consequence, our work together would soon have to end. Looking at Box, I could see that he was thinking the same thing. As the field leader, I could never send her into harm's way.

"We've got to stop the bleeding," Rick said.

"Yeah. Get me a tourniquet," I said.

"Hold your arm out," Rick gently demanded. I did, expecting to feel a soft cloth being wrapped around my arm. Box held my bicep, blocking Rick from my view. Then I heard the distinct sound of something hot contacting something that was not.

"Uhhhnnnn!" I cringed and grunted. I could smell my flesh melting, but I never pulled away, figuring that an Indian would know more about these things than I. The bullet—a 7mm slug according to Joey—deflected off a bone and exited at an angle. The damage to my arm was negligible, but the bone bruise, or fracture, prohibited me from making the climb up a tree with the satellite dish.

"We better step it up a bit," Debara advised. "That boy couldn't be too far from an adult."

"Let's just pray he's a part of the look-out patrol that Escobar told us about," Box replied.

"We're almost to the top of the hill," I said. "We'll call from there."

My legs and back were in spasm by the time we crested the hill. I asked for volunteers to climb the tree. There was no shortage of volunteers.

"No, Rick. We're gonna need you down here to boost lard ass up the tree."

"You've got Box," Rick said, suggesting that Box could lift Steven into the tree.

"It'll take more than Box to get him up to that first branch," I insisted.

"How 'bout me?" Quinn asked.

"You're too short. Look at the spread on those limbs," I answered. Joey began to ask about himself, when I replied, "The same reason."

"I can do it," Lourdes declared enthusiastically.

"Then do it," I answered abruptly. "Steven, wrap some cord around her waist—not too much—and lash the dish to her back. When the cord becomes nearly extended, we'll yell for you to stop climbing. Then we'll send Steven up. He'll match you step for step until you reach the top. That way, Steven climbs only as much as he has to."

"Okay. Let's go."

* * *

Lourdes climbed at a very brisk pace, pulling and hoisting herself ever higher with marsupial grace. I was convinced that there were ghosts in her past and that risking herself somehow made her feel that a debt was being paid. With each sacrifice came redemption. Within mere minutes, Lourdes had made her way far up the tree, and it was time to push Steven into the lower branches. I was unable to assist, so I watched as Box and Rick strained to boost him to the first limb. With legs dangling, Steven struggled to pull his torso to the height of the branch but could not do so. He hung, straight-legged and stiff, only six feet from the ground. In Three Stooges fashion, Rick climbed on Box's shoulders and then attempted to push Steven up the trunk of the tree over the limb. In a very undignified manner, and with his skin scraped pretty badly, Steven eventually succeeded.

Lourdes was much more patient with Steven than the rest of us on the ground. "Take your time. You can do it," she encouraged him. "Don't look down. Just keep climbing."

"Move your fat ass!" Box yelled.

"This proves we didn't evolve!" hollered Christina. "It would have taken more than a few billion years to forget this much about climbing!" she shouted, then burst out laughing.

"Don't worry! Just take your sweet old time!" Joey shouted.

"Why don't you get your ass up here?"

"That's it. I'm shooting his ass down," Joey said, loud enough to be heard. He then fired a round a few feet below the place Steven clung to the tree.

"What are you, fuckin' crazy?" I reacted in amazement. "You could have killed him."

"Yeah, well look at 'im climb now." Joey pointed to the tree, where Steven had made it halfway up.

"That was real bright, Joey," Lourdes yelled. "He's doin' his best, you know."

"Well now he's doin' better!" Joey claimed.

"The time we may have saved in his climbing may be lost in the time it takes the *campesinos* to find us," Debara said.

"Well, I'm not sure that that's such a threat. And by now that little fucker has told them everything they need to know about us. Half of Colombia knows where we are by now," I answered.

"So you're saying I did a good thing?" Joey asked.

"No, you stupid shit! Don't ever do that again! Or it'll be you that gets his ass shot!" Box threatened unequivocally.

Steven had made his way high enough up the tree to allow Lourdes enough free cable to make it to the top. "Are you there?" called Steven. Lourdes replied in the affirmative. "Now hold it up as high as you can above the tree!"

Lourdes did as she was instructed. "Oh, my God!" she exclaimed.

"What? What's wrong?" Steven asked.

"Nothing's wrong! It's beautiful!" she replied. "It's absolutely beautiful."

"Really?" Steven said, forgetting why it was I'd sent him up there in the first place.

"Really what? What are you two talking about?" I asked.

"She says it's beautiful! The landscape!"

"Shoot that motherfucker down!" I said sarcastically to Joey, loud enough for Steven to hear.

"I'm doin' it!" Steven shouted back. He then began talking to himself, saying, "I'm tryin' to get a signal. What does he think I'm doin' up here in a tree? This equipment isn't designed for this. No way this is gonna work."

"Stop your whinin' and do your job!" Box demanded.

Steven continued to mumble. "I don't see your ass up here. That's 'cause you can't climb. You can't swim either. You just scream a lot," Steven shouted back. "Wait. I got somethin'. Hello! Hello!"

"Aren't you supposed to use a code?" I reminded him.

"Damn it! Yes. That's right. 'The City Comes Alive at Four PM.' Over!"

Steven had made a satellite connection with Mena, Arkansas. He then attempted, in as few words possible, to come up with a plan to get us out. The biggest problem, of course, was that we didn't know our location. Steven broke away from his conversation to ask the pilot if he had removed the emergency transmitter from the aircraft. The pilot said that he had and that it was fully charged and ready to go.

"Great!" Steven responded. Now the awkward part. How to send an American military aircraft into the area, undetected, and extract us from the jungle. A helicopter moved much too slowly and carried too large a radar signature to cross the border unnoticed. A fast, sleek aircraft would be unable to maneuver in the tight jungle environment and would not have sufficient cargo space for us anyway. Steven was in the middle of discussing these extremely important details when he fell out of the tree. "Wooo! Ah shiiiiit!" he cried, crashing twenty feet through the tree branches to the ground.

"Are you okay?" I asked. He lay upside down with his neck twisted and electrical cord wrapped around his body.

"Oh, God, I think I broke something."

"What? What did you break?" I probed.

"I don't know. But I know I broke something."

"Let's straighten him out a bit and check for damage," Box directed.

We gently laid him flat and searched for lacerations or broken bones but found none. "Get your ass back in the tree," Box insisted.

"I can't. It's broken."

"You're fine. Now get up there."

"No. The SATCOM system. It'll take me a while to fix it."

"We don't have a while," I said gravely.

"The last thing he told me was to set the emergency transmitter ten minutes after he gave me the signal. Of course, I won't be able to receive his signal now."

"Great. If we set the signal too early, we could be detected by the Colombian Special Operations bozos. Set it too late and *swoosh*, there goes our ride! And if he doesn't receive your reply, he may not send an aircraft at all!"

I looked up the tree and told Lourdes to come down. I stared at the perch that Steven fell from and said, "How in God's name did you fall out of the tree? Would you please tell me that? In all my childhood I never once fell out of a tree. Not once!"

"So what do you want I should do with this?" the pilot asked, holding a little black box out in front of him.

"He said ten minutes, huh. Ahh, shit. Shit. Let me think." I sat on a log, unable to come up with a logical answer. Instead, I waited for it to feel right. I pictured the man in Arkansas trying to contact Steven. I added time for him to contact Langley, which would in turn have to make a secure call to an Air Force commander. Time would then be needed to detour a plane with a scheduled sortie and fly it to our general vicinity. I allotted twenty minutes for this to transpire.

"Okay. Turn it on." He did, and we waited with eyes and heads drawn skyward. Approximately fifty yards away was a tiny clearing, not large enough for a fixed wing aircraft to land, but large enough for a visual sighting of our team. We made our way toward it.

We stood poised on the edge of the clearing, hesitant to cross into the open. We squatted below the brush line, distressed over our inability to deal directly with the situation and decide our own fate.

"Hey!" Box whispered sharply to the pilot. "Fat boy." The pilot didn't respond.

"What should I call him?" Box asked Christina. She just shrugged. Box turned back to the pilot, who had stepped halfway into the clearing. "Get your fat ass back here!"

"Call me Mack from now on," the pilot said. He seemed a bit hurt. "Yeah, I'm fat. But you didn't see me wheezing after our little swim, did ya? No, you didn't."

"Wish we could say the same for your little hike through the woods. You sounded like a damn wildebeest," Quinn said.

"Try slop-hog," Joey added.

"Hey, you mentioned glands before," Lourdes said to Quinn. "Maybe he's got a glandular thing."

"Glands. That kills me," I said. "If glands were the problem, you would think that at least one Jewish prisoner during World War II would have been diagnosed with a glandular problem."

"They were starved!" Rick took offense with a loud whisper.

"Ohhh! So there *is* a correlation between eating and getting fat," I teased.

"I don't have glands." Mack said. "I just love to stuff my face." We all laughed. "Wait," he said, quieting us. "Shhhh."

"What is it? A plane?"

"Not quite."

"What then? Talk to us, damn it!" I said aloud.

"Hear that crackling sound?" he asked. We heard what sounded like a Harley-Davidson motorcycle. "Those are jet engines."

"I thought jet engines roared?" I said.

"They're near stall speed, aren't they?" Quinn surmised.

"Bingo!" Mack rasped. "This crazy pilot is flying by his ass to save our butts." He then shouted "There!" and ran into the clearing waving arms. Everyone followed except for Box and me. I was awestruck. I had never seen anything like it. Dark and foreboding, it glided across the tree line. In my mind, the operation had just expanded incalculably. The SR-71 program was one of the Air Force's most compartmentalized programs, yet here it was in support of Pseudo Miranda. The Air Force would now have a lot of explaining to do if anything were to go wrong.

Watching the SR-71 pilot risk his life for people he would never meet, I was never so proud of my country and the people who served it than I was on that day.

Moments after the pilot sighted us, he kicked in his afterburners and launched into the cosmos. Several seconds later it was out of sight. Anyone who witnessed this would have thought we were very important to someone, and someone very powerful, if we commanded such resources. This passing thought comforted me just long enough for the rescue craft to arrive.

* * *

We were soon on board one of Ochoa's helicopters bound for Guaviare, and eventually home.

Chapter 20

In Bellingham I found myself adrift and unsure of the direction life was taking me. I felt a bit concerned that Pseudo Miranda was floundering, knowing as I did that far more drug shipments got through than we intercepted. I applied to a number of local business firms, seeking a management position, but nothing panned out. I also applied to both the Air Force and Army officer training programs and awaited the results, although with indifference. I knew that the fix was in on the Air Force and that the Army would never want the likes of me.

I was living at home with my parents during this smokescreen period of my life. The neighborhood had changed ever so depressingly from when I was a kid. My father, Bennedict, had played a major role in developing a close-knit, happy neighborhood. My father was the linchpin that held the neighborhood together. Ironically, it was the introduction of drugs into the neighborhood that tore it apart.

He taught all the children around us to play a variety of games, for example. Many of the kids, I felt, adopted him as their own father. Especially the Ferrellis—Kenny and Joey—who lived across the street from us. Kevin and Paul Tagliaferri also formed a vital part of the clan. The neighborhood was ethnically diverse, but it seemed mostly Italian.

I vividly recall my father making hockey rinks for us with his hand-powered roller. Immediately after a snowstorm, he would be out in the backyard compressing and leveling the snow. I'd look out the second-story window late at night with my older brothers, Benny and Danny, as my dad labored. After rolling the snow, he would build a perimeter wall, then flood the interior to form a rink, complete with boards made of snow and nets. Having it in the backyard also offered the luxury of direct access to food, beverages and, of course, first aid.

My father was also the point man for developing and building the Little League and Senior League baseball and Pop Warner football programs in the town of Bellingham. The political climate of the time, which trivialized winning and learning and rewarded underachievement and nonsuccess, eventually drove my father out of organized sports. I can say without equivocation that the neighborhood, if not the town, suffered from the loss of my father's participation. To this day, whenever I visit my home town, I still bump into people who feel compelled to tell me what my father meant to them.

My mother Dorothy has always been the emotional foundation of the family. I credit her support and faith in me with my having gone to college. My mother was, and still is, there for me through thick and thin. And, as Freudian as this may sound, she is the most dependable woman I have ever known.

My first memory of her dates from the reporting of the assassination of President Kennedy. I didn't understand what saddened her, but I sensed that it was quite important. He was likely the last Democrat to receive any favorable press in the Bucchi home. Consequently, my mom called me Kennedy more often than Kenny from that infamous moment forward.

I acquired my sense of humor and extroverted personality from my mother, and my determination, resilience and pigheadedness from my father—a combination beneficial to the wheeling and dealing of the CIA, but not so becoming to the opposite sex. When times got tough, and they did, I could always rely on my parents to help me pull through. To them, I credit my life.

* * *

While waiting for a reply from the Air Force and Army officer training programs, I went on several more Pseudo Miranda missions. My travels included just two interceptions and no interventions during this period. On one of the interceptions, we recovered over a million dollars in cash, however. Apparently, the pilot determined that, pound for pound, cocaine was more valuable than cash. His decision, although nothing more than an interesting anecdote to us at the time, would irrevocably alter the course of Pseudo Miranda forever.

On April 15, 1985, a date etched in my memory because of IRS harassment, I was en route to Texas for another interception, but was diverted back to Massachusetts. Box met me in Paducah and informed me that George Lauder (CIA) demanded my presence in Boston in just two days. Box then flew off without revealing the exact nature of this pending meeting. All he said was that it involved the two of us traveling together to Panama in May.

I drove twenty straight hours, an hour of which I frustratingly spent on a scenic tour of Boston. When I finally arrived at the Quincy Market, located near the Boston Common and Faneuil Hall, I was completely exhausted. I walked in, expecting to be immediately greeted by Mr. Lauder, but was not. I was punctual, almost to the minute. It was 11:30 A.M., and the marketplace was hopping. I ordered some fried clams and devoured them in the main eating area on the first floor as I waited anxiously for Mr. Lauder to arrive.

A man approached me through the double doors at the end of the room. I had become very sensitive to people who seemed interested in me beyond a normal glance. He looked very Ivy League with his well-cut but crumpled brown suit and preppy tie. He was lanky, and had a face that sagged like his suit, only with more creases. Although attempting to be coy, he advanced directly to my table. Without a word of greeting or a handshake, he promptly started lecturing me on the proper conduct when meeting with Director Casey. My first thought was, "Not again." He spoke aristocratically, making sure to cram as many polysyllabic words into each run-on sentence as possible. In the middle of this excruciating lecture, I let out a contemptuous yawn.

"Did you hear what I just said?"

"You mean the Casey thing?" I said mechanically.

"It's that type of perfunctory response to a portentous matter such as this that will cause you great tribulation."

"And me without my thesaurus," I replied, eyelids drooping. "Look," I added, "I'm tired. I've driven 2,600 miles in three days. I haven't slept, bathed or brushed my teeth in over twenty-four hours. I've been living on Diet Cokes and Oreo cookies since I left Kentucky. And except for James Cagney, I've never been too awestruck by mere mortals. So if you would just wake me when he arrives, I would be most appreciative." I laid my head on the table between my folded arms and closed my eyes.

I was awakened with a thump on the head. The thumper, one Frank Dupero. I saw Frank infrequently during my short CIA tenure, but it was always a displeasure. On this, our first meeting, I responded to his rude welcome with a curt greeting of my own. I snapped my hand to his throat like a frog's tongue to a fly and, clenching his esophagus with the tips of my fingers, pulled his head down to meet mine. My fingernails drew trickles of blood as I reeled him in. With his desperate face next to mine, I said, "Anthony. What's yours?" I then released my grip and laid my head back down between my arms. He clutched his throat and gasped for air.

"You're damn lucky we're in a public place," he rasped.

"I feel lucky," I said sarcastically.

Mr. Lauder reentered the room and barked at me to look sharp because Bill Casey was about to arrive. "What the hell happened to you?" he said to Dupero, noticing his condition.

"Oh, here he comes," he said to me. "Try not to draw attention to him."

With Casey entering such a public place, Lauder was worried that I would do something untoward. I scanned the room, looking for the security men Casey would have with him, but even though I had become very astute at picking out people in a crowd, I couldn't readily detect them. When Casey sat down, I smirked, knowing how politically aware Bostonians considered themselves to be, yet here was the world's biggest spy walking among them, and they had no clue. Of course, in hindsight, I wonder if they simply weren't impressed.

"I don't have much time, so listen carefully," Casey muttered, never so much as removing his hat. And I did listen carefully, because of the characteristic mumbling; that went without saying. Mr. Casey then delivered a succinct briefing on the momentous changes in the operation. "Mr. Ochoa (mispronounced AW-choh-wa) has specifically requested you to meet with him at his ranch in northern Colombia before he meets with Manuel Noriega in Panama City next month. Mr. Escobar (mispronounced ES-choh-bar) was very impressed with you. That chance meeting you had with him has opened up new territory for us. That's good. But remember. This is the Supreme Don of the hemisphere. Escobar is a schmuck compared to this guy. Whatever Don Fabio says, goes. Get in good with him and the sky's the limit for us. He requested you by name!"

He then whispered loudly, "Do you know what that means?"

"That he knows my name."

"What?"

"Nothing. Go on, sir."

"We've been trying to get close to this guy forever. We've determined that he's the only one we can trust working with. But he's Colombian through and through. No American has ever gotten into his inner circle. Except . . . well . . . ." He caught himself before revealing something he shouldn't have. "He doesn't speak any English whatsoever, so pick who you want to accompany you."

"Lourdes."

"What? Oh, not now. Talk to George."

"What's this meeting about?" I asked.

"As you probably know, we're not doin' so well with our intercepts. Too many places of origin. Satellite problems, fuckin' Air Force, you name it. I want you to persuade the don to fly all PM . . . well, you know, through Panama." He removed a piece of paper from the inside pocket of his overcoat and showed it to me. "This is the operation's codename." The paper read, "Bottle Neck." He then replaced it in his pocket and continued, first muttering something incomprehensible. "He's gonna know this doesn't make much good business sense, so you'll have to convince him that PM dissolves if we continue to lose. Well, I wish I had more time with you. I don't. Do you understand what it is . . . ? Good. You're doin' fine—very fine work for us, Mr. Bucchi. Keep it up."

"Yeah, sounds do-able. When do I go?"

"George will handle that. Don't let the brevity of this meeting mislead you. This is very important to our country's security."

"No sir."

"George will fill you in on the Air Force stuff and the money issue, too. I gotta run." He stood up, and in a crouch shuffled out the door.

"The Air Force stuff?" I asked Lauder.

"Hmmm. Yes. You'll be attending the Air Force Officer Training School on the Medina Annex of Lackland Air Force Base in San Antonio, Texas. We will then send you for further training in Illinois."

"You're kidding me, right?"

"No we're not. We need to provide you and the others with airtight alibis now that this operation has achieved a new level."

"So I train and that's it, right?"

"No, that's not right. As long as this operation is in effect, you'll remain an active-duty member of the armed forces. In name only, of course. Everything will be taken care of once you've completed your training. While in training, you're on your own. This means that you could readily flunk out if you don't apply yourself."

"Why not just put the fix in there, too?"

"First we need to know that we can pass you off as a military officer. If you fail, we'll place you elsewhere and continue to do so until you fit in perfectly."

"So what's in mind for Box?"

"He's Langley. If anything were to go wrong, we'd fire him and accuse him of running the show with some other government employees in positions of opportunity."

"Like myself."

"Like yourself," he affirmed.

"There's that flapping noise again," I said.

"What's that?"

"Nothing. What's this about money now?"

"From now on, Frank here will relieve you of any money you acquire when you touch down in Homestead, Mena, or wherever."

"How does that differ from what we've been doin'? I mean, it's not as if were inundated with currency," I said, hoping to garner more information than I was getting. We had only received money on one occasion. An aberration at best, I thought. Then why this sudden change in logistics? In the past, one of us—typically Christina—would accompany the money to Tonopah, Nevada. The drugs, and on this particular occasion, the money, were then stowed underground, directly below a tower. Under this new scenario the drugs would still make their way to Nevada, but now any money that we acquired would go to parts unknown. The fact that the CIA might want some untraceable money to help fund other operations in no manner surprised me, nor did it bother me. The acquisition of money becoming the focal point of Pseudo Miranda did concern me, however. Warning sirens were wailing in my head, but I ignored them, hoping that Pseudo Miranda would continue its mission to curtail the flow of drugs into the country.

"There is no difference, so don't worry about it. Just do your job, and let us concern ourselves with the technical matters," Lauder assured me.

"Is that all?" I asked bluntly.

"No, just keep up the good work."

* * *

For the remainder of the month I was allowed to relax at home. Mostly, I went to some Bellingham High School baseball games, fished with my friend Mark Rizzo, played golf with my father, went "clubbing" with my eldest brother Danny, shopped with my mom, or just lounged around the house. It was nice for a while, but I soon grew restless. I wanted nothing more than to be thrown back into the fire and fly to Colombia. For all the horror and sadness I had experienced there, I still craved the pressure and excitement. Regardless of all the ethical dilemmas, I felt that we were doing what needed to be done and that it was important to U.S. security. I knew that Pseudo Miranda was not the be-all and end-all in the war on drugs, but it was a crucial step, and I was honored to be part of it.

Chapter 21

My patience ran thin, waiting to be contacted. I made myself available for message traffic for hours on end, hanging out in the malls or taking lonesome walks through the woods around Beaver Pond, but April rolled into May before a courier appeared with my orders. I was raring to go nevertheless, and, making up another plausible story for my friends and family to cover my sudden departure, I was off to Colombia.

I met up with Box and Lourdes in Arkansas. We had plenty of things to talk about, mostly questions from them about my meeting in Boston and what it all meant to the operation. Box seemed as caught off guard as I was about the procedural changes and the reasons behind them. "You got me," he said. "I completely understand the need to involve the general (Noriega), but all this stuff about money . . . I don't know."

"Why would they think there'd be more money in this anyhow? I mean it's not as if it'll continue to drop out of the sky. Don't they have numbered accounts in the Caymans for all that?" I asked. I was genuinely concerned.

"Of course. That guy must have had a need for cash. Maybe he didn't trust the Swiss system. I don't know, but I guaran-damn-tee that the rest of the pilots have it wired to an island," Box insisted.

"Then why Frank Dupero?"

"Who?"

"He's the guy taking the burden of the money from us."

"Oh, I don't know. But you can bet your noodles something's cookin'."

"Yeah, and I bet it has something to do with Noriega," I said.

"What are you two talking about?" Lourdes impatiently asked.

"If we knew, we'd be glad to tell you," I responded.

Box briefed me on the goals we were supposed to accomplish over the next couple days. With the assistance of a LORAN system in Acandi, Colombia, that the CIA had set up, the drug planes could safely fly out of Colombia and into Panama's Darien Valley, the location of Noriega's cocaine labs, and from there to the United States via designated guidance systems. This would provide a continuous beam to safely vector low-altitude flights into America.

My job was to convince Ochoa that the CIA needed to take these steps for security reasons and, off the record, to let him know the underlying motivation on the part of the CIA. This would enable us to capture the portion of the market that Pseudo Miranda established back in Zurich. Without these seizures, Pseudo Miranda would become defunct, and we would be forced to resume an antagonistic posture.

Ochoa would keep this sensitive information to himself and at the same time try to convince Noriega and the other traffickers that this was simply good business. Noriega was not to know that the CIA suspected he would try to capitalize on this opportunity and strike separate deals of his own, such as piggybacking drugs onto large shipments and accepting bribe money from the cartel in exchange for safe passage. Therefore, the CIA would pay Noriega for his assistance, and pay him well, in large amounts of U.S. currency. This would convince him that our government knew nothing of the outrageous compensation he extorted from the cartel. In this way, the CIA would avoid the potential for blackmail if Noriega were ever compromised. Noriega would be made to believe that the CIA was attempting to institute a better means of tracking drug shipments into America.

We had a most pleasant flight in a Lear jet through Panamanian airspace directly into Ochoa's sprawling ranch on Colombia's Caribbean coast. Mack was our pilot once again.

"You sure you know where you're goin' this time?" Box asked Mack. "Nicaragua, right?"

"Yeah," Box replied. "Head for Nicaragua and we're sure to end up in Colombia."

The runway at the ranch stretched for at least a mile, allowing the Lear plenty of room to maneuver. Two plain-colored pickup trucks converged on the plane as we taxied to a halt. The men casually exited their vehicles, secured our craft in place, and led us over to the trucks. From the runway I could view the ranch in all its splendor. The rolling hills reminded me of Maryland, speckled with cattle and spotted with trees and shrubbery. It all seemed so bucolic and ordinary, except that I thought I spotted buffalo among the scattered herds.

"Are those buffalo?" I asked.

"No!" Box said firmly.

"No, what?" I asked.

"No, we're not tipping them," Box insisted ever so seriously.

"Oh, my God!" Lourdes yelped, staring down at an elephant only a hundred or so yards from the runway.

"What's wrong with you people? It's an elephant. Haven't you ever been to the zoo before? Don Fabio's got lions, tigers, elk, deer, zebras, giraffes, chimps, monkeys, you name it," Mack said.

"How do they keep 'em off the runway?" I inquired.

"Sometimes they don't. But they've got electric shock and barbed wire," Mack added as a final note. Mack had to stay with the airplane, but the rest of us got into the vehicles.

As we drove up a staircased hill toward Don Fabio's low but expansive home, we passed a lake with an island in the middle of it, where carnivorous animals roamed. The Ochoa home was not unlike the mansions of Beverly Hills. Traditionally Spanish in style, there were many atriums, marble floors and vaulted ceilings, and the art was Spanish and likewise the furnishings. Overall, it had a much more traditional feel than Hacienda Napoles.

We were greeted by a young man with long, dirty blond hair parted down the middle. He spoke little English, so Box and I relied heavily on Lourdes' translation. From the moment I met him, he was the consummate gentleman. The interpretation of his words also told me that he was articulate and polite. This was Fabito, or young Fabio. He had a stately grace, although he was only a few years older than I was. He showed us around the house and the grounds, always more generous than demanding, more accommodating than leading. I felt that I was being coddled, however, as if he had some ulterior motive.

He took us to a garage where a brand new Porsche 911 Cabriolet sat nestled between several vintage Harley-Davidson motorcycles. Fabio made a reference to his brother Jorge, who at the time was imprisoned in Spain, asking what the CIA might be able to do about it. We gave no answer except to say that we would convey his concerns to our superiors. He seemed satisfied but guarded. He casually walked us to a fenced-in area where his father watched a horse being trained to prance about.

Except for Fabito, we were unescorted and appeared to have free rein to move about the ranch. Occasionally I saw people tending the landscaping and livestock, and a helicopter flying overhead, but never once saw an armed guard. I suppose the remote location allowed sentinels to be posted on the perimeter where they couldn't be seen. Oddly, this lack of security made me feel safer.

We came to a high-walled corral and stopped at the wooden gate. Don Fabio was in the ring with a fine-looking horse and another man, presumably the trainer. Young Fabio stood silent and respectful, waiting for his father's attention. I was reserved and patient, and quietly took in my new surroundings. From the look of the bleacher seats and the pen, I understood that this enclosure was a bullring. I saw no bulls, but my awareness of the Hispanic passion for bullfighting filled in the blanks.

My gaze returned to the horse and the men. Don Fabio weighed a good 250 pounds or more, and the horse's eyes widened as Fabio approached and got ready to mount. With his two-keg girth expansively overhanging his belt, Don Fabio grabbed hold of the reins and, with the trainer steadying the disciplined animal, rolled himself aboard. It took every scrap of discipline I could muster to keep from exploding with laughter. I knew that if I merely looked in Boxer's direction I would immediately erupt in a tearful cackle. I pinched my leg and imagined I was mowing my lawn when Boxer let out a snort of laughter. The rest of us couldn't restrain ourselves any longer and snickered and snorted with him.

Lourdes promptly covered, saying, "You mean to tell me you two finally got that joke? Unbelievable." She then said something to Fabio, and he appeared unfazed by our questionable behavior.

I said, still laughing," A pig that good you can't eat all at once! That's a good one, Lourdes."

We ceased our laughter as Don Fabio pulled his horse alongside the fence where we stood. He wore a hat, which cast a shadow across his face, and I strained to see him clearly through the nagging sun rays. He began to speak softly to me from his perch in the saddle. It soon became apparent that this would be as personal as we would get on this, our first encounter. I squinted at him with my head cocked. His chubby face and short, somewhat hooked nose, eerily reminded me of Marlon Brando. I felt awestruck. The obvious irony notwithstanding, it was the type of feeling I have seldom experienced in my life. I respectfully recited the CIA's interests, worrying endlessly that I had omitted something vitally important, and yet not wanting to take up the don's time. I realized, even before my departure from Vera Cruz that this is likely why Don Fabio never got down from his horse, an ingenious nonverbal way of communicating that I needed to be brief. Of course, there is no escaping the fact that he may have been insulted by our laughter.

He understood all of our demands but did not ask questions or convey his position on any of them. "Are we forgetting anything?" I asked Box.

"No. Wait!" He leaned toward me and whispered, "You know, this isn't any way to conduct a meeting. What have we accomplished? Is he gonna do it? How much, and when? We need something more concrete than a few stares and a nod or two." His whispers became more intense. "I can't go back to Langley with some stares and a nod."

At about that time, Don Fabio turned his mount and left, with Fabito in close pursuit.

"Now we'll have to wait for him to return."

"I don't think so," I said.

"What the hell do mean, you don't think so? We can't go without . . ."

"Sure we can. And we will." I turned and began to walk away. "We've got our answer. He'll do it."

"How do you know that? And how are we gonna know when we go back to Panama if he does?" Box challenged.

"Don't be ignorant. We found out about this meeting, didn't we? Anyhow, if he had immediately objected, he would have said so. Let's not force his hand before he's thought it out. If I'd pressed him for a yes or a no right now, he may have been forced to reject our offer. This way he can make any decision appear to be totally in his best interest. He knows he has to do this. But he doesn't want some young, snot-nosed American telling him that he has to. I want him to feel comfortable dealing with me. Right now he's gotta know that I completely understand what the appearance of our relationship must be."

"That's not how you dealt with Escobar," Box pointed out.

"Different people. You gotta make the call early. First impressions. Quick judgments will keep us alive in this business. Provided they're insightful, of course," I answered. "Oh, Lourdes. Good job back there. You saved our butts." I turned around to look at her. "How did you keep from laughing?"

"Did you see that poor horse?" she said sympathetically. Box and I began laughing once again.

"I should have guessed," I responded.

We started walking back in the direction of the house when a pickup truck pulled up alongside us. Fabito shouted from the bed of the truck, "Come! Come!" Box and Lourdes rode shotgun as I climbed in the back with young Fabio. He was all smiles, and he extended a hand for what appeared to be a congratulatory shake. He nodded repeatedly, making me feel somewhat uncomfortable. I felt like the unwitting entrée at a cannibal tribal dinner, not realizing that I was being cajoled into the boiling pot. I didn't want to return a smile, concerned that I would add embarrassment to my list of problems.

As we drove past the lake I noticed several large Quonset huts on the shore. I then inquired what prevented the carnivores from crossing from the island to the mainland for a snack. No matter how he attempted to explain, I didn't understand, which I demonstrated by shaking my head and shrugging my shoulders. I knew what it was he was attempting to explain, but I wanted a close up and personal look. What I got was a window into Fabito's ruthlessness. He tapped on the truck's rear window, and leaned over the side of the bed to signal the driver in another direction. When we came to a stop at the lakeshore, Fabito leaped from the vehicle and waved to a man on the hill. The man promptly ran down the slope with his loose-fitting clothing sailing in the wind. Fabito conferred with the man for a bit and sent him off. The man returned with a tiny lamb. Fabito carefully took hold of the lamb, cradling it in his arms. He caressed its head gently, demonstrating an authentic compassion for the cuddly creature. He then lobbed it into the water.

I gasped and then watched the lamb struggle to keep its head above water. Lourdes and I both knew what was about to happen. Lourdes kicked off her shoes and headed for the water, hoping to deliver the helpless lamb from the vicious piranha. I lunged for her clothing, catching two fingers in one of the belt loops of her fatigue pants. It was enough to slow her down until I could get a firm, two-handed grip on her. She lashed her arms violently as the water began to churn and boil around the pitiful lamb. Lourdes screamed and then cried, her body collapsing limply at my feet.

I grabbed Lourdes firmly by the shoulders, digging my thumbs into her shoulderblades, and said quietly but firmly, "Stand up and pull yourself together, right now. Do it, damn it." She barked loudly and attempted to brush me aside like a defensive end after the quarterback. I quickly locked my arms around her waist, pulling her backwards, as she flailed her arms and screamed defamatory remarks at Fabito. He never broke eye contact with us, nor did he demonstrate any emotion. I felt he was studying us, learning.

I walked Lourdes to the truck and turned to witness Box staring puzzled at Fabito, who stared benignly back. Having placed Lourdes in the front seat, I walked back to Boxer.

"Let's go," I said.

"You gotta ask why, don't you? Why are all these things necessary? The lamb was happily grazing—you know, content. And then he throws him into the . . . ." Box paused, then turned to Fabito and opened his arms wide, asking, "Why?"

"It's just an animal, for God's sakes. What's with you two?" I insisted.

"It's not about that! He could have simply told us! Don't you see? It's not just the lamb. None of it means anything to these people. You and me, we're just sheep."

"So for the price of a lamb we found out something very important about this guy. A small price to pay, if you ask me."

"Unless you're the lamb."

"Well, I'm not. Come on, Box. Do you think they surgically remove a lamb's leg to make leg of lamb? Huh? Anyhow, who ever said the lamb was a more important species than the piranha?"

"A lamb that good you can't eat all at once," Box said with a short smile. We both had a distracting laugh, ignoring Fabito as we trotted back to the truck.

Fabito escorted us to the Lear, where we found Mack sprawled out on the wing.

"You're gonna crack the wing spar, you fat ass!" I howled.

"Just gettin' an even tan," Mack retorted. "You meet the man?"

"Yeah, we sure did," Box answered.

Young Fabio was very pleasant with his departing comments. He assured me that his father would support the CIA's needs and apologized for the lamb incident. I knew the latter was devoid of sincerity, so I likewise doubted the veracity of the former. Nonetheless, I shook his hand and thanked him for his gracious hospitality.

Aboard the jet, some thousand feet over Vera Cruz, Lourdes voiced her anger at Fabito for torturing the lamb and at me for instigating it in the first place. "That was horrible. I can't believe you two."

"Shut up, you piece of shit!" I cursed her. "You hardly shed a tear for Jeremiah, and you have the nerve to cry over this! It's a sheep! I've seen you eat cheeseburgers, buffalo wings, and fish sandwiches. Is this lamb somehow different? It's not as if it's on the verge of extinction! It's a sheep, for God's sakes! You know, Baaaaah. Lamb chops! Lamb . . . You know, other lamb things," I said and then calmed momentarily. "You better damn well grow up, 'cause this won't happen again. Man is the only creature never to be killed. Period!"

"How 'bout the condor and the Bengal tiger or any other endangered species. I suppose if he'd tossed one of them into the water you'd be defending him," Lourdes countered.

"First of all, I'm not defending him. He's a sick bastard. But showing weakness in his presence doesn't accomplish anything. And second of all, if you wanna save the condor, make him part of the American diet. You don't see cows and chickens on the endangered species list, do ya? When's the last time you personally saw any of those animals, anyway?"

"I haven't. And it's probably because they're so scarce."

"Then you wouldn't miss them, would you?" I argued.

Mack called back, saying, "Not a day goes by that I don't mourn the loss of the Dodo bird." He then laughed sarcastically.

"Me too," I said. "And stop calling me a dego."

"You're right," Box said solemnly. "We should have ignored it. We should have walked away without any emotional outpouring. He won that round. It's gonna be hard to call his bluff in the future."

"That's why we have to reverse the tables on him some day," I said inanely, not knowing that such a day loomed in my future.

I returned home, but it wasn't long before I was en route to Panama City.

Chapter 22

I slept in the T-39 on the tarmac at Mena Airport for hours, while the pilot awaited clearance for takeoff. Latino pilots were practicing touch and-goes with their American trainers for hours on end. At one point I stepped out onto the tarmac for a moment to stretch my limbs and noticed a large prop aircraft at the end of the taxiway, directly in front of a large hanger, unloading a cargo of large, brown duffel bags. There were several of them. As soon as the unloading was completed, numerous large crates were loaded onto the aircraft. The engines cranked up, and the plane was soon taxiing. This all took place in minutes.

"What the hell was that all about?" I asked Mack as he came out to join me.

"Don't you know?" he said suggestively.

"Drugs?"

"Yeah. And weapons out."

"To where? The weapons I mean."

"That I don't know—and don't wanna." He lit a match for a cigarette and shuffled away from the aircraft. "Lots of drug money in this state," he said, still moving away from the T-39.

I walked along, not criticizing him for lighting a match near the air-craft. "Why here? I mean, wouldn't it make more sense to hide it in a place like New York or Miami?"

"Where do you think the biggest bond market in the country is? Here!

Right here! Low interest rates and no questions asked make for the perfect devil's pact. The state gets a lot of capital that would otherwise go to the Caribbean, and the traffickers have a safe way to launder millions of dollars. Everyone's happy. Except for us, of course. We sit on the ground for four fuckin' hours with our heads up our ass."

"That's a pretty amazing revelation coming from a guy who doesn't have two nickels to rub together."

"What's that supposed to mean? I have plenty of dough. Just 'cause I dress like shit doesn't mean I'm not flush with cash. You know, you oughta take some notes. I'd peg you for a drug dealer in a New York minute," he said.

"I'm not talking about your clothes! Well, actually now that you mention it . . . . No, I was referring to your girlie change purse. I'd wear an earring and an ankle bracelet before I'd be caught dead with something like that."

"You'd be amazed at how valuable a little change can be," he said ever so seriously.

"Yeah. From the looks of it, I'd say you've dropped some change in every candy machine across the South."

"Oh, was I ever that young?" he quipped. "Next time you need to make a phone call and don't want your boss listening, remember that we had this conversation."

* * *

We finally got some runway time, and were on our way to Panama. I met Box at Howard Air Force Base, and we took off again into the darkened sky for Panama City. The two of us were alone on this excursion, apparently because Fabio and Noriega insisted on having their own translators. Box asked the question that I'd hoped he had the answer to: "Is Don Fabio already in Panama City?"

"You know, this is all too Helter Skelter for my liking," I complained. "If he is already there, who knows what they've already discussed."

"What does it matter?" Mack called back. "They can talk to one another any time! As long as you get what you want, be happy!"

"I hate to admit it, but he's right," I said.

"What?" Mack asked.

"What is it we want?" I screamed forward to the cockpit.

"That's not what you said! You said I'm right! Anyway, why else would you be going to this meeting unless you wanted something?"

"Yeah! But you know what it is we want, don't ya!" I kept on.

"I just fly the plane."

"He knows," Box deduced.

"We're beginning our descent into Panama City. Tuck your carry-ons under your seats or in the overhead compartment, fasten your seat belts and place your seats in the full upright and locked position. And, of course, thank you for flying Pan American Airlines."

"Why bother?" Box began with some sarcasm of his own. "Two-to-one odds our bags will be scattered all over Latin America the way you land the aircraft."

"You crash one aircraft, and you're branded for life," Mack shouted.

"We probably should fasten our seat belts, though. You know, so they can identify the bodies," Box quipped.

"What? They're gonna get us confused?" I said.

"We could burn," Box replied.

"So. You'll still burn black, and he'll turn into a pool of blubber oil."

"Yeah? What about you?" Box asked.

"I'll still look good."

Mack announced our approach, saying, "Okay! Here we go!" It made me nervous that he would treat an everyday occurrence like a landing as a monumental event, but then we dove like a kingfisher, perpendicular and precise. My organs fell slower than the rest of me, tossing my stomach up into my rib cage. The bottom of the aircraft seemed to fall away like the trap door of a gallows. My feet stammered in search of the floor, looking for something firm.

"What the hell are you doin'?" Box screamed. "Hey! Hey! You're killing us back here!"

Mack remained quiet.

"He passed out!" I yelled.

"No! Don't say that! Get up front!" Box desperately screamed.

I rose to a crouch and immediately plunged forward. I put my arms out to catch myself, smashing against the metal divider between the passenger compartment and the cockpit. The aircraft leveled without warning, providing me with a practical lesson in Newton's law of gravity. Now on my back, I let out a breath of relief. "Thank God," I said with a gasp.

"Ohhh!" I wailed, my body whirling sideways, and my face smashing into the metal seat support. Gravity made it difficult to push myself out from under the seat, but a twist of the joy stick sent me rolling back into the aisle. When the aircraft suddenly leveled, I was suddenly thrust head-long into a seat back. I turned about, my personal odyssey at an end, only to hear Box laughing hysterically. I imagined how I must have looked and began to laugh with him as the aircraft touched down.

"What the hell was that all about?" I wondered aloud, still giggling.

"Who knows. But I'd pay to see it again," Box laughed.

After taxiing to a halt, Mack came to the rear of the aircraft. "What the hell happened to you?"

"What?" I said, vainly patting my face for injuries. The bridge of my nose was painful to the touch. Glancing at my hand, I said loudly, "I'm cut! Shit! Box! Does it look bad? Did I break it?"

"With a beak like that, who can tell?"

"You went from Italian to Jewish in a single trip," Mack joked.

I reamed him out: "Do you have your pilot's license? What the hell was going on up there? Come clean! You were a crop duster before you became a Company man, weren't you? Up there, demonstrating all the moves that made you famous. You're so fat, the plane probably noses over whenever you let go the stick! You fat piece of . . ."

"I was told to conduct an emergency landing," he said, dumb-founded.

"Oh. Sorry," I said, feeling stupid.

"Fatness runs in my family, you know," he explained, his pride slightly bruised.

"The problem is no one runs in your family," Box teased unsympathetically.

*　*　*

Three jeeps with military personnel aboard closed in on us, traveling in a V-shaped configuration with their emergency lights flashing. There was no need for subtlety, since we were meeting with the head of state. They drove directly to the Caesar Park Marriott Hotel, located right on the shore of the Gulf of Panama. In fact, the hotel seemed to float on the water. Water flanked the walkway into the hotel and ran flush to the building's foundation, where it flowed around the sides. The lobby was an elegant tropical atrium. A railed balcony ran along three sides of it, offering visitors a romantic view of the palms below.

Box and I were quickly introduced to a gentleman known to us as X-7. I was later told that his name was Mark, possibly John, Butler. On first appearance he looked mustached and blue-eyed, and later brown-eyed and clean shaven. His height and weight also changed moderately throughout the night, making a description ambiguous and imprecise. He would function as a liaison between Ochoa and ourselves. This was a condition set by Noriega and agreed to by Director Casey. The CIA's only counter-requirement was that Box and I visually identify Ochoa and Noriega before the meeting took place.

We took an elevator to the top floor with an armed military escort, who surrounded us as we walked down the hallway to the room where the two men waited. X-7, bearded, and with hair halfway down his back, met us in the hallway and instructed us to fold our arms in front of us before he took us to see them. We nodded when we were satisfied that we had a positive ID. I had only seen the general in photographs, so I was concerned that I would not be able to readily identify him. My worries were soon eased because I immediately recognized Pineapple Face, as Noriega was affectionately known. Box and I both nodded at once, and were then escorted back to the lobby.

Over the next two hours, X-7 came down to the lobby just once, and then only to ask Box a logistical question of little significance. X-7 returned at the completion of the meeting to tell us that everything had been agreed upon. He gave us no specifics. He just slipped away into the black, still night.

* * *

Having envisioned myself playing an instrumental part in intense negotiations, I departed with feelings of uneasiness and disappointment. Yet there was a certain comfort in knowing that there was at least one critical element of Pseudo Miranda I wasn't ultimately responsible for. Nonetheless, things were steadily becoming more convoluted, and there were distinct signs that they would become even more so. This decision would ensure a bigger take than we had been getting before. How would the traffickers react at the distribution level? I had a bad feeling.

Chapter 23

Box and I connected with Debara, Joey, Rick, Steven, Lourdes and Quinn at Howard Air Force Base. Debara informed us that we were to strike a Colombian lab near the Meta River, east of Bogota, in the lowland Llanos region where we had gone before to see Pablo Escobar in Puerto Triunfo. Stretching into Venezuela, Llanos is filled with faded green meadows, caterpillaring hills and sparse shrubbery, with an occasional stand of trees. The tall grasses mark the breezes' path like the brush strokes of a velour seat cover.

I made the command decision to have Mack fly the mission in place of the pilot who flew the others into Panama. Mack knew that the real reason we busted his balls was because we knew he was a drug trafficker. Knowing this, Mack didn't hesitate to jump into the cockpit of the C-123 and begin his function checks and preflight preparation of the aircraft. Box and I quickly changed out of our "civvies" and into our military fatigues. Debara briefed us on the specific objectives of the mission, which included destroying all the ether located at the lab. According to Debara, this particular lab was the ether storage site for several larger laboratories in the area. The cartel kept the cocaine production way down to exclude it from targeting by the CIA. This way, whenever we hit another producing lab, we would in no manner cripple that lab's ability to hastily return to the business of manufacturing cocaine. Under the guidelines of Pseudo Miranda, cocaine precursors were treated the same as the product itself.

This situation here gave us an opportunity to affect several labs with a single blow. Having heard this information, I knew to expect the worst.

An encrypted message soon came by way of the SATCOM, telling us to rest up for an early evening launch at 0530. We made use of some Aerospace Ground Equipment (AGE) to get comfortable, and slept for a few hours.

"Cockadoodledo!" cried Mack, his version of an early morning wake-up call. "Rise 'n' shine, Dixie cups!" He cranked the engines and wailed, "Feed the tires and kick the cat! By golly, we're on our way!"

"Maybe switching pilots was not such a good idea," I muttered.

*   *   *

We flew east across the Gulf of Panama, turning slightly south as we vectored off the Acandi LORAN system. Turning east once again, we crossed the Gulf of Urabé and maintained an easterly track across northern Colombia. The aircraft shook and flexed, sometimes threatening to buckle, as we narrowly cleared the mountain tops. The towering trees on each peak appeared to rise up and clutch at the belly of the plane. We perceived in a distant mountain valley ahead of us two enormous lakes of listless blue, which split into five as we drew closer, like parameciums dividing under the microscope. As we came near, they sparkled grandly. Soon we could see the Magdalena River slicing through the Andes, and we turned to follow its course south, toward Bogota. We pursued the main branch of the river, passing directly over a large mirrored body of water, chewing up the miles quickly. Because we were traveling the opposite direction of the current, the Magdalena appeared to splinter as we neared the headwaters.

The flying became unprotected when we left the mountains and started across the wide-open plains of the Llanos.

"I sure hope you know what you're doin', Quinn," Mack called out.

"Why? What's wrong?" she asked.

"This." Mack pointed through the windscreen. "No way of evading radar out here."

"I don't know what to tell you," Quinn said. "These are the coordinates I was given. Can't you drop down lower or something?"

"We're only a thousand feet off the deck. I don't go any lower unless I know the area better."

"No. Don't go any lower," I said. "Box says Escobar's got a lot of air traffic controllers on the payroll out here. They contact his people before notifying the authorities as standard operating procedure. Just fly to where you're supposed to and call out if there's trouble."

"Roger that, captain," Mack said.

* * *

We soon arrived at the long grass runway on the Guaviare River. Mack expressed his concern that there would be no service facilities at this locale for the C-123. Knowing the extent of Escobar's resources, I wasn't in the least bit worried about being stranded in Llanos. But the airstrip didn't have a tower, and according to Mack, no one made any attempts to contact us by radio. We taxied unsurely to a spot that Mack arbitrarily decided was safe. While the engines wound down, we waited tensely for some sign that the authorities were aware of our arrival. An hour passed, and still no one attempted to contact us.

Then, while most of us were gathered about the cockpit window planning our next move, two military jeeps loaded with armed troops charged rapidly toward us. They drew up in front of the nose of the plane, purposely blocking us from making any kind of move. I rushed to the back of the aircraft, commanding Mack to lower the cargo door.

"Come on! Come on!" I shouted to myself, impatient with the door's slowness. I twitched anxiously, waiting for the door to drop just low enough for me to jump safely to the ground. When the door opened a bit, I could see three rifles pointed upward at me. I changed my mind about leaping out of the aircraft.

"What the hell is going on here?" I screamed forcefully. "Is this how you greet . . . Do you know who we are?" I looked over my shoulder, careful not to make any fleeing motion. "Lourdes! Lourdes!" I called.

She answered with a hoot, "Here! Here. I'm right here. You want me to interpret?"

"No, I want you to strip naked and do the cha-cha." I turned to the authorities and said, "Tell these gentlemen who the hell we are."

She whispered, "Who are we?"

I grinned nervously. "You're killing me," I said with my teeth clamped together. Facing the police, I said calmly, "We are close, personal friends of Pablo Escobar. He's expecting . . ."

"El Padrino? El Padrino?" they said. Their chatter drowned out what I was saying.

"What are they saying?" I asked Lourdes softly.

"The Godfather."

"Really? The Godfather? Can't let this pass." I climbed down the sloped door and yelled for Steven to bring his radio. Their weapons were still aimed aggressively at us, even as Steven unthreateningly shuffled down sideways to where I was standing.

"Call him," I said sharply. "Go ahead. Call him."

"Who?" he asked.

"You two . . . Escobar. Get him on the phone. And ask him if this is the way he treats his loyal friends. Go ahead. Call him."

Steven handed the satellite dish to me, and I in turn handed it off to Rick. Standing in the great wide open, Rick twirled it about until Steven found a clear signal to the predesignated channel. Finally, from an unsecured telephone line at Langley, Steven was told something rather amazing.

Looking into his blanched face, I asked what was the matter. "Strange. I don't see how it's gonna—help—I don't—I don't . . . ," Steven muttered.

"What?" I asked.

"He said just have 'em look at the pilot."

"Oh, God. Please don't tell me he means the pilot I got rid of?"

"Shit. I didn't think to ask."

"It wouldn't matter anyhow. Say, where is Mack anyway?" He was conspicuous by his absence. I searched about curiously, finding everyone but him right before my eyes. "Do you know our pilot?" I asked the leader.

"Which one is he?" Lourdes translated for him.

"Mack! Somebody get Mack, ASAP."

Quinn soon returned with Mack, having persuaded him with a little hand twisting. When the authorities did not recognize him, Mack seemed quite relieved. The officers then gathered us all together and searched the plane. Meanwhile, I asked Mack why the Colombian authorities would know who he was.

"You probably left the person they'd recognize in Panama," he responded.

"Don't give me that shit. You were scared out of your gourd a minute ago. Now clue me in before it's too late."

"I don't know. Really. Are you sure Langley understood you were being held up by the police?"

"I'm not sure of anything. What do you mean, 'held up'?"

"These guys will rob us, torture us for information, and kill us," he said frankly. "We better do somethin' quick."

"Shit. I could blow them into the next century with these." I lifted my untucked shirt above the belt and exposed two grenades in my left pants pocket. My arm obstructed the view from the front, making it impossible for the officers to see them. Mack never looked down, trusting that I had what I said I had.

"Grab one," I told him quietly. "Be casual. When I say 'now,' you toss yours into the plane, and I'll throw mine at the bozos in front of us. Okay?"

"Mmmmhuh," he answered.

"Wait," I said. "These are the good guys. I can't . . . we can't do this. Are you sure they'll rob us?"

"What do you think they're doin' out here in the middle of nowhere?"

"Catching drug dealers," I stated quietly.

"Do what you want with your ball; mine's goin' in the hull."

I became overcome with fear, my mind racing. I needed time to think, time to gather my wits about me. I needed a delaying tactic, something simple to buy time. "They want drugs, I'll give 'em drugs," I thought.

"Lourdes! Translate. You're looking for the cocaine?" I said openly. "I can give you tons! My offer is ten percent, and a guarantee that I won't have you killed."

"Have us killed, *gringo*?" The short, dark-skinned man said in Spanish. "We want it all, and maybe we don't have you killed."

"Told you," Mack said.

"Wait. Just wait," I cautioned. I walked carefully up the cargo door to talk to the dark-skinned man. With my left hand still in my pocket, I asked, "Would you like me to show you how we hide it?"

"Yes," he answered.

I lured the five men to the front of the plane, where I furtively removed the pin, marginally controlling the handle in the process. "Here," I said, pointing to a small opening in the floor where loadmasters secure their cargo. As the man in charge knelt forward over my right shoulder, I planted the grenade into his chest and said smugly, "You lose." He could readily see that it was a live grenade, and he cooperated when I pulled him to his feet. I turned him methodically so that everyone could see his dilemma. They raised their guns crisply and trained them on my head.

"I let it go, we all go! Boom! Boom!" I threatened. I used sound effects for understanding. "Drop 'em! Drop 'em. I'll kill him! I'll kill us all!"

They argued tumultuously, unable to agree what course of action to take.

"Lourdes!" I wailed.

"Yes! I'm ready!"

"Tell 'em I'll let them go unharmed!"

She yelled it out three or four times before they made their way out the rear of the aircraft. The man in my grip said nothing, even as his men drove off in the vehicles. "Let's get the hell outta here!" I yelled. I tossed the man out the rear of the plane, having already confiscated his MAC-10. He flapped his arms for a second, then spiraled face down into a small pool of water, where he lay in humiliation.

"Bap! Bap! Bap! Bap! Bap! Bap! Bap! came the sound of gunfire in the distance. Then a large explosion. The man in the puddle lifted his head timidly, water dribbling off his face. He clenched his eyelids, trying to determine his condition. We were all in the cargo bay, unable to see what was directly in front of us. All of us except Mack, that is. He had a bird's eye view of the pandemonium.

"Holy cow!" Mack said. "Come look at this!"

I didn't need to. The man in front of me told the whole story as he scurried desperately away from us, futilely attempting to escape the soldiers who had decimated his men. It was Colonel Borda and his army. As the man fled, I couldn't help but feel empathy toward him. Three pickup trucks pulled up, corralling him like Indians circling a wagon train. He knew that his life was over; it was only a question of how tormenting it would be. "Joey," I said in a normal tone of voice, "can you hit him from here?"

He craned his neck to the right and said, "Pick the anatomy."

Colonel Borda stood beside me, assuming that I was enjoying the entertainment as much as he. "It's good?" he asked in English.

I ignored him, feeling comfortable and safe in his presence. By now, his men had tied separate ropes from a jeep to each of the man's feet. Borda said, "Make a wish."

"Now," I said, never blinking.

Joey fired two quick shots. The man fell backward. The trucks churned mud high into the air, like molten lava spewing from a volcano. They pulled in opposite directions, shredding the body irregularly. Even from our distant vantage point, I could see the shower of blood that was released. The vehicles spun toward us, dragging the torn carcass, smearing blood across the thick grass.

"Did you hit him?" I asked Joey.

"Twice between the shoulder blades. He didn't feel a thing." A pause, and then, "God, I hope not."

"You're no fun!" Borda exclaimed.

"Service our aircraft and get a helicopter to us now!" I demanded.

"I come with you, you know," he said.

"I know. Believe me, I know."

Box said, "Why were we abandoned again by you idiots? I thought we worked all this out. Remember? No surprises! This is bullshit! What if they'd killed us? Huh? What then?"

Lourdes translated for Borda, saying, "We didn't know that you were landing at this particular runway today. When they came, we hid out in the woods, like we always do. They were on you before we knew that you were even here. We couldn't attack without killing you also. This was good the way we handled it, don't you think?"

"No, I don't think! And someone's gonna damn well hear about it!" Box insisted, referring to someone in Langley, not Colombia.

"You won't tell Mr. Escobar," he said.

I saw a weakness, and moved in. "You delay us or cause us any more harm, I'll have Escobar make a wish with you. Understand?"

He nodded.

"Good! Now let's go."

As we gathered our gear, I asked Mack why the Colombians were working on the tail section of the aircraft. He said, "Haven't you seen them do that before? They're changing the registration number to match one of their own. They do it any time we bring one of ours in. In case it's discovered."

"You mean they have a C-123 in their arsenal?" I was flabbergasted.

"Of course. It's one of the more common CIA planes."

"I don't follow you," I said, now even more puzzled.

"Arr! You crack me up!"

* * *

We flew the helicopter west by southwest up the Guaviare River to the base of a low mountain range. We touched down in an open field surrounded by hills, which had me wondering if there was indeed a lab out there.

"Why here?" I asked. "There's nowhere to hide one."

"Quinn!" Box said stoically.

"We're in the right place, I promise you," said Quinn. "Keep in mind, these coordinates don't land you on top of the snow. We should be due north about five hundred meters or so. That means it's just over that ridge right there," she said, pointing to a line of trees on the hill facing us.

We walked easily up the slight incline, dropping to our bellies as we neared the top. Crawling through the tall, airy grass was almost relaxing. As we transitioned into a thinly wooded area at the crest of the hill, we advanced cautiously, in a crouch. When the lab came into view, we were spread in a line seventy-five feet across. There was tropical growth and an oasis, probably man-made, next to a long, wood-framed structure. Between the forest where we were concealed and the lab there was a short, open field consisting of nothing more than grass.

Through the dense forest undergrowth, I could make out people hastily rolling barrels into the center of the clearing. We had already made positive identification with IFF, so there was no doubt that they had chosen to fly the ether out instead of destroying it. If they had wanted to destroy it, they would not have needed to move it. And with IFF confirmation they knew that they were in no danger of arrest, making destruction of the ether nonsensical. They were indeed trying to salvage as much as they could before we took half. The clock was ticking, making safety a secondary issue.

Positioned at the center, I looked right and left while giving orders. I didn't bother to resituate anyone, because there was no time. I worked with them where they were. Using hand signals as I spoke, I said, "Joey! Debara! Secure the rear of the building!" I looked right. "Rick! Steven!"

I then said to myself aloud, "Shit, Steven! What the hell you doin' out there?" Now calling to them in a low but carrying tone, I said, "You two make a long swing to the right!" Finally, I said to Lourdes and Quinn, "Cover all of us on our approach! Lourdes, you and Quinn remain about fifty yards back and support any retreat we may have to make. Okay?"

"Roger. We got your cover," Quinn said boldly.

I signaled with the swirl of an arm for Rick and Steven to go. I would have preferred a sharpshooter to support both flanks. However, as it was, I only had Joey protecting the right flank. When Steven and Rick made it safely to the trees, I sent Debara and Joey. Debara smiled at me, as if to say all was well. I gravely demanded that the others shoot anything that appeared threatening—orders I would never have given had I felt comfortable with Debara's position on the field of battle. My fears diminished as they too made it to the base of the trees without incident.

"Ready, Box?" I asked.

"As I'll ever be. Let's do it."

We stormed down the hillside, separating as we neared the edge of the woods. We darted lightfooted through the trees, screaming "Miranda," while directing our weapons at the campesinos in the clearing. They shuddered uneasily, appearing more reticent than aggressive. We boldly pressed them from two sides, pinning them against the front of the building. Our commands were threatening and domineering, in a way only bank robbers could appreciate. Rick and Steven closed ranks from the sloping right side of the hill where the structure sat. They brought with them a contingent of nonbelligerents, who they added to our group. Box and I inspected the containers that the campesinos had intended to airlift out. Piled high and wide were about two thousand drums of ether.

Then there came a gunshot.

I instinctively dashed to the rear of the lab, where I found Joey prancing up and down with his M-16 pressed to the base of a man's skull. I didn't see Debara, but I wasn't concerned. Joey appeared to have everything under control. One of the prisoners must have fled, and Joey had fired over his head. I was confident that was what happened.

"Joey! Joey!" I shouted. He looked at me. "Calm down. It's okay," I assured him.

He frowned and then stared past me. He shuddered, and his knees buckled slightly. He began to twitch like a fidgety child.

"What's wrong?" I asked somberly. "Why are you acting so skittish?"

"Ahhh!" he screamed and beat the man he was holding in the face with the butt of his weapon. The man fell down.

"Stop it!" I hollered. He did so immediately, and collapsed beside the man.

"Oh, sweet Jesus. Look at her. I was . . . I . . . I was just . . . Oh, God. Look at her," he stammered.

Box came up behind me, gently placing his arm around my shoulders. "Don't turn around, man. Come on. Let's go for a walk." He started leading me away from the building, saying to Joey, "Blow it up. Blow it all up."

I spun out of Boxer's arm and looked at her, or what was left of her. I nearly collapsed. Debara's body was so mutilated it was hard to recognize her. I traced her body with my eyes, attempting to personalize her death from this amorphous glob of organs and body parts. The shotgun blasts must have come at extremely close range. One complete side of her waist was torn away, the pellets embedding whole chunks of flesh in the wall. Her blood covered the structure like paint from a spray gun. Debara's shoulders snapped inward, contorting her elbows and back, and with the impact of striking the pipe and the building her chest had folded, causing the bones to give way. Her skull, wedged in the gutter pipe, dangled by a piece of skin from what remained of her neck, her milky brown hair still shiny as it flowed gently in the breeze. This was no longer Debara Allen.

I stood over her for a time, my hands pressed to my face, trying to decide how to extract her from this impossible place. I reached out and then pulled back, jittery and in shock. I couldn't bring myself to help her. Rick responded to my numb desperation by yanking down the pipe and trying to balance Debara's remains on his knee. The others assisted him as soon as they realized that he couldn't handle the various sections and pieces by himself.

I don't remember much after that. What I do recall is that I could vividly see her comforting smile as I went up the hill to the helicopter. Reality soon slammed the door on my reflection when Rick passed by, Debara piled in his arms. I climbed aboard in a trance. I vaguely recall Borda's offer of sympathy.

The hill exploded.

I cried off and on during the trip out of country.

One of the axioms of this business is "Never return home with the mortally wounded." But the axiom was ignored; no one wanted to do the harshly necessary in my presence. Rather than leave her in an unmarked grave, we did the unthinkable and brought her home.

The flight out of Colombia was the loneliest time of my life. Tucked in a ball in the corner of the helicopter, I stared without focus across the open cabin bay. Although the others tried and tried, their words of encouragement and sympathy couldn't soothe me. Only then, as we flew her dead body home, did I realize how many plans I'd made for our future together. In the vacuum of my own loss, I couldn't know the extent that the others had suffered too. My selfishness and alienation would have detrimental effects far more reaching than I could fathom. But for now, there was only this whirlwind of emotion to deal with.

*   *   *

We landed in the Darien Valley of southern Panama to have the tail of the C-123 repainted with its former U.S. registration number.

Just before landing at Howard Air Force Base, Box delicately informed me that we would be leaving Debara with the CIA agents stationed there, and they would properly dispose of her remains.

When the aircraft set down, Mack explained the situation to an agent of the Air Force's Office of Special Investigations (OSI), who had come to debrief him on transportation issues, not the disposal of a body. Rick readied her for departure. I tenderly took her from his blood-stained arms and carried her onto the tarmac. I was soon met by two OSI agents and a CIA representative. They were beside themselves that we had brought back the unexplainable. Responsibility for disposing of Debara's remains became the topic of argument. I stood, broken, my sanity fleeting, as they battled like children. When the CIA agent attempted to gently take her from me, the two OSI agents yanked her heartlessly in the opposite direction. They literally pulled her apart. I have no memory of the remainder of that day. Box told me that I simply fell to my knees and cried.

Chapter 24

In late May I was home in Bellingham. My parents told me that the Army recruiters had been calling but had been unable to contact me because I hadn't given them a number where I could be reached. My mom also said she was concerned about me, especially when I went on the road, because I didn't check in with her and she had no way of knowing if I'd had an auto accident or if I was all right. A fictitious military career was sounding more and more sensible.

I called the recruiter in Boston and told him that if I were chosen for their officer candidacy program, I would not accept unless they offered me a career in the Army's Central Intelligence Division (CID). My reasoning was simple: slots were so prized in this career field that they would never go for it. I was wrong. I called, they agreed, and I now had a major predicament.

It would look rather odd for me to turn down such an opportunity, especially since I had majored in criminal justice in college and was supposedly unemployed at the time. I told the recruiter that I would accept his offer only if the Air Force turned me down. I had to follow up with them too. Actually, I expected the CIA to be aware of all these developments and to make sure the Air Force held a place for me in their next class.

I received a call the following day. I had been selected for their next Officer's Training School (OTS) class in San Antonio, Texas. I was pleased to later discover that I had legitimately qualified for the program, even without the CIA's assistance.

My father and brother saw me off from the recruitment center in Springfield. It was the only time in my life that I can recall my brother telling me that he was proud of me. It lifted my spirits and made me realize that I needed to succeed in San Antonio. Regardless of the underlying reason for my going, doing my best and succeeding became paramount. Like Tonopah, OTS was to become my only reality for the next several weeks.

* * *

Although there were no torture boxes or walnuts at OTS, it was in many ways more difficult for me. I had a poignant revelation when, after four weeks of training, my flight commander called me into his office to tell me that I was by far his most natural leader but that I had to learn to follow. Under his unique tutelage, I learned to listen to more than the words that were being spoken. Near the end of my training Captain McKinney wrote a letter to my parents, expressing his belief that I was one of the finest young officers he'd ever met and that I had excelled in many different categories of leadership, including counseling. Later in my Air Force career I would become a very effective counselor and leader, which led to many Outstanding Unit Awards and personal decorations.

* * *

Officer's Training School culminated in graduation ceremonies on Friday, September 13, 1985. I felt I was an officer in the Air Force, sworn to defend my country from threatening nations. One part of me wanted to fade into CIA obscurity, while another part wanted desperately to continue combatting the drug epidemic. I was torn. I missed my friends and worried about their well-being. For almost four months I hadn't heard a thing about the operation.

I drove my Corvette to Chanute Air Force Base in Rantoul, Illinois. For six months I would receive training in the Aircraft Maintenance Officer's Course (AMOC). I decided to enjoy the down time before returning to the dangers of Pseudo Miranda. What I hadn't expected was to fall in love once again.

Her name was Christine Burnam. I met her in Champaign, Illinois, where she waitressed at a local nightclub. By coincidence, she was in her final year of college, and a part of the Air Force ROTC program. When we met, I didn't know or care. She was quite a looker, and very personable. During my six months at Chanute, we grew extremely close, but memories of Debara still haunted me. In almost every manner possible, except for intimacy, I was open and sharing with Christine. I just couldn't seem to get beyond my love for Debara.

In November, I received my first contact since May. Box personally came to Illinois to tell me that the two of us were to meet with Noriega in Panama and persuade him on behalf of the CIA to talk to Ochoa.

The topic of discussion would be money. Noriega was piggybacking drugs onto Pseudo Miranda shipments. Piggybacked drugs were subject to a higher rate of confiscation than the prescribed fifty percent. The reason for this was simple: piggybackers didn't have the luxury of spreading their production equally over all shipments. They took space as it was afforded them, whenever it was afforded them.

Noriega was to inform Ochoa that, as a condition of flying through Panama, the pilots would need to be given half their money up front, in cash, and they would carry it with them throughout the mission. Noriega would sell this proposition to Ochoa as a way of giving the pilots an incentive to avoid detection by PM intercept pilots. Under Pseudo Miranda, a pilot had no reason to avoid contact. He wasn't subject to arrest, and he would be paid, regardless of the results.

The theory was that the cartel pilot, if captured by the Pseudo Miranda pilot, would drop the money first, because it had far less value per pound than cocaine. If we on the ground reported no money dropped, the Pseudo Miranda pilot would escort the drug pilot to a predesignated area and force a landing, where the CIA would then seize money. The pilot, it was decided, would not attempt to fly out of the country after being escorted indefinitely by the Pseudo Miranda intercept craft because his load (money) would cause high fuel consumption, making a safe landing highly unlikely.

*   *   *

The base commander gave us students five days of vacation during Thanksgiving week. This was logically the week I would accompany Box to Panama.

I drove to Murray, Kentucky, and joined Box there. We flew down to

Kelley Air Force Base in Texas, where we boarded a jet bound for Panama. Mack did not go with us on this expedition.

Box went through a laundry list of problems that the CIA had been having with the operation. Over the past six months teams had only gone into Colombia three times, and in each instance, they failed to hit a laboratory with any sizable amount of cocaine. Box said that the Colombians jerked them around continually on each trip and delayed them beyond reason. He told me that they sorely missed my presence. It struck me as curious that even though people tended to die when they went on missions with me, they preferred that risk to failure. Box also told me that other team members had been made to train in second occupations, which limited their ability to go to Colombia as often as they would have liked.

*   *   *

We arrived in Panama City late that evening. We were alone on this trip because Noriega demanded his translator handle the translation both ways. A chauffeur met us at the airport and drove us to the bay, where we waited for an armed military escort to arrive. Next we boarded a small speedboat bound for a large yacht anchored in the bay. The warm Caribbean air streamed past us intoxicatingly as we glided across the almost rippleless, smooth water. Lights from other vessels glowed in the distance. We raced toward a lone spot of brightness on the blackened canvas of the sea. The water surrounding the large yacht appeared oily, the ship's lights unable to penetrate its nighttime darkness. I felt adrift and secluded. The sheer isolation seemed designed to give the general the psychological edge.

Box and I soon found ourselves below deck in the air-conditioned comfort of Noriega's den. With its wood finishing and marbled floor, it was more tastefully decorated than I'd expected. Box and I sat on a couch that ran along two adjoining walls. Mauves and pastel greens accented the furnishings stylishly. Not a place where bad things happened, I surmised.

When Noriega entered the room, Box and I stood, if for no other reason than to pay respect to the de facto leader of this nation. He wore full military dress, and he wore the uniform well. He spoke disarmingly. Of all the important people I'd met, he was surely the most articulate. Not so much the words he chose, but rather the manner he delivered them. His points were clear. What he said, however, reminded me that this was the discourse of a thug, not a Martin Luther King.

Physically he appeared plump and soft, and his face was pockmarked with terrible acne. The rest of his features were nondescript, but his eyes—those cold and calculating eyes—were steely and fixed. He could speak endlessly without moving them. A man who could lie in this manner was without conscience.

"I wish to establish a large lab on the Rio Quindio," the general said bluntly.

"Does that flow into the Gulf of San Miguel?" Box asked.

"In the Darien jungle. Near Colombia," he explained.

"Why would we wish to add to our problems?" I asked him, hoping to lead him into suggesting that it would be an easier way of controlling the flow of drugs. This would be a lab that we would be unable to strike, for fear that he would use it to gather evidence of our complicity in the drug trade, which he could later use against us.

"You would have an easier time controlling your borders with so much cocaine coming from here. Don't you agree?" he argued diplomatically.

He knew of the deal we had struck with the cartel, but we couldn't insinuate that we understood what he spoke of. We acted confused and told him that we would make his demands known, no matter how outrageous, to our superiors. He knew that he would get his lab, and he seemed to know why we could not answer.

"General? The money issue. Can you do it?" I said, cutting to the chase.

"The don is just a short distance from where we last met. I will speak with him tomorrow. He will do this. But without my lab—safe from your DEA, mind you—it won't last very long, I'm afraid."

"Yes, sir, I understand. But I cannot make a decision of such gravity without first consulting my superiors. You understand that?" I repeated.

"Yes, I do. But you must understand that I have a country to run. It takes money."

Neither of us acknowledged the implication that he needed money to do what it was we needed him to do.

"Just so I understand, though," I started. "This lab. The one in the Darien jungle . . . Do you intend for it to produce cocaine above and beyond what's already being produced in Colombia? Or will it replace other labs? Or do you even know yet?"

"No. This will be the only lab north of Antioquia, I assure you."

I almost choked. If he was even partially correct, this would make things infinitely easier for our team. I very much wanted to agree, especially because I knew he would be speaking with Ochoa tomorrow.

As I made mental notes, he added, "You've already destroyed several labs. If I'm wrong, you'll destroy this one." He laughed.

"Protection of the Panama Canal is still paramount with our government. If you set up a lab in the Darien Valley, do you intend to resupply ether through the canal? Because I'll tell you right now, no one will go for it. We can't protect you if it's discovered that you're doin' that," I said.

"Then what do you propose? If you allow me this one thing, that is?"

"Resupply through Colombia. That way we're assured that your lab isn't producing cocaine above and beyond what we've already got," I answered directly.

"Agreed." He stood up to shake hands. "I will expect to hear from you soon, then. Feel welcome to stay anywhere in Panama this evening at my expense. Thank you for coming."

* * *

Box and I were bursting at the seams with elation but didn't want to show any outward emotion until we were in the air, bound for Howard Air Force Base. We declined Noriega's offer to stay overnight in Panama City because we had gone there for what I'd considered questionable reasons to begin with, and we weren't going to heighten our sense of dirtiness by celebrating with the proceeds of the drug trade.

Once on the plane, Box said, "Can you believe it? With that ether agreement, we will wipe out a quarter of our problems for sure. What the hell made you think of that?"

"I'm really not sure. I think you mentioned something about the Panama Canal being used for ether shipments in the past. I figured that if all his efforts went to supplying his own lab with ether, it's got to have some effect on the Colombians down there. The problem is, there's probably a million things I didn't think of."

"Yeah, but we got much more than we thought we were gonna get. If the money starts flowin' in, and we take far less trips to Colombia, then it's been a grand slam, I think."

"I suppose," I said.

*   *   *

As we taxied into Howard, I was disturbed to see other team members sitting in three jeeps, waiting for us to shut down.

"Not again," I said solemnly.

Almost the whole term was there: Christina, Joey, Quinn, Lourdes, Rick, Steven, Jesus, and even Tina. Tina was Debara's permanent replacement.

Rick briefed us on a gigantic shipment of cocaine that was being gathered in the mountainous region just south of Medellin. According to intelligence reports, young Fabio intended to ship several tons of cocaine simultaneously through different routes in hopes of pushing more than fifty percent through our safe channels. Our mission was to intercept it before shipment and take half. We would have to strike quickly if we were to have any chance of success. This would surely be our most precarious endeavor yet, and arguably the most important.

We flew out immediately, even though Box and I had had very little sleep. The aircraft was a C-60. It was very old and quite narrow. Its green, flat paint was oxidized and cracked, and it had the same trailing tail as the C-47, but it was significantly smaller in every way.

Although I had complained repeatedly about the inadequacy of the transportation, I kept my fears and prayers to myself. Our flight took us directly to the Ochoa ranch in northern Colombia. There we boarded two Titan aircraft and flew to a grassy field just north of Medellin. When we landed, the ground was quite saturated, and the planes slid sideways a bit before coming to complete stop. There was absolutely no resistance to our movement.

I had the aircraft serviced with fuel to give the appearance that we intended to fly elsewhere in them. At the same time, I had Lourdes instruct the pilot of my plane to radio for a helicopter and explain to him that we wanted to fly as one group to Llanos. The pilot was eager to assist, relieved that we were not headed for a place called La Loma, where the Ochoas had created an enormous stockpile of cocaine. It had occurred to me that our flight had been trouble-free most likely because the cartel knew that we were headed for the Llanos region and that most of the laboratories there didn't have substantial amounts of cocaine, due to the stockpiling in La Loma. Therefore, no matter where we struck in Llanos, they would not suffer much damage.

*   *   *

We waited at the edge of the woods for our helicopter to arrive. The ground crew had pulled the Titans and the fuel truck off the grassy runway and covered them with green-and-brown tarps. Large pools of water dotted the grassy runway, while droplets hung from the branches of the trees surrounding the clearing. Our feet swished through the wet grass. A light mist clung to my face. I was beginning to feel a little miserable.

When the chopper arrived, we scurried across the open field without delay. Quinn climbed in front, while the rest of us dove into the rear. My legs dangled in the open air as we lifted off.

Quinn quickly gave the pilot the coordinates to La Loma, our real destination, causing his face to turn wan with terror. She radioed back on the intercom, "He won't go."

"Don't let him on the radio," I desperately demanded.

"How? What should I do?" she asked, somewhat panicstricken.

"Can you fly one of these things?" I asked.

"Yeah, I think so."

"Can you or can't you?" I yelled over the microphone.

"Yes!" she declared.

"Put your gun to his head and tell him to fly us there or you'll kill him. Oh! Make sure to tell him that you can fly this damn thing, or he'll consider it an empty threat."

"Is it?" she asked, worried.

"No!" I said emphatically.

He took the threat seriously and flew us to La Loma. The ascent above Medellin was steep and splendid. The city below seemed to rise out of the low-lying jungle, and crawl slowly higher to the base of the mountains. Soon we left Medellin behind and were flying over dense wilderness. It was midmorning when we dropped down and landed at a large ranch with exotic animals running freely about. There was also a long, tin-roofed structure stacked with drugs.

"Oh, my God," Rick said in astonishment.

"Would you look at that? Would you just look at that?" Box added.

"There's got to be a fifty tons of cocaine there. Or more," I said, equally astonished.

"I think more," Rick said.

"I don't like the way this feels," warned Lourdes.

Just then, twenty vehicles came roaring toward us, the men riding them toting automatic assault weapons. Our presence was neither expected nor welcomed. When the pilot informed the leader that we were there under the auspices of a bilateral agreement with Don Fabio Ochoa, he struck the pilot in the face with the butt of his rifle. I attempted no further conversation.

The men pushed us to the ground and seated us back-to-back in a circle of sorts. Another pickup truck soon arrived with Don Fabio and young Fabio. When I saw them, I rose to my feet and demanded answers from the bandit who struck down the pilot. He immediately raked the stock of his gun across my face, snapping the bridge of my nose. I deliberately provoked this in order to gain a sense of indebtedness from the Ochoas. With my nose gushing blood, I was helped to my feet by none other than Fabito himself.

I took the rifle from the bandit and turned away from him. Without looking, I whipped the weapon backhand over my shoulder, striking him squarely in the face. All of his people laughed hysterically, making me feel as vile as he.

The Ochoas walked with us to the storehouse of cocaine. It was crammed into duffel bags and stacked in a pile six feet high by four feet wide, which extended a hundred and fifty feet or so beneath an open-sided structure constructed of 4 x 4s and wooden poles, covered with tin roofing, and camouflaged under grass and brush. It was obviously temporary, and served the purpose of hiding and protecting the drugs, mostly from the elements. We walked slowly down the length of it.

When we reached the halfway point, I paused and said, "We'll take it from this point on."

Deep gasps could be heard from behind me. "Never," Fabito said. "This is not a single shipment or a production lab. This is a storage facility. Many shipments will come from this location and this stock-pile."

"It doesn't matter at what stage of shipment or production we find the product. We have an agreement that we can take half. This is half, and we are taking it," I said clearly.

"No!" he shouted, now standing in my face. Speaking in Spanish, he continued to yell. "This is our country! This is our resource! We are sovereign."

I stared directly into his eyes, yet addressed my response to Don Fabio.

"Are you changing the rules, Don Fabio? Because I wouldn't want to bring such news back to the States."

"We are men of honor. It has been agreed upon. You've outplayed us this time, so take what you can," Don Fabio said, knowing that it would be theoretically impossible to carry half the cargo in the helicopter. By the time we returned, the drugs would be gone.

"Okay, everyone," I said to my people. "Let's load the helicopter as tight as she'll pack. Leave room for two people in the back. We'll fly loads to the coast or over the jungle. Split the bags and let it fly."

Fabito pleaded with his father to stop us. "They will now intercept half of the remaining cargo when it enters their country. They will cheat us as they always have."

"Will you intercept half this coca when it comes to America?" Don Fabio asked quite innocently.

"Don Fabio, you have my solemn word this will not happen," I answered earnestly.

"They will inform the DEA, and they will steal our coca!" Fabito yelled while stabbing his finger at me. "They will then say that it was not taken by them!"

"If you fly it through our safe zones, it will go untouched. But if you don't trust me and fly it elsewhere, you will undoubtedly lose it all, because I will personally tip off the DEA," I firmly declared.

Don Fabio began to laugh uproariously as he prepared to depart. He asked his son to accompany him, and they both drove off, leaving us to labor over the destruction of the massive pile of cocaine.

It had occurred to me that the Ochoas might be putting one over on us. By dumping half this shipment, we in essence guaranteed safe passage for an equivalent amount. What if most of what we were dumping wasn't in fact cocaine? Or even more insidious, what if it were only half pure? Then they would be cheating the U.S. out of tons of cocaine seizures.

The dilemma was that we didn't have enough testing kits. I needed a way to positively identify each bag. I knew the answer, but I didn't know how to go about implementing it. Then it struck me. I would find volunteers.

"We can test about a one hundred and fifty bags with the kits, but the other hundred need to be tested orally. I'll need four people to do the tests in shifts. Who wants to test the remaining hundred bags or so of cocaine?" I could hear myself saying it, but I couldn't believe it was me.

There were no shortages of volunteers. I selected Lourdes, Steven, Quinn and Tina. I needed Joey to remain sober because of his shooting ability. Christina had been an addict in the past, so I didn't want to subject her to a possible relapse. And Box didn't volunteer.

"We've got a bunch of coke heads!" Box spluttered

"We're just making necessary sacrifices for our country," Lourdes said all too altruistically

"Sacrifices!" Box huffed with a sarcastic shrug.

"I want no more than five bags tested per person per trip. Get it?" I demanded. "Place only an infinitesimal amount on your gums above your teeth. Just like you were taught in training." I paused at their snickering. "I'm not fuckin' around here! This is some serious shit! I don't want anyone getting high and doin' somethin' stupid that might endanger the lives of the rest of us!"

I calmed down a bit. "Now. Does everyone know what it's supposed to feel and taste like?" They began to chuckle once again.

"Great. I want to know the general quality. And don't test on the same spot in your mouth more than once in a short period."

*   *   *

I had the Titans assist us with the challenge of dumping the cocaine. After one trip to the coast and two to the jungle, we decided to simply fly over the local area and pour the cocaine into the air. The swirling wind tended to blow the powder back into our faces, so we were forced to don masks and shield our eyes. We slept and worked in shifts, never for a moment leaving the drugs unattended. The entire campaign took the better part of two days to complete.

The disposal went well. The Ochoas were remarkably hospitable, bringing us food and drink every day and offering us comfortable quarters to sleep in. We refused the quarters, because the rules of engagement would have allowed them to remove the cocaine while our backs were turned, provided they didn't take it forcibly.

Once the Herculean task was completed, I had the Titans refueled one last time, and we prepared to leave La Loma. Fabito came to bid us farewell. This was not the same man who had lambasted me days earlier. He offered his hand in friendship, saying, "My father's word is his honor, and I trust that yours is also."

"I assure you," I said.

"This is just business. I'll ship all this," he said with his arms thrown open, "by the end of the year."

"We'll be watching this area very closely. If it comes from this stockpile, we won't touch it." I pointed up to the heavens. "We have very sophisticated satellites up there. We will know absolutely if a shipment comes in from this particular batch of coca. Any further buildup in this area will be detected also. So I ask you, Fabio, please ship all of this immediately, and none other."

"Agreed," he said with a nod and a smile.

The flight home was most satisfying. Everything had gone perfectly over the past few days, but there was something missing. We weren't the talkative bunch that we once were.

"So? What's everyone been up to?" I asked jubilantly. "Doesn't anyone want to know about the Air Force?"

"Oh, yeah. It's lieutenant now, isn't it?" Christina said. She seemed happy that the silence had officially been broken.

"Oh, don't be so formal. My friends call me sir."

"Ahh. Too bad Box is in the other plane. He'd be calling you LT and shit," Joey said. "Vietnam, right?"

"I'm not sure; he's never quite said," I answered.

"So? How was it?" Christina impatiently inquired.

"You know. I never thought I'd be thinking this, albeit saying it. But most of these Air Force guys are pretty on the ball, you know. I mean it. Too bad I'm not actually gonna be one of 'em."

"How've you been dealing with Debara's death?" Lourdes asked.

The smile fell from my face, even as I tried not to let my pain show.

"I'm fine," I responded. "So what have you been up to, you little shit?"

"I'm so sorry . . . ," Lourdes began.

"So, you're an officer and a gentleman now. I bet you're a handsome boy in that uniform," Christina interjected, insightfully changing the direction of the conversation.

We gradually fell back into our familiar ways, but there were still lingering issues not yet dealt with, Debara especially.

* * *

I awoke on Sunday in Rantoul, Illinois, with every muscle in my body aching with pain. It was bizarre, sitting there in my apartment, knowing that my body ached from the cocaine I'd wrestled with in the Colombian jungle only the day before. It was then that I realized that it was going to become more difficult to keep my lives separate. This Air Force stuff and my new girlfriend were going to complicate things. I had no choice about the Air Force, and I wasn't about to shed the girlfriend.

As I relaxed and watched the football games, I found myself laughing at how crazy my life had become, and not regretting it for a moment. I smiled when I thought of the pride my parents would feel if they could see what I'd accomplished. And I cried when I thought of the pain my parents would feel if they could see what I'd done. I sat alone, and watched the football games.

When I finally met Christine's family, I was pleased to discover that her father was a Senior Master Sergeant in the United States Air Force. It was a relief to know that her family would understand the nature of the military and, in turn, the nature of my job. At the time, I expected that the CIA would send me on secretive missions throughout the world, ostensibly for the Air Force. In this way, I figured, Christine's parents would not ask many questions if Christine were to become my wife. Of course, I'd decided that I would eventually tell Christine everything.

The Christmas season soon arrived, and the students of AMOC were unofficially given several days off. If you didn't take the leave time, you had to remain at Chanute for most of the holidays to paint. I didn't wait to be told a second time, and went home to begin loading the Vette for an unexpected Christmas in Kentucky.

I had just finished packing when a courier arrived with a message for me to meet Box at Paducah Airport that evening.

I made it to Paducah in about five hours. It was late afternoon when I pulled into the main terminal parking lot, expecting Box to greet me, but he didn't arrive until two hours later.

"Let me in," he said, rapping on my window.

"Not enough room. Just tell me what you need." I was abrupt.

"I'm freezin'."

"Good. Then you'll be short."

He looked in at the crammed passenger seat, his breath fogging the window. "Damn, man. It's cold out here."

"Cold! Are you crazy?" I said. "You want cold! Try Chanute this time of year. I'm freezing my cannolis off up there. Now what is it you want?"

"You need to fly outta here after Christmas. They need to speak with you at Langley."

"Headquarters? Why the hell do they . . ."

"No. I'm sorry. I mean Langley Air Force Base."

"What! Why there? What's goin' on, Box?"

"I don't know exactly."

"Do you know generally?"

"I don't know exactly."

"What's goin' on, Box?"

"They spoke to me in Washington. At the old Executive Office Building. Spoke? More like interrogated me. About our meeting in Texas, remember? I don't know what's happening. Whatever it is, though, it appears we're smack dab in the middle of it. I wanted to tell you, but I didn't want you to appear coached. You know, you need to tell 'em that it was my responsibility to tell Casey, not yours. You tell me things, and I'm supposed to tell them. Okay? Okay!" He sounded pressured.

"No. Not okay. I'm not leaving you to twist in the wind. Screw 'em. I don't owe them jack shit."

"See! That's why I didn't want to tell you in the first place." He spoke rapidly. "I knew you'd start worrying about me. Just do what I told you to do!" Then, changing direction, he said, "Damn it. I'm freezin'!"

"Why are you so up tight about this? It's just a stinkin' meeting for cryin' out loud."

"Take this stuff seriously," he said gravely. "These guys can be meaner than the Colombians."

"Where's my plane gonna be?" I asked, steering him away from advising me.

"It'll be in the same place. The twenty-seventh. T-39." He redirected. "Do you understand what's goin' on here?"

"Quite frankly, Box, no, I don't. But I really don't care. It sounds like a problem bureaucrats worry about, not field agents. You see? I'm goin' there because I have to, not because I think it necessary or anything. Can't you see? The vice president was only positioning himself back in

Texas. He's a good man, I think. A smart man, who wants to take a bite outta crime. He's not gonna point the finger if this hits the fan. He's simply gonna clam up. If he wanted us stopped, he'd have done it. Damn it, Box! He could just do it! Boom! Just like that. Everyone running around covering their asses really sucks. And I'm not about to cover mine with yours. I believe in what I'm doin', Box. And damn it, you should too. I hide what I do because it would be impossible to do otherwise. But if it's discovered by the public at large, I'm not gonna shirk responsibility for what I've done. Look, Box, if you can't defend it right now in your own head, you sure as hell won't be able to later on in public. If you ask me, the CIA's involved in things closely related to Pseudo Miranda that they can't defend, even to themselves. And that's why they're running scared."

"Yeah. I guess you're right. But please, for God's sakes, don't give that speech to the bureaucrats in Langley."

"Don't worry. I'm just gonna sit and listen."

"Good."

* * *

My aircraft landed at Langley Air Force Base before I knew it. At this juncture, I was the only passenger on board. There had been other passengers, but they must have gotten off at other stops along the way while I slept. I was scratching my forehead and rubbing my face when a late model Lincoln, black on black, pulled alongside the plane.

"Time to go!" the pilot called back.

"Yup. Hey, thanks for not waking me with Navy landings."

"We aim to please!" he said perkily.

The driver of the car actually held the door open for me. I felt kind of important arriving in what appeared to be my own personal jet and then being whisked away by chauffeured limousine. Of course, I also knew that a convicted criminal's door is held open for him. Just before he's carted off to death row.

I was under the impression that the drive would be short. However, after traveling Highway 17 for about thirty minutes, I determined that we were headed back to Maryland. Probably some remote location, where the DEA had confiscated a house or something. I woke up about an hour later and discovered we were on Highway 95, still heading north.

Langley, I thought. That must have been why Box didn't say "Air Force Base" when he first mentioned Langley. I wasn't the least bit worried. I wanted to stroll the hallowed halls anyway.

I fell back asleep and didn't awaken until I heard the gate guard ask for identification. When he handed it back to the driver, I noticed little red tags clipped to notches that were cut out of the card. We entered the White House from the side, across from the old Executive Office Building. I pressed my face to the window for a better look. The Marine guard spoke on the phone and then asked me to surrender my military ID. I passed it through the window. We drove around a winding driveway, stopping about three-quarters of the way to the building. Two gentlemen approached the car and discretely escorted us across the lawn and down a walkway. I paused momentarily to look at the Washington monument all aglow in the distance.

We quick-stepped it up a wide, L-shaped staircase and into the south end of the building. From the main hallway, located at the middle of the house, we passed by an elevator, still walking briskly, and descended a straight flight of stairs to the first floor. With the library to one side, we continued our descent into the basement. The basement corridor seemed narrow and featured an arched, low-slung ceiling. To the right there was a small walkway and a door. I entered the room, turning left, and was surprised to find a tight, confining room.

This was the Situation Room. For being in the White House, it was not all that impressive. In addition to being cramped, the furnishings were strikingly plain. There was a computer on each end of the long and narrow conference table and an easel at the head; that was basically it. Both walls were draped, concealing what I'd guessed to be maps and diagrams. Just as I pulled back the curtain to take a peak, Mr. Casey walked in.

"Leave that alone," he said sternly. He looked as rumpled as ever. He wore no glasses this evening, and was without that massive school ring. He appeared tired. Not in the conventional way, but as though he was running out of the energy to live.

"Director," I said in acknowledgment.

"Mr. Bucchi," he started, sitting at the head of the table with a Marine colonel. "We've got a problem." He then mumbled something incomprehensible. "This Texas meeting. Why did you keep it from us?"

"He's your boy, sir. Claire George. I . . . I don't fill him in on anything. As for the vice president, he should be talking to you, not me."

"The . . . no. You didn't speak with . . . You don't . . . You didn't see him. I'm asking about the man you spoke with."

"Yeah. Claire George. I said that."

"So why didn't we hear about it?" the colonel asked. He was a CIA agent's worst nightmare. He was, in essence, a tightly controlled man attempting to play in the no-holds-barred world, often called intelligence. I, on the other hand, was a no-holds-barred man playing in the tightly controlled world of the military.

"You didn't hear about it because you're just a schmuck, Colonel. And I don't answer to schmuck colonels."

Bill Casey laughed briefly and then said, "No, you don't. But you do answer to me."

"Give me your telephone number and I'll call you next time," I said facetiously.

"You can reach me at the (703) 482-7676 number or the 6363 number simply by saying 4PM," Casey said. "Call secure."

I couldn't believe he actually gave me a number. I had just been kidding with him. Of course, that is how this whole thing started in the first place.

"So. Did you bring me all the way out here just to harass me?" I asked.

"We're not harassing you! We're just trying to hold this thing together while idiots like you keep tearing it apart!" the colonel retorted.

"You're right. *We're* not. Because it takes a hell of lot more than you to shake me. So just keep your mouth shut when it comes to me or I'll slap you around and stick a dress on ya."

"Excuse me, Lieutenant," the colonel said.

"Only in name," I replied.

"No, I'm afraid that's not quite true, Mr. Bucchi," Casey added. "You'll be stationed at Randolph Air Force Base in San Antonio after this assignment. It offers a very convenient location to stage interceptions, and your close proximity to Kelley Air Force Base will allow you to readily fly out on intervention missions. Also, your position as an aircraft maintenance officer provides you with certain benefits that other career fields don't. For instance, you'll have easy access to a T-39 if we need you to leave suddenly. We've also had that squadron deploying to Hondo for some time now, offering you the perfect excuse for going there from time to time. So you see, it's the way it needs to be." He made a grumbling noise and leaned backwards.

"You should buy a house as soon as you can. In San Antonio. If you marry that girl—ahh . . . ," he searched through a file with a Top Secret stamp on the cover. "Christine. That's her. Lovely choice. That would be a nice touch."

"A nice . . . ," I started, in shock and disbelief. I had begun to tell him where to stick it, but then remembered where I was and who I was talking to. "Great. Two full-time jobs," I said in frustration.

"No, I don't think so," Casey replied. "You'll be tapering off on the drug exchanges. I wanna concentrate you on the diplomatic stuff. Maybe an occasional tough seizure. But for the most part, diplomacy."

"Diplomacy?"

"Yes."

"Sounds good to me," I responded, feeling relieved in a way. I loved what I was doing and would never have slowed down unless forced to do so.

"Oh, Mr. Bucchi. Before I go, one last thing. This whole thing—Pseudo Miranda, Mena, Noriega. It doesn't go any higher than here, okay?"

"Far as I'm concerned sir, it doesn't go above me."

"Good. Very good. Oh, and by the way, excellent job in Colombia and Panama last month. Excellent work. Superb."

*   *   *

On the way back I began to sew together the pattern of events for the past several months. The operation had become more entrenched than I was led to believe it was supposed to. My original understanding was that we were to carry out the operation for a few years, after which we would have enough tactical information about South American cocaine trafficking that we could persuade the cartels to significantly reduce their production. The theory was that in four years they would have made profits that would otherwise have taken twenty years to make, and, with the threat we posed to their personal security, that they would gladly scale back their efforts by at least half. This expectation may have been a bit idealistic on my part, but certainly not unreasonable. But Pseudo Miranda began to exist for its self-perpetuation and, forgetting the original motivation, growing bigger and more important than the ideals it served.

I arrived in Paducah the following morning, tired and confused. It suddenly struck me while walking toward my car that I was an Air Force aircraft maintenance officer, but I couldn't even change the oil in my car, and now I would be supervising hundreds of people charged with maintaining multi-million-dollar jets. I knew then that I would need to do more than get good grades over the next few months; I would actually have to learn something.

I was surprised to bump into Box on my way to the main airport parking area. He had one eye closed and a concerned grin as he tentatively approached me.

"So. How'd things go, Ace?" Box asked.

"Well, fine, I guess. I'm officially a full-time officer. I'm getting married and we'll be living in a new home I'm buying in San Antonio. I wasn't told how many kids to have yet. Maybe the next time you see Bill, you could ask him for me."

"Oh. Sorry about all of that. I should have told him," he said sympathetically.

"No, you shouldn't have! Would you get the door?"

He opened it.

"Thanks. That was Claire's . . . Sounds like a woman's name, doesn't it? Anyhow, that was his job."

I was about to close my door when Box said, "How about the games? You didn't find that unbelievable?"

"The what?"

"The games." He saw that I was unresponsive. "The . . . oh, boy." He walked around the other side of my car and got in.

"Okay. Get this. They want us—as a team, mind you to travel to Colombia and play some drug trafficker reps in sporting events. Something to do with building better relations and cutting down on violence. It's crazy."

"Play games?"

"Yeah. Can you believe that shit?"

"In Colombia?"

"Yeah. I mean, it's crazy."

"What . . . what . . ." I shook my head and threw my hands up. "I don't have a response to that." I was flabbergasted. "What sort of . . ."

"Soccer, football, bullfighting, and I think baseball," he answered. "Those are the ones they've decided on so far."

"I guess they forgot to mention it. They were probably too busy telling me what position to have sex with my wife in."

"They told you that?" He seemed legitimately stunned. "No! What? You're kidding, right?"

"When do these games . . . ? God, I can't believe I'm saying this. When do they . . ."

"Soon. But no dates yet. Oh, yeah, another thing. You and I have also got a date in Medellin at the Intercontinental Hotel. The Rooftop Lounge or something. In a couple weeks. It'll be on a weekend, so don't worry. You may have to call in sick one day, though. We'll see."

"Any other surprises before I leave?"

"No. That's about it." He looked at me, pulling on his hair. We both began to laugh at the absurdity of it all and didn't stop laughing until we said good-bye.

I didn't hear from Box for several weeks, but, as luck would have it, he showed up on a day I was supposed to take Christine into Champaign for a day alone together. I wanted to call her, but neither of us could come up with a sensible excuse. I decided to spin the wheel and wait until the next time I saw her to explain. Big mistake.

"It's the Company's way of keeping me single, isn't it," I commented to Box.

"I'm sure with your track record it wouldn't take much."

"I'm serious, man. I might as well be dating you. I see you more than anyone I've dated."

"Come on, now. You know the Company's policy on dating people you work with," Box said, tight-jawed. He then smiled. "She'll understand. Whatever you tell her. Hey, look at me. I'm married."

"I'm sure in your case the Agency felt there was nothing to worry about. I guess they just didn't count on anyone being desperate enough to sleep with you. But I suppose if they were caught off guard by the Berlin Wall, how much greater a surprise could this have been?"

"Are you done?"

"Yeah, I think so."

"Good, because my wife wasn't desperate! She's very pretty and quite smart," he said defensively.

"If she's so smart, why's she married to someone in this screwed-up profession?" I became serious. "Why would anyone, Box? You tell me that, because I wanna know. Why would anyone marry me? Look what the hell I've become."

"It hasn't always been like this for us. I've never come home with nightmares." He inhaled deeply. "She's scared. She doesn't want me to leave the house any longer. She knows what I'm doing now isn't the same as before. It's so obvious. It's all about her face now. I hate what I'm doing to her." He paused to drink some water. "But I've got to see it through, you know?"

"Oh, I know all right. But at least you're married. I'm either gonna die doin' this, or I'll be too old to marry when it's over."

"Hey! Let's not get all down and shit. We're goin' to a party and then a bullfight. When's the last time you had a weekend like that?"

*　*　*

Box drove to a small airstrip outside of Chicago, where we boarded a small, twin-engine prop bound for Mena. There we hooked up with some of the others and transferred to a T-39 before continuing on to Howard Air Force Base. The rest of the team joined us there. The flight into Colombia was the smoothest imaginable. Mack was not with us, though, and his fate was a mystery to us all.

We landed on the same grassy airstrip outside of Medellin that we had used before. This time, however, we flew the C-60 all the way in. When we slammed down, I could feel the struts bottom out. The aircraft's nose swung left and then right, jolting us in our seats. I could hear the brake disks grind as we bounced across the field, and then we screeched to a stop. Tina was visibly shaken by the episode.

"Rookie," Quinn teased.

"What? There have been worse landings than that?" Tina asked excitedly.

"Oh, I guess we may have had one or two that rivaled that," I said.

"Well, it could have been worse," Tina comforted herself. "We could have crashed."

We all exploded in laughter.

*　*　*

We flew a short jaunt to a runway on the outskirts of Medellin. There were a number of hangars with some expensive aircraft outside the doors.

We left the aircraft and traveled aboard trucks to the southernmost part of Medellin. We moved rapidly along a curving dirt road high into the mountains. The drivers appeared confident that no one would be traveling in the opposite direction, as they haphazardly allowed their vehicles to drift across the road through each turn. Then the landscape opened up, the tree line pushed back from the roadway, and the terrain began to look familiar.

"Are we . . . ?" Rick started.

"Looks like it," I said.

"What?" Box began. "Oh, yeah. La Loma."

* * *

The sun had long since set by the time we reached our destination: a palatial estate on the peak of a hill, overlooking Medellin like a castle looking down upon a kingdom. It made me feel uneasy about getting too cozy with our enemy partners.

The estate didn't appear as colossal as Hacienda Los Napoles. Rather than sleeping one hundred twenty people, this modest home could only accommodate fifty or so. We slept in exquisite quarters. Each of us was given our own room, all on the north side of the house. My bed was Victorian, and the furnishings were all handcrafted and delicately sturdy. There was a sunken Jacuzzi, a fireplace in the bedroom, and in the bathroom an oyster-colored bathtub that was three feet deep. It stood alone at the center of the Spanish-tiled floor and was raised a foot or more. Staircased to the corner was a fancy glass shower. The bathroom window was three-dimensional and offered a picturesque view of a flower garden.

The first day (Saturday) we spent eating traditional Colombian cuisine, horseback riding, and touring the countryside. We were captivated by the dwarf horses that roamed freely about the ranch. I spent hours petting and playing with the cuddly creatures.

In the evening we went to the party at the Intercontinental Hotel. Box and I were the only ones invited to attend this lavish affair. From the moment we walked into the Rooftop Supper Lounge, we were treated like celebrities at a Hollywood premier. Although the Ochoas were lightly complected for Colombians, and I was quite dark (likewise Box) for a *gringo*, we nonetheless stood out. We were a curiosity, and were treated as such. Box was noticeably uncomfortable in the lime-light. I, on the other hand, thrived in it. I was, and still am, at my best under pressure.

It was here that I met José Ocampo. Although he was average in height, his big, curly hair made him seem much taller. He was obviously a work-ing man but pretended to be an aristocrat. Nevertheless, all the coke money in the world couldn't turn his blue collar into blue blood. He didn't im-press me as a leader or a businessman. Too frequently his conversation would slide into his native slang, often too crude for interpretation. The advantage to dealing with Ocampo over the others was the fact that he couldn't help but speak his mind.

Pablo Escobar was extremely personable for a notorious killer. He introduced me to Crystal champagne at this affair, and laughed grandly when I told him that it tasted no better than Martini and Rossi. Ocampo had provided the bountiful spread, which included delights for all palates. Escobar found my very particular eating habits amusing. I devoured the beef and crustaceans but avoided the vegetables and appetizers altogether. We all sat at the head table along with the Ochoa clan, surveying at least a hundred of their closest friends.

The evening moving along quite nicely until one table of rowdies raised their glasses to salute the cartels.

"To the *gringo* coke mine!" one of them cheered.

"To the *coca* crop!" another one exclaimed.

I wasn't about to let these in-your-face toasts go unchallenged, so I stood up and raised my glass. Their upturned faces expressed curiosity at what I might have to say.

"To extradition!" I cried.

Box literally fell over in his seat.

There was no reaction. I continued to hold my glass of Crystal raised in the air.

"The extraditables!" Escobar proclaimed first in English, then in Span-ish. Everyone cheered, and Box heaved a sigh of relief.

*   *   *

Box and I soon found ourselves becoming rather friendly with the lot of them, in spite of what we knew them to be. There was dancing, and several performers entertained the crowd. A space in the center of the room had been left open for this purpose. Sometime around midnight, I saw a man armed with a hatchet move to the center of the room.

"He's got an ax!" Box cried out.

I grabbed a large carving knife and vaulted over the table. The man squared to face me, and Box joined ranks with me to do battle with the assailant.

"No! No! No!" Fabito screamed. Through a translator, we learned that the man was part of the entertainment.

"Oh. Sorry," I said, feeling quite foolish.

The laughter that ensued amused us as much as it did the cartel. We returned to our seats and waited for the performance to start.

"I hope he juggles them," Box said.

"Sure you do," I chided him.

"It's always some sadist in the back row cheering on the chain saw juggler."

"Yeah! Isn't it great!" Box exclaimed. He was like a kid at his first baseball game.

A second man with a hatchet came forward, exciting the crowd even more. Box turned to me and said, "Two! They're gonna toss 'em back and forth. This is great!"

When the entertainment began, it became evident that this would not be an innocent juggling act. The two men circled around the room no more than five feet apart, waiting patiently for an opportunistic shot. They kept their backs to the outside, facing each other. Although they never came near us at the head table, as they shuffled past the tables on the sides, the guests would lean away or crawl over one another to stay out of range of the swinging hatchets. The perverse laughter of the drunken crowd was an obscenity.

I knew that Box was feeling deceived and violated because I was too. We had temporarily deluded ourselves into believing that these people could still appreciate the good things in life.

The man who had come out first, alarming Box and me, jabbed his weapon into the air repeatedly as a feint, then heaved it at his competitor, missing him entirely. The hatchet gashed the wall and fell to the floor. Everyone started to pound on the tables in rhythm—three quick raps and then another. They continued that sequence, and the intensity of the pounding steadily increased. The noise reached a fever pitch and remained there for at least a minute. With no baiting or feints, the second man whirled his ax at the first man, missing him by a Lilliputian centimeter.

The hatchet, however, hit a woman no more than twenty-five years of age, who had been shoved behind the intended victim by the crowd. It struck her on the front of the shoulder blade, virtually severing the arm from her trunk, and she screamed in pain as she collapsed to the floor. My instincts were to help her, even though she had been acting as depraved as the rest of these degenerates. By the time I reached her, they were sprinkling cocaine on her wound to deaden the pain. Someone took the carving knife from the prime rib platter and sliced the final membranes holding her arm to her body. She smiled and giggled throughout the ordeal, a result of the cocaine going up her nose before I arrived.

Box and I asked Fabito if we could be driven back to La Loma, and he politely complied.

Chapter 28

The next day, Box and I took our hangovers and the rest of the team to Vera Cruz. Along the way we decided who would participate in the bullfighting extravaganza. I volunteered myself and Box, deciding that it was best to pull a string than push it. Box took immediate exception, as I'd anticipated.

"No, thank you. I've already had my fill of bulls chasing me. Another 'horned cow' in close pursuit would probably trigger a posttraumatic stress thing. You know, it's bad enough you looped me in the first time. Then once again with that climbing thing in Nevada . . ."

"For which you never got off the ground," I interrupted.

"Doesn't matter. You still sucked me in, like you always do. Well, not this time. And don't try any of that 'It doesn't matter what he says, he's doin' it anyhow' stuff. I hate when you do that to me. I'm not . . . there's no way I'm gettin' in there with a . . . No way."

"Okay. We need a couple more volunteers," I said.

"No. See. There you go again. I'm serious this time . . ."

"I know. I'm not including you," I responded.

"Yeah? Then what's this 'couple' shit? Couple means two."

"Okay already. Do I have a *few* volunteers?"

"Sure. I'll do it," Joey said without hesitation.

"Me, too," Quinn followed.

"Oops. I forgot to mention it. No girls. Colombians don't like that sort of thing when it comes to this macho bullshit sport," I explained.

"Hell, I'll do it," Rick said. "You just hold a thing out for the bull to run through, right? How dangerous could that be? I just don't see how they grade such malarkey."

"Well, Steven. I guess it's yours, my friend," I said.

"All right, already. I'll do it," Box complained. "Steven. Great. It'd take me a month to explain that one."

"Hey!" Jesus shouted, crouched in a corner of the plane. "What am I, chopped liver?"

"No! Don't even think about it, Box!" I explained. "You've already volunteered. Case closed."

"You tricked me." Box acted betrayed.

"Yup, I did."

* * *

Several trucks came to take us to the game. It was a ritual that I had grown quite tired of. Not that I was opposed to getting chauffeured around. I simply wanted to be more in control.

"Oh, my word!" Christina reacted with consternation. "Elephants!"

"What?" Lourdes began. "You've never been to the zoo? It's an elephant, for Pete's sake. Don Fabio's got all kinds of animals. Zebras, giraffes, buffalo, llamas, you name it."

"Lamb," I said sarcastically.

"Yeah, lamb." Lourdes caught herself. "Funny."

"What?" Christina and then the others asked.

"It's too complicated to get into. Just don't ask what keeps the carnivores on that island out there." Box pointed to the lake off in the distance.

* * *

There were many people, both men and women, gathered at the bullring. Most were spectators. We hadn't brought any bullfighting attire, so we simply wore what we had on: camouflage fatigues. Had we known that they would make such a big deal of these games, we would have come more prepared. As it was, though, I didn't think it mattered whether we won or lost any of the events. I just wanted to get them over with.

Young Fabio, who reputedly collaborated with Mr. Casey on setting up these ridiculous events, trotted over to where we were standing.

"Are you ready?" Lourdes translated.

"We just let the bull run through a towel, right?" I asked, broadcasting my ignorance.

Fabito's laugh told me that he thought I was kidding. It also told me that I was in deep trouble.

"What do you suppose was so funny about that?" I asked.

"I think you have to jab them with little arrows, don't you?" Christina replied. She sounded unsure.

"Oh, no!" Boxer's blood pressure began to rise. "I almost got killed when I shoved one of those bad boys. Now you want me to prick and prod one. You're crazy!" Box directed his anxiety toward me. "You're nuts. I'm gonna get in there, make an appearance, and run around a little bit. Then I'm going right over that fence. It's not as if we can win anyhow."

"So who's asking you to do anything else?" I stated. "You won't see me throwing my *sombrero* to the crowd. Let's just make an effort and have some fun."

"Hey, Ves," Christina called to me, grabbing my attention. "Looks like your kind of fun," she said, marveling at a bull that rippled and bulged with muscle. Its monstrous head bore huge horns that jutted out like sharp batons. With head hanging low, the flaccid lips dripped saliva and collected dirt. As the bull breathed, each pant stirred the soil beneath its face, and it oscillated to and fro in search of something to hurt. Wavering at first, it suddenly burst forward without warning, circling Fabito on his horse. Fabito played the master bullfighter, frustrating and confusing the bull as he whirled lightly about the ring. He was elegant and sophisticated in his tight white pants and red-on-black vest. His long blondish hair floated behind him in the breeze.

Another rider guided the bull to its pen. Fabio rode over to us and politely asked if we would prefer to go first. He explained that the bull would be more difficult to contend with after he got stabbed three times by the first rider.

"Rider?" Box asked, his blood pressure reaching the maximum allowable limit.

"Yes," Fabito answered. "This is equestrian bullfighting." He then galloped away to the other side.

Box stared me straight in the face for several seconds, then said, "I can't ride a horse, and I've never fought a bull, and this ain't happening. No way."

I stood quietly for a moment and then answered, "You can ride."

"That was a parking lot, you moron!" he quickly fired back.

* * *

The rules of the game were simple. There were four riders per team. Each rider got three needle-tipped arrows, about the length of a lawn dart. The arrows were yellow with either green or red feathers, depending which team you represented. The riders had a minute and a half to insert their arrows (one at a time) into the bull, forward of the shoulders. Fabito assured us that this would not permanently harm the bull. Needless to say, this was never a concern to any of our players.

Fabito went first.

"Everyone shut up!" Box yelled above our chatter. "I wanna see what he does." Box leaned over the railing to watch Fabito fight the bull. Young Fabito hastily placed three arrows strategically into the neck of the bull.

"That's it?" Box wondered aloud. "The bull hardly did shit!" Box strutted to the horse he was supposed to ride.

"Like taking burgers from a drive-through."

We all cheered him on. "Go get 'em, Box!" we yelled encouragingly.

"Stick it to 'em, Box!" I called in support.

"All right, Box!" Lourdes wailed. "Think he'll get 'em all in?" she asked me.

"Hell, no. The bull might, though," I said with a smile. "Go get 'em, Box!" I hollered.

Box walked the horse out to the center of the ring. He kept perfect rhythm with the animal. As the horse sank down, he rose up, and when the horse rose up, he dropped down. The bull tore from his pen and charged past him. Boxer's style was the exact opposite of Fabito's. Whereas Fabito moved about the ring, Box stayed still. As the bull ran by his mount, Box awkwardly leaned over and stuck it in the ass. When the bull reared about to make a second run, Box was still facing the other direction. He acted imperturbable, almost to the point of insanity. He hummed softly to himself as he took out another arrow from his belt. The bull attacked. It passed him once again, taking another arrow to the butt. The bull was annoyed, and the horse acted jittery, obviously sensing something that Box didn't. All of a sudden the bull gored the horse in the chest, knocking it to the ground. I never knew a bull would do that.

Boxer's leg was trapped under the dead horse. The bull stamped and snorted, getting ready for another assault.

"Holy shit!" Joey yelled.

"Get up, Box," I repeated softly to myself.

The bull charged with malice.

"Help!" Box screamed. "Help me!" he screamed again, terror in his voice. My eyes flashed between Box and the bull, knowing that there was nothing we could do.

"For God's sakes, somebody help me!"

Two deafening gunshots and it was over. We lost the round, but they lost an expensive bull. Young Fabio seemed to take pleasure in destroying the bull under such outrageous circumstances because, not unlike the hatchet incident, it was entertaining. In truth, if it had been someone other than one of us, he would have let the bull mutilate him.

The next game was baseball. We were a little more prepared for this. I had my glove and spikes with me, but the Ochoas provided the rest. The field was completely makeshift: The base paths were grass instead of dirt and the outfield was unleveled turf, which made for some rather stopgap play. The pitcher's mound, however, was graded and groomed properly. I hadn't thrown a baseball in earnest for more than a year, so we warmed up for about an hour before finally taking the field.

Lourdes, with her lanky and flexible body, played first base. I was on the mound with a ninety-mile-an-hour fast ball and a slight tendency to clock people with it. Rick played center field. His previous baseball experience came in handy because Christina in right field and Tina in left had only played a little. At third base, we were rock solid. Joey could snag anything that came his way. He was a virtuoso—the Venus fly trap of ground balls. Filling in the rest of the infield were Quinn at short and Jesus at second. The sad catcher of my ninety-mile-an-hour fireballs was Box.

We assumed we would annihilate them as they would have annihilated us in bullfighting. That is, if the bull had not died. But by the fourth inning neither side had gotten a hit. They did have a player advance to first base. Actually, he wobbled to first. He had the audacity to laugh when Box took one in the cup. I kind of forgot to shake off a fast ball that

I'd changed to a curve. Anyhow, he wouldn't laugh at our misfortune or hug the plate again.

In the fifth inning when we got to bat Jesus led off with a blooper single over second base. I shagged the first pitch to deep left and was already around first base when the dope head made a no-look catch over his right shoulder. Joey was picked off before he could make it back to first base.

After that I got into a groove, picking off the corners of the plate at will. We still hadn't scored, though. I was amazed. These cartel guys were the equivalent of the high school potheads who wore army boots to gym class, but we couldn't score on them. Several of us tore the threads off the ball when we got up to bat, only to have it caught in some unorthodox manner. The Colombians, on the other hand, had yet to hit the ball out of the infield. And that was good because, except for Rick, I had little confidence in our outfielders.

Pitching at the top of the seventh, the final inning in PM regulation ball, I struck out the first two batters and beaned the third, although purely by accident. My arm was exceedingly tired and sore, but I knew I would never pitch another day, so it didn't matter. By this time, I was counting my blessings that the umpire was better at calling balls and strikes than they were in high school. I was pitching to the number five batter. After two consecutive fast balls that went for called strikes, I got lazy and pulled a sophomoric move. I threw a change-up curve. The batter hung on it, then plastered the ball to deep, deep left. Tina snapped up from her crouch, hesitating for a second before she vectored toward it. By the time she closed in on the ball, the lead runner had rounded third for home. When she dove for it, I knew it was a home run.

"Damn it. Why did I throw that?" I grunted in self-disgust.

"I don't believe it!" Joey declared as Tina rose from the playing field with the ball in her glove.

"Throw it in!" I called to her, the runner having not tagged up. "Holy cow! I can't believe you caught that!"

Everyone was jumping up and down as she lobbed it in, easily catching the runner off the base, who made no real effort to return to first. It looked like we had just won the pennant. It was good for us to cheer together this way. Usually we had very little to cheer about. It also did a lot for Tina, who had felt like an outsider for a long time.

The game took on a whole new meaning with that catch. We finally realized that we had to win. We had to show them that we could win, that we would always endeavor to beat them, and that they were indeed the enemy.

I led off the bottom half of the seventh. My whole team was up and cheering. It was the biggest baseball game of my life, yet there would be no trophies, no scholarships or contracts, not even a picture in the news-paper. It was more important than all that. It was as if we were playing for our country's honor.

I waited for the count to go three and one, when the pitcher threw a low, inside fast ball. I croaked it down the left field line, only to have the third baseman leap out and grab it. Rick was next. He drilled one to the gap between short and third, only to have the third baseman dive into the grass and pick up a one-hopper. His quick throw to first nailed Rick by half a step.

Box was up next, and hope for avoiding extra innings dwindled. Box swung for the trees at the first two marginally good pitches. The next pitch was outside of the strike zone by at least a foot, but Box teed off on it, barely nicking the top of the ball. It trickled toward the third base line. The third baseman charged the ball, picked it up bare handed and threw it all in one motion. The throw was perfect, arriving at its destination about the same time Box did. Box rammed the first baseman, bowling him into the grass and crashing down on top of him. Safe at first.

Joey then stepped up to the plate. At that moment I wished I had placed Rick in the fifth batting position and not little Joey Bali. He was a gifted infielder but not much with the stick, I thought, having already watched him hit some ground balls to the pitcher and the second baseman. He appeared to know what he was doing, like clicking the dirt from his cleats with the bat and rubbing dirt in his hands, but the results were always the same. I sat back down resignedly.

The first pitch was a hard, outside fast ball, about waist high. Joey clobbered it with an inside-out swing, knocking it into right field, the only field that had a defined home-run line. This was a stream that flowed across right field, and the ball fell with a splash into the water. I was in complete shock. Everyone but Box and I stormed Joey at home plate. Box walked over to me after crossing the plate and said, "If being gay means doin' that?"

"If that's all it meant, I'd be for it too," I said with a grin. I then said to Joey as he came toward me, "Hell of a hit, my man."

"Ditto," Box added.

"You two and your generalizations," Joey said.

I brushed his shoulder lightly and said sarcastically, "Let me get that chip off there for you."

He swept my hand away and smirked vaguely.

"What do you suppose that meant?" Box asked.

"I'm not sure. But to be honest, I don't care. He hit the homer. Can you believe that?"

"I got a hit, you know," Box said.

"A what?" I said loudly. "You're not calling that a hit. Please! You fight bulls better than you play baseball."

"What do you mean? I stuck two darts in that thing!"

"In his ass!" I explained.

"Bull! Right in the throat! 'In the ass'? You're crazy."

"You know, Joey may be confused about his sex, but you're confused about everything else. Throat? Gimme a break. I'll give you throat."

Joey called back to us, "Are you two gonna stay and argue, or come back to the States with us and celebrate!"

"Ask the matador!" I replied.

*   *   *

On the way back home, we congratulated each other, heaping accolades on Tina for her catch and Joey for the home run. It was one of our better days, that's for sure.

"Does anyone feel as strange about all this as I do? Playing sports against the Colombian drug traffickers?" Rick asked.

"I like it, but I don't," Jesus reacted. "You know?"

"If it'll stop people from dying, I'm all for it," I said.

"Is that what it's supposed to do?" Christina wondered. "How?"

"I don't know," Box said. "But I guess it can't hurt. Maybe if we know each other better, we'll be less likely to . . . shit, I don't know. Let's just accept this triumph as our own reward. If we leave Colombia feeling this good anytime, don't question it."

"Good point!" I agreed.

*   *   *

Silence prevailed on the last leg of our journey together. We were exhausted, so we huddled together like puppy dogs and slept. I was thinking of Debara, however, and couldn't sleep. How I wished she could share in this victory. I closed my eyes and could still see her smiling back at me. I missed her, now more than ever.

Chapter 29

Between January and April, Christine and I spent almost every day with each other, and I was seriously in love. In fact, I was so sure of this relationship that it frightened me. My graduation was set for the first of April. Christine had already decided to put in for Randolph Air Force Base as her first posting after graduation. If she was unable to get stationed there, we discussed the possibility of getting married to ensure that we could spend our lives together.

During that time we carried out very few Pseudo Miranda missions. Of the interceptions I went on, only one had what might be considered negative results. While in southern Texas on a milk run, we were sitting around the IFF antenna, out of harm's way, awaiting the arrival of the drug plane that would drop the cocaine shipment over our position. Steven received word that the aircraft had been intercepted and was heading our way. We could expect to see it in ten minutes. However, Quinn, who was holding our only pair of night-vision glasses, suddenly announced our impending doom. "It's here already! We're dead! Run!"

"What's wrong?" Steven asked. Two words too many. While the rest of us fled without question, Steven fuddled with the communication cord and became entangled. He quickly freed himself, only to have a two-hundred-pound bag of cocaine strike him on the right leg, snapping his femur like a twig.

We had to set the bone. We didn't have any painkillers, but Steven didn't scream during the entire ordeal. I placed a rifle under his chin to restrain him, while Rick popped the bone back into place. He groaned and grunted, his eyes running with tears, but he never once cried out. It was a painstaking task to deliver him from the field in this condition. Had it occurred in Colombia, we would have been prepared with morphine. As it was, he just had to grit his teeth until we got him to a hospital. Steven was out of commission for the next three months.

*　*　*

After graduation, Box informed me that he and I were to accompany Rick, Christina, Joey, and Quinn to a large *finca* in Colombia west of Medellin, on the Pacific coast. The Medellin cartel was having a party.

The house was contemporary and sophisticated. Lustrous white in color, it capped the mountaintop like snow and commanded a breathtaking view of the ocean and shore. Armed guards patrolled the entryway to the mansion, and a gun-check girl politely relieved all guests of their instruments of death. This honor system made me feel trusted, even though everyone also had to pass through a metal detector on the way into the house. The floors throughout the place were covered in elegant, polished black marble, and modern paintings, vases and sculptured arrangements decorated the walls and alcoves and furniture. The rear of the house was a continuous wall of glass that looked out on a large pool and an enormous patio.

I was disillusioned by the number of Americans I saw there. Some I recognized as film stars and celebrities from the music industry but could not place their names. The women were the most beautiful I'd ever seen gathered in one place at one time. As the music played out, the guests consumed large amounts of cocaine and alcohol. We didn't mingle much with them.

Box and I concentrated our diplomatic efforts on Don Fabio, young Fabio, and José Ocampo, our hosts. We hoped to make them understand the inevitable course that Pseudo Miranda would take; that is to say, at some point in time, once the coke lords were all billionaires, courtesy of the U.S. government, we expected them to voluntarily discontinue the cocaine trafficking. Ochoa seemed amenable.

We were all relaxing by the pool and considering this when suddenly a dark-skinned, tall man came over to Don Fabio and whispered something in his ear.

"If something happens," I said to Christina, "You give me all the English."

Two men then stormed into the party, dragging a third. This man was much older—probably in his fifties—and looked soft and plump. He recoiled fearfully with each poke and prod from the other two. The man who whispered to Don Fabio now approached him and began to beat him.

"He's saying something about theft," Christina advised. "Shouldn't we do somethin'?"

"What? Want me to jump 'em and wrestle their guns away?" I asked sarcastically.

"They all get what they deserve," Box said.

The tall man drew his handgun and stroked the man's face softly with the barrel, teasing him. The old man begged him to spare his life and got down on his knees, insisting he had done nothing wrong.

"Don't anybody panic," Box said. "He won't kill him."

The tall man then fired a single round in the man's forehead, spilling his brains on the cement. He then grabbed the dead man's feet and twisted him into the pool. I watched in disgust as several women jumped into the pool and began to play with the floating body. "Time to go," I said. I then nodded to Don Fabio and said, "Don Fabio."

I had heard the murderer's name, a name that I had heard once before. I was frightened at what I was thinking about doing. On the way out, I knelt inconspicuously to pick up a single shell casing.

At the door, the gun-check girl handed back our weapons. I pressed the empty casing into my clip. Although the shell was the wrong size, it looked authentic enough from the rear of the clip. I then showed her the rear of the clip and snapped it back into my Colt .45. Placing the gun to her head, I had Christina tell her to give us back our bullets. She promptly unlocked the safe, and we loaded up.

"What the hell are we doin'?" Box said angrily.

"We can't let this pass. I just can't," I said.

"Have some sense, Booch! We should leave right now."

"Do what you want," I said, determined to make right that which I couldn't.

* * *

The moment I went back in the house I passed through the metal detector, and bells began to ring loudly. I continued walking until I reached the patio, but security forces swarmed me before I could make it outside to the pool. The others had also been cut off inside.

"Don Fabio!" I called.

He said something to his men and I was allowed through, but without my weapon. I was able to convey to him that I needed Christina to translate for me, so he had someone get her. I asked his permission to meet this killer squarely. Ochoa informed me that the man was his production chief and that he was doing what was necessary. As we discussed the matter, caretakers were busily cleaning up the blood at our feet with something that smelled like gasoline.

"This is the way we do things," he said.

"I understand, Don Fabio, but this is the way we do things also. You wouldn't want a coward working for you at such a high level, now would you?"

"What if you are killed?"

"So be it." I waited. "No retribution whatsoever."

The don signalled the man who had taken my gun, and he responded by handing it back to me. The don then backed away, a gesture of nonintervention. I remembered this from my classroom training in Nevada. I intended only to destroy the man's credibility by bluffing him into displaying his true cowardice, not kill him. After all, I thought, nobody duels anymore. The man acted confused. "Don Fabio? What is this? Who are these people, Don Fabio? Are they your friends? Can I kill your friends?" The man's gun was tucked in the front of his pants.

Don Fabio did not answer.

"What?" he screamed at me.

I didn't respond.

"I'll kill you!" he yelled. "You . . . you . . . you are dead!" he spluttered in Spanish.

I held the gun at my left side, muzzle pointed upward in his direction. I depressed the safety mechanism with my pinkie and placed my index finger over the trigger. With my hand held straight down over the weapon, the untrained eye could not recognize that it was ready to fire. My fingers were stretched, and I could feel the cramping pain between them.

He went for his gun.

I squeezed off a single round, striking him in the chest. My gun recoiled, snapping a bone in my hand. The back of his chest exploded with blood, spraying a mist halfway across the water. He keeled backward over the corner of the pool, his head bouncing off the concrete. I picked up my weapon in my right hand while cradling my left, and walked over to where he lay. By now he was mired in a puddle of blood. I grabbed his shirt and dragged him into the swimming pool. His apparent girlfriend, one of the women who had toyed with the other floating corpse, attacked me with flailing arms. I grabbed her by the hair, and twisted her into the pool too.

"Play with that," I said, and walked away.

I couldn't look any of my teammates in the eye on our journey back home. I felt evil and dirty. I didn't mean for it to happen, I kept telling myself. But I couldn't deny how good it felt, and that's what scared me. I would soon find out that sin has its own punishment—punishment brought on by our acts, and not by God.

The man I had killed went by the name of Hitler's Savior. The name I carried with me after Debara's slaying. The name Joey kept repeating. The name of the man who vanished from that lab on the hill. The name of the man who killed Debara.

* * *

After we had already stowed our weapons in Mena, Arkansas, I decided to divert the aircraft to Englin Air Force Base. The pilot complied without argument, calling in a fictitious in-flight emergency (IFE) as we neared the base. We left the plane in the transient aircraft parking area and called a taxi from Base Operations to take us from the airfield to Biloxi, where Box quickly rented a car, and we were on our way to New Orleans for a little R & R.

My attitude over the past few weeks had not fostered team unity, and I was rapidly widening the ethical gray area of my life. No one adamantly opposed my spontaneous decision to go to New Orleans, but everyone seemed concerned about my motivations.

"Partying on Bourbon and Canal Streets," Rick said, sounding upbeat. "Any particular reason?" He directed this question to me.

"No, I just wanna party till I drop," I answered. "I have a lot of good memories about that place." Ironically, memories were what I wanted to drown—in a Hurricane at Pat O'Brian's.

"Sounds good to me!" Joey said excitedly.

"Yeah, real good," Christina echoed, although dampening the mood.

"What's with you?" Quinn asked in a snotty way.

Christina switched gears. "Nothing. Let's have some fun. We've earned it, darn it."

"You're darn tootin' we have!" I exclaimed loudly. "Bourbon Street!" I yelled till they all joined in.

We stayed at the Holiday Inn. Sometime during the evening, we hooked up with a crowd of people—mostly women—at a bar a few blocks away and took them back to our hotel. Of the four rooms we had, two were adjoining, and we were able to party on through until morning uninhibited. About 2:00 A.M. as the party raged on, I retired alone to the room across the hall. I sat at the desk and removed a kilo of cocaine that I had emancipated from the party in Colombia. Staring down at it, I wondered why I had taken it in the first place. I then pondered what mysterious grip this innocent-looking powder had on so many millions of people. I carefully sliced the thick cellophane packaging to get a whiff of it. I lowered my head to the pile on the desk like Al Pacino in *Scarface,* when suddenly Christina barged in unannounced.

"Don't let me stop ya," she said. "Your first time?"

"It might have been if you hadn't stormed in here."

"Oh, please. Go ahead, knock yourself out. Don't let me ruin your indulgence." She walked over to me and said loudly, "Go on! Go on, you hypocritical bastard!" She then grabbed the kilo and smashed it in my face. "Here! Get a big snootful."

I smacked her arm away and grabbed the fallen kilo, heaving it against the door. "What the hell's your problem? You psycho bitch!"

"What's my problem? You. You're my problem. Ever since Debara's death you've been acting as if you had a license to do whatever the hell you want to do."

"What are you talking about? I haven't changed . . . Have you been sniffing any of that Rush junk from the French Quarter?"

"You didn't have to kill that man."

"He murdered a defenseless old man! In front of us no less! We allow that—even once—and they'll have us. They'll have us forever. I don't know what shooting you witnessed, but I sure as hell didn't see it that way. Killed? Right. You say it like I committed a crime. The only crime I'm guilty of is running a sanitation service without a license."

"I don't care what he did! Or what you call it!"

She then pleaded. "Don't you see? It's not about justice. If that were the only standard we had to achieve, then fine. But we have to be above that. This crazy operation requires that we be above that. Above equal. Above instinct. You killed that man. And then you threw his girlfriend in the pool after his dead body? My God, Ves. What level were you seeking there?" She paused to back away from me.

"No. No matter how fair and just it was to challenge him, you met him—you met them—at their level, on their playing field."

"That's easy for you to say. You stand behind God as an excuse not to act. Well, I acted, damn it! Right or wrong! Good or bad! I did something."

"Walking away *is* doing something! And don't you dare lecture me about doing! Every day of my life now—and in the future—I ask if what I'm doin' is right. And then I go out and do it! It's easy for you. You don't have to wrestle with a conscience every minute you're out there. Well I do! And it's hard."

She thought for a moment.

"Do you think that I didn't want to kill him? Do think any of us didn't get sick when he toyed with that man before killing him? You didn't kill that man because it was right! You killed him because it made you feel better!"

"Who the hell do you think you are? You wanna be judge and jury? Take it somewhere else, because I don't need it! You want reasons . . ."

"Yeah!"

"Good! Because I've got plenty of 'em! He was a cold-blooded killer! They're all cold-blooded killers!"

"That's right!"

"That's right! And that's why Jeremiah and Debara are dead!"

"And what's that make you?" she shouted.

"His name was the Savior! Hitler's Savior!" I shuddered and trembled.

"What?"

"Hitler's Savior! Hitler's . . . Oh, God. Debara." I fought back the tears, as my voice faltered.

"You mean he was the guy that killed . . . ?"

"Yes! What does it matter? What does any of this matter?"

"It matters. You're not the only one hurting over her, you know. We all miss her. Not a day goes . . ."

"A day? Not a day. Not a second goes by that I don't die inside." I paced about the room. "I see her smiling on that hill. I smell her hair in the jungle. I hear her voice constantly! Right now I hear her. I'd waited my whole life for her. And now . . ." I swallowed tightly and then switched momentarily to thoughts of my new love. "And now I've found the most perfect girl. And I can't let her in. And I don't know if I ever will. You miss her every day? Is that what you said?"

"Go on feeling sorry for yourself."

"How can you be so . . ."

"But remember there are people that count on you."

"Don't! Don't give me that about needing! How about me? Huh? What do I get? Who can I count on? I've got nothing! Nothing! So take your . . ."

"Nothing! You selfish little prick! While you're there . . ."

"I don't wanna hear . . ."

". . . While you're out there venting your anger, the rest of us are looking over your shoulder, making sure you're safe! So don't tell me you've got no one! There are fifteen . . ."

"Thirteen."

". . . Thirteen people who are counting on you! They'll go anywhere with you! They trust in you! And no matter what you think, they'll die for you. So don't tell me you've got no one. Because there's a Vesbucci I would have died for. And I think I still would."

"Save the pep rally speech for Lourdes. I've grown up a lot in the last few months."

SMASH! Christina whacked me over the head with an empty beer bottle. I collapsed to one knee, half hurt and half shocked that she would do such a thing.

"Oh, my God. What'd I do?"

Box flew into the room. "What the hell happened?" he asked.

"Christina broke a glass," I said.

"What?" he said with a raised voice.

"Just leave, Box." I was short with him. "Everything's fine. Really."

I stumbled to the bed and lay my head on the pillow. "Nice wrist action," I said.

"A misspent youth, I guess," she said mildly. "I'm sorry." She touched my head.

"Ow."

"Well, it serves you right."

"Yeah, I suppose it does." I sighed deeply. "I guess I've made a debacle of this whole thing, huh? Don't answer. I know I have. Everything has just gotten so damn confusing. It seems like only yesterday that we were just a bunch of trainees trying to get through camp. All of a sudden people are dying, and you can't tell the good guys from the bad guys. If anything, you're right about that. If we don't exceed normal standards of behavior under these trying circumstances, then we'll never be able to tell the good from the bad. It's just sometimes I think about her, and I forget how to do what's right."

"You don't forget. You just choose not to."

"Damn, girl. You don't let me slide on anything. Okay, you're right. I know when I'm screwing up. It's just that it's so easy to screw up out there in the jungle. You're right, you're right. No more excuses." I exhaled loudly. "God, how do I put it all back together?"

"I don't think you can put it back together. But I agree that asking God is the place to start. And finish, for that matter. Do you want me to get some ice for that?"

"Yes, please." As she started out the door I said, "Seedy?"

"Yeah?"

"Do you think God approves of anything we're doin'?"

"I think you have to ask yourself what your motivation is. I don't think anything done with pure motives can be bad. And I don't think anything done that appears to be good on the surface can actually be good if done for the wrong reasons. It removes the powerful hand of God from the picture."

"Like giving Mafia money to the church."

"Exactly, . . . I think."

"Are your motives pure?"

"No. But I think they're as close as they've ever been on anything. How 'bout you?"

"I don't know."

"Wait there. I'll fetch some ice."

Chapter 30

We made numerous successful interceptions and interventions over the next several months, some that I was a party to, and others not. We had become expert in the field, developing preemptive techniques and strategies that made such delicate matters seem perfunctory in nature.

It was now the summer of 1986. I was in the house that I was told to purchase, but my girlfriend Christine had disappeared. She gave no reason. She simply cried and said that I couldn't call her any more. Although I tried and tried, I never got any answer when I called, and I never spoke to her again.

With summer passing, I readied myself for another mission into Colombia, scheduled for the Labor Day weekend. As soon as Box called, I hung up the phone and was out the door. I couldn't find my house keys, which made me late, but I drove my De Lorean to the Hondo airstrip as fast as I thought I could push it. I sped into the almost abandoned airport, peeling rubber down the taxiway, and skidded to a stop beside the Cessna 400 twin-engine prop we were flying. Box was waiting impatiently outside the plane for me, slapping his thigh with exasperation.

"You're gonna be late to your own funeral!" he vented.

"To me," I said, pulling my gear from the car, "that sounds like a good thing."

"Hurry!" he demanded, sticking his head back into the aircraft to speak with the pilot. "Hurry! Come on!"

I slipped past him in the doorway and went directly to a seat in the cramped rear quarter of the aircraft.

"Let's go!" Box called to the pilot. "Where have you been?" he snapped at me.

"I had to wait around for an FCF on a CND," I answered, knowing it would drive him mad.

"A what on a what!"

"Oh, I'm sorry," I taunted him. "I forgot you've never served in the armed forces. A Functional Check Flight for a Can Not Duplicate discrepancy on a jet. You know, like the CND aircraft we handed the mechanics in Alexandria."

"What CND?"

"Remember? We faked a problem to get them to allow us to land at Englin Air Force Base."

"Oh, yeah. Man, you've really corrupted me."

"Yeah, right. You were such an angel when I met you."

"Well . . . I just hope we're not late or nothin'."

"Why? Are we on some sort of an unusual deadline or something?"

"No, not really. Well, sort of." He collected his thoughts. "We've got a big shipment of paste just sitting in southern Colombia."

"Oh, I get it. We need to strike it before it gets divided up to several labs."

"Correct. One problem, though."

"What's that?"

"It's right near a river called the Piranha. And you know our luck with those little critters," he said. It seemed quite prophetic later.

In Panama we met up with the others: Christina, Joey, Rick, Quinn, Lourdes, Steven, and Tina. We were all sporting darker complexions and leaner figures, the result of too much equatorial sun and too many jobs. Not to mention the nervous stress. We didn't appear withered, but there was an emptiness in our eyes. We were now veterans of the drug wars, whether we liked it or not.

We picked up an additional Cessna for the journey into Colombia. I sat comfortably in the copilot seat as we hugged the contours of the land, flying above jungle and green pasture, dropping jarringly when we hit pockets of air and soaring like eagles when we found heated updrafts. Every now and then we would catch the eye of a lonesome farmer, who waved circumspectly, as we dropped to treetop level for concealment.

The clouds then rolled in, blurring the various features of the land-scape. The forms of mountains and lakes and jungles grew almost indis-tinguishable. The torrential rains then came, enabling us to blend in with the radar ground clutter, while at the same time heightening our chances of becoming ground clutter ourselves.

Our planes finally touched down somewhere in the Llanos for us to transfer to helicopters for the final leg of the journey. Colonel Borda climbed into the cockpit with the pilot because we didn't need a naviga-tor of our own to direct the pilot to the first stop. We would soon be in Leticia once again.

Now, all packed aboard one helicopter, we joked about our ride thus far and loosened up before the pending mission. We were roughhousing in the back of the helicopter as if we had no concerns about our immedi-ate future. In the act of laughing, I looked around at my friends and wondered how long I would have them, never once considering my own mortality. I worried how their loss would affect me.

The commotion in the cramped cabin inexplicably died down, as if in homage to Jeremiah, and Debara as well. The main rotor kicked up dust from the ground outside, which infiltrated the cabin and eddied about in a whirlpool. We waited for the right moment to exit. With our faces thinly coated with dirt and the rotor blades slowing to a weathervane's pace, we strolled out to greet the children. Borda was already doling out the coins when Rick gave him a critical, somewhat intimidating stare. Borda immediately turned the bag upside down and shook it. When he could demonstrate to Jeremiah that the bag was empty, Rick nodded and walked back to the group.

"It's good this way!" Borda bellowed. "I won't miss the trip!"

I had no intention of ditching him this time while he indulged himself with some desperate woman, so I was glad to see Rick honor Jeremiah that way.

Fuel was brought to the helicopter in large drums pulled by a pack team, which made me extremely nervous about the possibility of fuel contamination. "How do you think we fueled you the last time you were here?" Borda asked through a translator.

We ate cornbread and some unusual form of chicken soup before ready-ing ourselves for departure the following morning.

"Let's go," I said, sitting beneath some trees, soup bowl in hand.

"Where's Christina?" Lourdes asked.

"What's she doin' over there?" Box asked, gazing across the street at Christina. She was chatting with a young girl, maybe fourteen, who appeared to be pregnant.

"Seedy! Come on! Let's get a move on!" Box yelled.

"No, we can wait," I interjected.

"What? She's just shootin' the shit with some chick," Box protested.

"Some pregnant chick," I emphasized.

"Okay. Some pregnant . . . Oh, yeah. Right," he remembered. "Well, I wouldn't give her long," he advised.

"No, but we can spare a minute or two." I turned back and looked at Christina. "She sure is a good person, huh?"

"Not again, okay?" Box said.

"Not again, what?"

"You know."

"What, I can't compliment a woman without there being some sort of implication?"

"Exactly."

"Shut up. Here she comes."

*　*　*

The course was the shape of a 7, with each leg approximately a hundred miles in length. On the first leg we would not tip off the people at our intended destination we were coming, but the vector of the second leg would. To avoid this, we invited Borda to transmit messages at will by not placing anyone in the cockpit with him and the pilot. We then ran slightly off course north of the second leg so that Borda believed we were steering away from the *coca* paste storage site. After we were convinced that Borda had given notice to the *campesinos* at the target site that they were in the clear, we radioed forward to the cockpit and advised the pilot to set down near a lab in our immediate area—one that CIA intelligence had plotted out earlier. Quinn then moved to the front, and Borda to the rear. Quinn instructed the pilot to reverse our course from a northerly to a southwesterly heading.

Borda was furious, spitting profane utterances about my character.

"Box," I said unemotionally. "Shut him up."

Box scooted over on his butt and grabbed hold of Borda's military shirt. As Box reared back to pound him with his fist, Borda submitted and shut up. "Yes! Trouble!" Quinn radioed back. "Pilot says we've got a GOES unit on our ass. Advise."

I studied Colonel Borda's facial expressions when I told him of the warning. He didn't impress me as a man concerned about going to jail.

"Ignore it!" I told her. "Drop down to treetop level and increase speed! Roger?"

"Roger, sir!"

"Lower, Quinn!"

"Copy that lower, sir."

"Max throttle!" I demanded, my eyes fixed on the colonel's.

"Copy that max throttle, sir! Max throttle!"

Moments later the skids scraped the canopy. "Pull up, sir?" Quinn suggested.

"No! Well, maybe just a hair!" I answered.

Box scooted across to my side of the chopper, plopping down beside me. "What do we do if he's (the pilot) telling the truth?"

"Go to jail."

"Good. I thought you were gonna say shoot 'em down."

The second leg of the journey was quick. The helicopter slowed on its approach, and it turned sideways per Quinn's instruction, offering those of us in the rear a clear view of the site. A nondescript structure occupied the center of a jungle clearing before us, its perimeter protected on three sides by a snaking river, and by the jungle on its fourth. Barrel upon covered barrel spilled from the structure. They were stacked haphazardly, engulfing most of the clearing. Their contents: a thick, sticky, gray substance called *coca* paste.

I placed Joey and his M-60 machine gun in the center of the helicopter's doorway. The pilot descended parallel with the storage facility, keeping us in constant eye contact with the site's occupants. We descended from the chopper on either side of Joey, breaking outside of his direct line of fire, while covering the perimeter.

I was in the lead position, cantering past the *campesinos* to the left of the structure and behind it. "Clear!" I called to the others.

Rick now crossed to the opposite side to face me. "Everything looks hunky-dory here."

"Good," I said. "Let's dispose of this shit and get the hell outta here."

I searched the forest for any immediate signs of danger and then quickly refocused on Rick.

"Stay back here. Be on the lookout for anything out of the ordinary. We'll dump all the paste in the river and be on our way."

"Wouldn't I be more useful up there? Those containers look kinda heavy."

"Good point. I'll send someone back to replace you."

I moved hastily to the front and told everyone to pitch in and start moving the barrels.

"Lourdes, go to the rear and replace Rick."

"Could you send someone else? I sort of forgot my contacts," she explained.

"You sorta forgot your . . . How far can you go before you realize something like that?"

"I'll go," Christina volunteered.

"Fine. It doesn't matter. Just go. We need to get this shit done already."

I grabbed Lourdes by the shoulder. "Under no circumstances are you to fire that weapon. Understood?"

"Yup."

Down at the river, Box and Rick stood knee-deep in the water and dumped the goop into the current as quickly as we rolled the barrels to them. We got a good assembly line going and spun the empty barrels behind us while we passed the full ones in front of us. Barrel upon barrel rolled by, and then suddenly Lourdes grabbed hold of an empty one.

"Steven," she said. "You're getting them confused."

I had a real bad feeling. "Tell me you haven't been rolling the empty ones into line with the full ones. Please tell me that."

Steven searched frantically for a full barrel, yet found none.

"We emptied them all, didn't we?" I asked, even though I already knew the answer.

"Shit!" he yelled.

"Box! Don't pour out the rest of those!" I admonished him, then said softly, "We may have a problem."

"What?" Box shouted. "Have we dumped half already?"

"Oh, yeah," I said, barely audible. "And then some."

"You here that?" Joey called from the chopper.

"What?" I asked.

"That!" he replied.

I began to hear what sounded like the faint purr of a cat. The sound grew and became more distinct.

"Take cover!" I yelled.

We scattered to one side of the structure, with Christina still in the rear. Now hidden in the brush, we watched nervously as the chopper approached.

"What the hell is that guy doin'?"

"Who?" Box asked.

"Borda." I directed his attention to the storage building.

"He's near the IFF, I think," Steven advised.

"Shit! Joey!"

"Got him," he said, firing one bullet into Borda's skull.

The man had attempted to change the IFF codes, which told the occupants of any PM aircraft that we were not a part of PM and therefore the enemy. We would then have been forced to wage war with the cartel. Borda knew the consequences of such a decision, but I'm not sure I did, even as I called to Joey to shoot him. Whatever actions Joey took, though, he took because he believed I wanted him to, and therefore I was ultimately responsible. To this day I'm not actually sure if I wanted him to kill Borda, but I'm reconciled to the fact that I ordered it.

The small Huey helicopter passed directly overhead, toward the rear of the building, at a high rate of speed. With so many barrels strewn about, and the *campesinos* tucked away in the structure, I was sure that our uninvited guests would be alarmed. If the codes were changed—which we weren't sure of yet—there would soon be trouble.

"Check the IFF, Steven!" I said.

"It's changed," he called back. "Damn, Joey. Good shot."

"Hey!" Joey shouted. "Listen! No sound! I think our visitors are on foot."

"Okay! Let's go!" I commanded.

"Look!" Steven said, pointing to the river. It looked like tons of paste had collected on one of the banks against a fallen tree.

"Joey! Blast that shit outta there!"

As he shredded the tree and blew apart the paste, I asked Box, "Where the hell could they have set down?"

"On the bank of the river? I don't know. They probably just flew out of earshot."

"I hope you're right."

Joey completed his task, and we were ready to go.

"Let's get a liftoff."

"Bap! Bap!" Two shots were fired at the side and back of the structure. Then some return fire. It was Christina fending off the intruders.

"Let's go!" I shouted. We scurried for cover, firing into the wooded area on the bank of the river. "We need support cover for Seedy! Rick! Box! Get up there!"

"Lourdes! Steven!" Box called. "Follow us!"

As they made it around the structure to the other side, I fired my modified 30-06 at anything that moved to suppress fire. Christina had positioned herself on the point, and was unable to take refuge closer to the building.

"Joey! Joey!" I called out.

"Yeah!"

"We're assaulting! Let's go!"

I didn't need to look for him to know he was attacking with me. Joey knew no other gear than overdrive. He was ready to give his life on every mission, especially if it meant saving one of us.

As I ran, my feet struck the dank earth rhythmically but almost without sound. They moved without my willing it. I would feel my eyes looking toward their destiny, but they were not connected to me. My head was a movie camera, zooming in on the moment. Adrift on the wind, I was momentarily invisible. Shots were being fired toward the others, but none toward us. I stopped and my legs became real to me again. I could hear my breath and feel my heart. I was no longer invisible. Joey broke left and took position behind a tree. We fired, striking three of them before they surrendered. Only one of them had been killed—the one Joey shot, of course.

"How are we?" I hollered, keeping a watchful eye on the prisoners.

"It's Christina!" Box replied.

"Oh, no." I dashed toward the team, leaving Joey to guard the prisoners. They were all huddled around her. I gently pushed through and found Christina cradled in Steven's lap. As I knelt beside her, Steven placed her in my arms and said that he would radio a distress call to Langley.

"Oh, Seedy. Is heaven calling you?"

"Yes."

"Heaven's been getting much prettier lately." I laughed nervously.

"I'll say hello to her," she said softly, and her eyes began to close.

"Don't go. Stay and talk a while. Please."

"I'll see you again some day, Ken. Please don't blame yourself. I've been ready for this day for the longest time. Remember, only the dead bury their dead."

"I don't understand."

"I love you," she said, gently closing her eyes, and went limp in my shivering arms.

"I love you, too," I whispered.

I carried her body to the chopper and laid her carefully inside.

"Lourdes," I said, still choked up, "stay with her."

As she passed me, I hugged her, feeling the barrel of her .22 rifle. It was warm. Christina had been struck in the abdomen by a small caliber bullet, and I could tell by the sound of the return gunfire that our adversaries used heavy-caliber assault weapons.

"We'll get through this, Lourdes."

I went back behind the building and told Joey to lend me his weapon.

"Rick, line 'em all up against the wall. Tie that asshole (Mandoza) to the overhang." Mandoza had replaced Hitler's Savior as Ochoa's production chief.

Box stepped in front of me. "What do you plan on doing with that? I hope it's not what I think. We're not about that."

"Step aside, Box." I turned to the others. "Everyone step aside!"

Box reluctantly moved backward, probably hoping that I was merely scaring them. I could hear the silence. My heart beat with pessimism; it methodically hammered out doom to my temples. "Let the dead bury their dead," I thought, my finger clenching the trigger. But I didn't shoot the prisoners. I fired over their hands and up to the roof beams, blasting the structure to splinters. Shell casings flew like popcorn. With each gunshot came release. I felt exalted, like my hideous intent, my soiled motivations, had been exorcised from my spirit. The gun finally stopped cycling. It was done.

With the dim sounds of moaning and crying in the background, Box and Joey came to my side. Joey pulled firmly on the gun a few times before I released it.

"I hope we don't run into any more problems. That's the last of the sixties," he murmured, referring to the ammunition.

"I knew you wouldn't kill them," Box said.

"How could you? I didn't know myself."

"Because I know how much you wanna see them again some day."

"Yeah. Let's go, my friend."

I walked over to Rick and said to him, while facing Mandoza, "Cut this piece of shit down."

Mandoza never cried, and hardly flinched throughout the ordeal. The building behind him was destroyed. The *campesinos* were covered in rubble, but none the worse for wear, except for some abrasions.

"We can't take her, you know," Box advised.

"I know," I responded. "Get the windscreen cover," I said to anyone, as I carried her to the river. We shrouded her in it, and stood waist deep in the running water. After everyone said their farewells, I said, "Lord, into your arms," and released her to find her own way, her own grave, somewhere downstream in the Colombian jungle.

Chapter 31

Yes," Box said on the phone.

"Yeah. Is this Box?"

"Yeah." I could hear a tremor in his voice. "I've got somethin' bad to tell ya."

"What?" I sensed, after all we'd been through together, that this must be bad. "What's wrong?"

"It's Rick," he sobbed. "He's dead."

I didn't speak. I couldn't.

"Did you . . ."

"Yeah. Yeah, I heard you. Uhhh . . . How? How Box? Oh, for God's sake, Box. Oh, God. I can't take it anymore."

"Suicide. They're tellin' me suicide." There was a lull and then, "Hello. Are you still there?"

"Yeah, I'm still here." Another lull. "Where is he? Can we see him? I wanna see him. We need to see him, Box," I said in a glum tone.

"I know. I've already set somethin' up. We'll have to be blindfolded. You know, knowledge about each other and all. Anyhow, call in sick tomorrow, and I'll see you in the morning at your house. Okay?" He spoke despondently.

It had only been a couple months since Christina's death when Langley began putting pressure on Box and me to withdraw the team from the operation. Withdrawal could only be accomplished, per the rules established in Zurich, by transmitting, via satellite, the phrase "Miranda is alive and well." This would be accompanied by a code word, also sent by satellite from Mena and changed weekly, that verified that the operation was indeed terminated. In addition, the code word had to be issued during the final interceptions themselves. This combination was established to preclude the outside possibility that someone apart from Pseudo Miranda would attempt to pirate a shipment.

Box and I agreed to drag our feet until all fears of disclosure subsided in the CIA and the Reagan administration. Casey was more than a bit concerned that the revelations of the Iran-Contra affair would compromise the secrecy of Pseudo Miranda. I felt no direct personal link, and therefore no commitment to these goals. Box and I did not act within a vacuum, however. After consulting each of the remaining members at an unauthorized "family meeting" in New Orleans, we found everyone to be of one mind.

I came home to find that a couple of uninvited guests had dropped in. I parked my De Lorean in the driveway, choosing not to pull it into the garage, and immediately detected the garage door, which leads to the house, ajar. I had been meaning to fix the problem I was having with it not closing properly, but now I was glad I hadn't.

Slipping quietly into the house, I made my way back to my bedroom, where my Colt .45 lay beneath my pillow. On my way past the kitchen, I smelled aftershave. I knew where they were. I pulled back the slide on my gun. To muffle the distinct sound, I kept my hands beneath the pillow and faked a sneeze. I crept back down the hallway, turned on the kitchen lights from outside, and got the drop on the intruders through the serving window that led to the dining room.

"Game's over, boys," I said smugly. "Drop the guns. Drop 'em!"

One of them said, "There's two of us. You drop the gun!"

"You're a very stupid man," I said with a pause. "Okay, let's play that hand. Raise your fuckin' weapons. Come on! You want me? Raise 'em! You think you can beat me? Huh? Raise 'em!"

They kept the guns at their sides.

"That's what I thought. Now drop 'em."

"You'll kill us."

"I could kill you both four times over, so what's it matter?"

"I don't wanna die for this," one said, stammering.

"I'm not gonna kill you," I said sympathetically.

"Really? Thank you." He sounded surprised. He then looked at the other guy and said, "Drop it." They placed their weapons on the floor.

"Hands where I can see 'em."

They raised them above their heads, blaming one another for their obvious ineptitude.

"Shut up," I said. "You talk when I tell you to talk."

And talk they did. They had been sent as messengers to demonstrate the Company's ability to reach out and touch me. We were to make every effort to finalize the operation as soon as possible. My deadly mistake was equating the CIA's resolve with the caliber of people they sent to intimidate me.

* * *

Box came to my home, and we drove to Hondo. The windows of the Cessna we flew were covered so we couldn't see outside. We landed twice, probably to impair our ability to calculate the distance traveled, before finally touching down at our destination. We were blindfolded and driven to Rick's apparent residence, where the blindfolds were then removed. It was a very modest home, and, although it was nighttime, I could tell that it was in a southern state, probably Arizona. We were directed into the living room by two men who were already in the dwelling.

There he sat, his head leaning over the top of the recliner and his arms hanging casually at his sides. The blood had long since dried, clumping together in his long silky hair. The entry wound was to the right temple. It was small and sunken, and folded inward like the mouth of a toothless old man. The exit was clean and precise, the result of a small, fast-moving projectile fired at close range. The blood sprayed decidedly downwards and in a tight, controlled pattern, slightly off kilter with the present placement of the body. He looked so peaceful, so calm.

"Could you leave us alone please?" I asked the men.

"Sorry, sir. We have our instructions."

"It's funny how people choose to do things differently when they kill themselves, isn't it, Box?"

"I'm not sure I . . ."

"You know. Like sitting higher in the chair than would be normal." I turned my attention back to the agents in charge of disposal.

"For God's sakes, can we be alone here?" I cried. "Couldn't you have at least had the decency to check to see whether he was left- or righthanded first? Do you know what you've done here? Do you know what kind of man this was? Of course you don't. How could you? You don't run in circles where people actually sacrifice themselves for something. You have no idea what sacrifices this man has made. Sacrifices that afford you the privilege of being here today to kill him!"

"Step outside, gentlemen," Box started, "before I kill you with my bare hands." They left the room.

Box and I sang what we could of the Cheyenne Anthem and then kissed him good-bye.

"Good-bye, my friend," I said, barely able to see through the tears. "You deserved to go out with more honor than this. Oh, God, I'm sorry."

Box and I were totally silent during the return trip. When we were finally back at my house, Box said, "They wanted us to know they killed him, you know."

"I know." I waited, and then said "It's over, you know. We've gotta end it."

"I know." He looked me in the eyes. "Are you gonna be all right?"

"Huh?" I sighed. "Yeah, I'll be okay."

"Damn it!" he screamed.

"I know, Box." I sobbed. "I know, man."

"Well. I'll be in touch."

"Box," I called. "Are they gonna kill us all?"

"I don't know."

"Let's vow now—today—to go down with dignity and honor. I don't wanna go that way—the way he went. I don't want any of us to. Will you promise me? I mean, if you know before me. You'll give me—us—that chance?"

"What is it you think?"

"I don't know anymore. I don't care. Promise," I demanded again.

"Get some sleep. You don't know what you're saying."

"Promise."

"Promise what? What do you think? That I knew about this? That I let him die?"

"Did you?"

"Are you serious? My God, you are."

"I don't know what to think anymore."

"As God is my witness, I swear that I would never allow anything to happen to any of you. My God, what has this done to you?"

"I believe you." I bowed my head. "Good night, Box."

"Good night, Ken," he said hesitantly, and then walked off.

"Box!" I called to him. "I know you didn't."

*   *   *

Over the next several months, there were only four intervention missions. Langley wanted us to concentrate on making interceptions that had already made it to the first-level transfer. Their reasoning was complex, but in its simplest terms it went as follows: With the cartel already in possession of the first half of the code that released the U.S. government from its commitment to the operation, the Colombians were very reluctant to have us pass on the second half of the code, which officially terminated the operation altogether. They were able to elude us in Colombia by vacating their labs before we arrived, leaving us no way to confirm the end of PM with them. They were also careful not to tag any of the preshipped cocaine with their individual identification symbols. They started using these ingenious tactics after we caught Ocampo's people at a lab in Colombia and discontinued his participation in Pseudo Miranda. However, because he was able to still piggyback shipments, it essentially had no effect on the amount of cocaine coming into America. It simply put us one step closer to ending the operation. Because shipments coming in had to be tagged, interceptions at the first level made more sense. We would have people to give codes to, and, based on the tagging symbols, we would know where those codes were going.

I was informed of two simultaneous shipments that, if they reached the mules on the ground, would serve our purposes. That is to say, we could easily distribute the code words to the traffickers, informing them of the official termination of Pseudo Miranda. I had been adamantly against such an interception, but I was weakening beneath the stress and Langley's coercion. Their threats had become more and more intense with the passage of time. On one occasion, Box and I had to flee for our lives in a 308 Ferrari through the mountains in Cumberland, Maryland. Box would take half the team to Florida, and I would take the other half to southern Texas. These were the final two interceptions our team would ever make.

Joey!" I called in utter desperation. I got no response. I heard gunfire outside the house. The ambush had begun. Quinn, Jesus, Lourdes and Ming were fighting for their lives outside, while Joey and I scrambled to survive inside. The guy I called Fossil? Well, he was probably already dead, the likely result of having his head separated from his shoulders by Quinn—she always took orders quite literally.

"This way!" Joey yelled. He fired his M-16 for suppression, and continued to call for me as he made his way up the stairs.

I ran toward him, tripping on the raised floor as I scurried in a semicrouched position for the staircase. I could now see Joey clearly, as he leaned over the railing and continued to riddle the room with bullets.

"Go!" I screamed, almost at the top of the staircase. He darted down the hall and out of sight. Return fire followed my path up the stairs. I now knew the caliber of murderers I was dealing with: Professional killers would have fired ahead of me and let me run into the stream of bullets. I went nearly halfway down the hallway, then dove into a side corridor to dodge a fusillade of bullets, slapping a preloaded clip into my weapon.

The shooting ceased inside. In the pause I could hear the frantic cries of my friends and sporadic exchanges of gunfire.

"Joey! Ves! Joey!" Quinn hollered.

"Run! Get outta here! I replied. I knew they wouldn't, though. "Joey,"

I said softly, peaking around the corner to see if our assailants were lurking. No one there.

"Joey?"

"Mmmm."

"Joey?"

"Hhhhnn. Yeah. Over here."

I glanced down the hall again before scooting across it to the corridor on the opposite side. I saw his legs first, his feet turned outward, more like a person resting than fighting under fire. I stood up, turning my back to the wall opposite Joey and sliding down to the floor. I now had a good vantage point to detect the approach of any more attackers and to face Joey at the same time.

"What's up, buddy?" I asked, drawing back his protective vest. A bullet had penetrated the seam and torn through the front of his abdomen. His pants were already drenched in blood, and he was fast losing consciousness.

Gunfire erupted once again down the hall, but it didn't seem to matter any longer. I numbly leaned out from the side corridor and fired two quick shots into the attacker's stomach with my .45 automatic. He fell back against the wall and sat, somewhat upright in the middle of the hall, with his shotgun only a few feet in front of him.

The gunfire outside had diminished to a trickle. I was sure my friends had gone.

"Joey? Hey, buddy. I'm gonna take you out of here." I bore no illusions about our present state, and said this only to ease his suffering. "I'm gonna lift you now, okay?"

"Give me your gun," he mumbled. "so you can grab me better and I can cover your ass."

"You're the expert in these matters," I said. "Hey, Joe? We did the right thing, you know. And I wouldn't . . . I couldn't have had a better man at my side when it ended."

"Go out like James Cagney, Ken."

I handed him my Colt .45 and slung his M-16 around my shoulder. I gently lifted his arm and placed my head under his shoulder. As I positioned myself to pick him up, I heard another shot. It jolted me backward, pounding my head and back into the wall. The ensuing burst of blood and flesh led me to believe that I had been killed. The M-16 was firing down the hallway, and I wasn't sure how. Blood poured down my shirt, but I wasn't yet sure what had happened.

"Joey," I said, broken in spirit. I hugged him, pressing my face to his. His blood was very warm. I could feel life slipping away. Wiping his blood from my eyes, I removed the Colt from his grip, wrenching back his finger that still depressed the trigger. He had made the ultimate sacrifice.

Now in the center of the hall, I stood ready. I wasn't there to do battle; I was there to die. I wondered why no one had come to kill me. I walked wearily to the man sitting in the hall. He was still alive. In my half-lucid mind, I bent, kissed him on the top of the head, and said that everything would be all right. His hands stretched to the floor, and he attempted to pull himself to his shotgun.

"You need to kill me that bad?" I asked and handed him the weapon. I backed away and faced him. "Top of the world, ma," I said softly, already missing life.

He fired, striking the side wall.

He gasped several times, trying to gather the strength to fire again.

"You're gonna die, and you still want to kill me?" I asked him incredulously. I was debilitated, the fight gone out of me. "No greater love," I thought. "Joey," I said scrupulously. I knew then that I couldn't give up, a thought that would have served me better had it occurred to me a few seconds earlier.

As I went to relieve the wounded man of his shotgun, he fired. At extreme close range, the pellets didn't expand, but slammed like a slug into my torso, launching me several feet in the air. My back bounded off the wall, and I tumbled to the floor on my face. It took precious time to catch my breath. Hoisting myself up by gripping the hole in the wall created by the first shotgun blast, I laughed painfully at the sweet taste of blood on my tongue.

I aimed at his head, sadness in my heart. I couldn't kill anymore. But he could. He fired again, this time with an empty weapon. Then shots fired blindly from around the corner struck the wall next to me. By instinct, I fired three shots into the corner of the wall leading to the staircase. I heard the sound of a person tumbling down the stairs.

I saw a vision of my mother crying at my funeral in the window at the opposite end of the hall. "Into your hands, Jesus," I said, and then crashed backwards through the window. My right shoulder collided with a solid object, which flipped me a hundred and eighty degrees as I fell to the ground below. My left knee, which was already less than perfect, buckled inward like Gumby's. My vision became blurred and unreliable. I was feeling less than human, a contorted pile of incongruent limbs.

I felt a dull pressure at my shoulders and my legs being dragged roughly across the grass. I was being pulled, Quinn on one arm and Jesus on the other. Was it over? I didn't know for sure. We came to rest at the back of the yard. Quinn and Jesus still held me up. I faced a metal fence.

"Whatta we do?" Lourdes asked, quite scared.

"Run," I heard myself gurgle.

"We're in charge now, Ken," Quinn said. It only now occurred to me that they all seemed to know my real name.

I then heard a lot of voices chattering in the distance. I couldn't tell if they were speaking Spanish or not. Quinn and Jesus gently lowered my body to the ground, my face turned to the right, looking in Lourdes' direction. I saw, as if in slow motion, her weapon fall to the ground.

"No!" I yelled.

I heard no sounds but the sounds of Quinn and Jesus being thrown against the fence with a crash. I had my eyes clamped shut, but when I opened them, I could still see Lourdes standing there. Two men, speaking Spanish, threw her to the fence and began stripping her clothes off. Although I tried and tried, I couldn't move. My mind some-how did not seem connected to my limbs. I was fading in and out of consciousness. Lourdes never once screamed, nor did she resist. But that didn't matter to these animals. They began to do unspeakable things to her. I heard laughter from everywhere as they continued their abomi-nable acts.

"Please don't forsake me," she cried softly. Or did she?

I had my left hand tucked beneath my body, and in it what felt like a gun. My hand was completely numb, so I wasn't sure whether the gun was actually still there. I felt the phantom sensations of a man with sev-ered legs who still perceives his feet are still there. I just wasn't sure.

When they began to slice her skin off as a prelude to killing her, I grunted loudly, forcing my rear end off the ground and arching my back. I then squeezed what I prayed was a trigger and watched in relief as the bullet struck my dear friend in the side.

The angered men hurled me into the fence and beat me about the face repeatedly. I hardly felt a thing, even as they tore off my vest and stabbed me several times with a knife. I simply wasn't there any longer.

Faint sounds of gunfire reverberated in my mind. Or were they imagined? My tormentors lifted me up, throwing one of my forearms over the top of the fence, which pierced the flesh like a meathook, and left me hanging like a side of beef. My skin quickly tore, and I fell heavily to the earth once again. More voices speaking Spanish, and then loud blasts. The two men assaulting me were hurled against the fence, painting it a rich shade of scarlet. Then there were the muffled sounds of rotor blades.

I listened to my breathing and remembered how my uncle George and Christina had sounded in their last moments. I was dying, I knew that, but how would it feel the moment my heart stopped? I felt hands take hold of me and slide me through the morning dew. I saw the bodies of my friends and enemies laid out in a row, steam rising from their corpses. Now on a stretcher, I was lifted above the fog crawling over the Texas hills like a thin veil, softening the horror that lay below.

I could hear a hollow thump, and then another, and another. I checked my breathing. It was me. The thumping—it was me. They were attempting to resuscitate me. But I wasn't dead. A bright light shone in my eyes.

"Come on, sir! You can make it!" someone said.

"But I have made it," I thought. "It's over now." I listened to the soothing sound of the rotor blades and felt warmly about the faceless people who were doing so much to help me. And then, darkness.

I opened my eyes. A brightness rushed in. I felt incredible pain. I drifted back to the darkness.

I opened them once again, this time fighting back the pain. I sank back into the darkness.

I reemerged moments later, or so I thought. Three days had elapsed since the ambush.

"Yes! It's me, Mr. Dix!" Mr. and Mrs. Dix often took care of the team whenever we gathered in Florida. At first I had trouble deciding what I was, never mind who I was. My faculties returned in an avalanche after about a half hour of listening to Mr. and Mrs. Dix.

"Oh, my God," I cried with a scratchy, dry throat. "They're dead. They're all dead." I lifted my hands to my face but screamed from the pain.

"It's your arm. Don't move it. You've received a lot of injuries. It'll take time," Mr. Dix said.

"Time? Time for what? I've lost everything." I caught my breath. "How long before they come for me?"

"Who?" Mrs. Dix asked.

"The people who did this!"

"It's over now," she answered.

"Mr. Casey passed away while you were . . . well, you know," Mr. Dix said.

"Where am I?"

"The Galloway's . . . Lake Austin," he replied stumblingly.

"The Galloway's? What's that?"

"Fine patriots. They've helped keep you alive, and they ask no questions," he explained.

"What happened to Box and Tina and Steven . . . the others?"

"I don't know. I swear, I don't know," he said truthfully. "Get some rest. You need to build your strength. Oh! And don't worry, it was arranged to extend your leave by two more weeks."

"That's a real fuckin' load off my mind," I said sarcastically.

"Good night."

*　*　*

For the next few days, a nurse came in twice daily to refill my intravenous bottles, check my vital signs, and administer cortisone shots as needed. She told me that I received some internal injuries, but that she wasn't sure how extensive they were.

"Don't you wonder why I wasn't taken to the hospital?" I asked curiously.

"I'm paid not to ask. Now you just do your job and get well."

She also said that my knee and shoulder would be permanently deformed with arthritis in a matter of a couple years. And that some day in the not too distant future I would be tormented with back problems. Just the kind of bedside manner I needed.

After about a week I was slowly regaining my strength and had stopped taking my meals intravenously. I was also allowed to sit in a wheelchair and go outdoors. It was only then that I could see where they had taken me. The Galloway's was a mansion that sat immediately on the lake. The lot next to it was empty, and directly behind the house was a tall hill with a sheer rock cliff that rose like a wall at the back of the grounds. On the lake there was a boat house that appeared to berth at least two vessels, perfect for fast getaways. I was filling my lungs with the refreshing air when I noticed an American flag hanging from the front of the house, and I wondered what it now meant to me.

I was in my room resting when Mr. Dix came in with some news. "There's some people out front who'd like to see you."

My heart churned like a locomotive. His smile told me what I had wanted to hear for days.

"Box," I whispered.

"Booch," he said gently.

Tina and Steven were with him. They had all survived. But how?

"You remember that guy in Panama with the wigs? Butler?" Box said.

"Yeah, I do."

"Well, he heard about this plot to ambush us, so he phoned someone in Langley. Whoever he spoke with—I'm guessing Lauder—knew only about those of us in Florida. When we got the warning, we told the courier about you guys. But before we were able to get someone to you, well . . ." He paused, saddened. "You remember that guy Mandoza?"

"I saw him," I said. His face flashed in my mind. "He was the one who saved me, right? Why?"

"Ochoa."

"Why?"

"Escobar's people were sent to kill us, and for some crazy reason, Don Fabio didn't want it done. I have no idea why."

We talked into the late afternoon. No one wanted to say good-bye, but good-bye it was to be.

"Well, Kabooch," Box started, "we've gotta be off."

"Where? Why so soon? When will I see you guys again?"

"It's over for you, Ken. You've given more than ten people to this country." His voice weakened. "It's over."

"Oh, Box. We've lost so much. And what did we accomplish? There's got to be more. How can I walk away like this?"

"Don't do this," he said, weeping lightly.

"What? What am I doin', Box? What happened over the past three years? Did they die for something? Did they?"

"Damn it! Look at you. You're all busted up. You're not the same Vesbucci that started this operation. None of us are. But you have a chance. You're out. They've given you a new lease. Pick the pieces up and start over." He then added, "Someday this will all seem much clearer. Give it time."

I turned to Steven. "You made it through. Who'd have thunk it?"

"I'll miss you. More than anyone, I'll miss you," he said, all welled up with emotion.

"I'll miss you too, scarecrow. You're a brave man, Steven. I just wish I'd told you that before, when it mattered."

"It matters," he replied.

"Tina," I said, "we could never have won the football game without you." We both strained a chuckle. "I wished you'd have been with us from the beginning. We could have used you, and you really would have liked Debara."

"I know I could never fill her shoes," she said.

"You did fill her shoes. And she'd be the first to tell you that. God bless you for saying that, though."

Box wheeled me to the end of the dock, where their boat was tied. He sniffled profusely and brushed back tears.

"I know I can be real pig-headed, but I want you to know that I have never met a finer, more qualified agent. I mean that." He sighed. "I'm never gonna work with anyone like you ever again. I know that. And I tell ya, not a day goes by that I don't think about that."

"Thanks, Box. And stop calling me a *dago*." We all laughed, although it was strained. "You're the best, Box. Pure and simple. I pray we meet again some day."

"Hey!" he whispered loudly. "Do you hear that?"

"What?" I asked.

"The music?" he said, a great big smile rolling across his face. He then began to dance. Even Tina joined in, although she had no idea what he was doing.

I spread my arms and swayed back and forth, not hearing music, but happy to have been associated with such people. As they cruised away in the boat, they saluted me with the sign language for 4PM.

Epilogue

In 1989, while stationed in Korea as a captain in the United States Air Force, I was contacted by representatives of the CIA and told to feed disinformation to reporter Carl Bernstein. I did as I was asked to do and met with Mr. Bernstein at his New York home. After the interview, I was satisfied that my job was done.

When I was told that Bernstein had spoken with Frank Rubino, then Noriega's lead defense attorney in the drug dealing case against him, about our visit together, I became quite concerned. I then notified the DEA and told them what had transpired. Dan Moritz, the CIA agent who convinced the attorney to prefer charges against Noriega, immediately took my call from Korea, and had me speak hypothetically about Pseudo Miranda as he taped our conversation. He then sent DEA agents out to speak with me on four occasions about the operation. Agents Tom Raphenello, Steve Grilli and Dave Sir assured me that they had extensive knowledge of the operation and that they wanted desperately to head off any attempts on the part of Rubino to introduce this operation in court. In no uncertain terms, Dan Moritz stated that if Rubino were to prove the existence of Pseudo Miranda, General Noriega would walk.

Months later, while I was a student at Squadron Officer's School, after receiving my second commendation medal for meritorious service, agent Ed Wezain and another unidentified agent from the DEA, CIA agent Sutherland and agent Ron Humphrey of the Office of Special Investigations (OSI) interrogated me for six hours. The point of the conversation was their demand that I sign a perjured statement, which said in essence that Pseudo Miranda never happened. When I refused, the OSI threatened me with a psychiatric discharge, even though I was highly decorated and had a flawless record. In fact, during the eight years it typically takes to advance in rank from captain to major, only about half of the officers are selected for Squadron Officer's School. I was selected in the first year that I was eligible. I agreed to see their psychiatrist, Captain David Horwood, M.D., who found that I tested normal on all empirical tests and interviews. But Horwood declared that if the OSI found what I was saying not to be true, then I must be suffering from delusions. A perfect example of military circular reasoning.

Throughout the following year, the OSI pressured everyone in my chain of command to let them pursue their perverse military psychiatric prosecution. At the end of a year of humiliation, the final review board (the only one I actually got to meet in person) returned a diagnosis of sane. They even went so far as to say that the OSI had a remarkable level of interest in what should simply have been a medical case and that they had systematically altered evidence and manipulated the system. The OSI, concerned about the implications, went behind closed doors in Washington, DC, with the review board and supposedly gave them some new evidence, even though this board was not allowed to consider any new evidence. I was never given the opportunity to see this "new" evidence and was summarily drummed out of the Air Force with a 50 percent disability.

During the time these events took place I was able to acquire some very persuasive evidence that not only supported my testimony but convinced the final review board that the OSI had been lying all along about my mental health.

The DEA, in response to a Freedom of Information (FOI) request I made concerning Pseudo Miranda, initially said they had no records pertaining to it. Later, when they became concerned that I might be called to testify in the Noriega trial, reissued a response, in writing, to the original request. They admitted this time that such an operation had indeed occurred and that I was involved in it but that they could not release associated documents to me. They cited several security reasons for their denial to release these records.

In November of 1990, Frank Rubino, while appearing on the "Larry King Live" television show, evoked my name and the operation as being closely tied to his client.

Carlos Lehder, in a letter to me from his prison cell in Marion, Illinois, identified Pseudo Miranda as a ". . . drug proyect (sic) of the United States."

I have since passed an extensive polygraph examination, administered by a highly recognized expert in the field and retired FBI agent, Francis M. Connolly. I also was given a clean bill of health after taking a battery of psychological tests, which were likewise administered by a recognized leader in the field, Michael A. Turelo, M.D.

I was interviewed on camera by Sam Donaldson of "Prime Time Live," but when his producer failed to conduct an interview with another party involved in Pseudo Miranda—someone I took the risk of securing for them, I refused to be the only one on camera speaking about this operation. I was now very exposed and flapping in the wind. All the Agency had to do was swoop in with the appropriate threat and it would be over. They did. They threatened to harm my fiance's brother in Alaska, and I was compelled to do what they demanded. I sabotaged the ABC segment, and I have been blacklisted ever since. It seems that the free press isn't much different from the government. Nevertheless, given the same choices, I would do the exact same thing again without batting an eye. I also spoke on several occasions with Lowell Bergman, who had appeared on "60 Minutes" and was famous as "The Insider," but, as with Carl Bernstein, I was never allowed to be fully veracious with him.

A woman by the name of Pilar Rivas contacted me several times on behalf of Carlos Lehder in regard to my dealings with Manuel Noriega. She was also speaking directly with Manuel Noriega and attempting to get him to tell her things that would provide Lehder with enough testimony against Noriega to enable him to strike a substantial deal with the U.S. government. Frank Rubino did not know of these conversations with his client until I informed him of them. Noriega surrendered critical information to Rivas, which Lehder later used in Noriega's trial.

As the years passed, I saw many stories surface on things such as Mena, Arkansas, Whitewater, and the crack cocaine epidemic in Los Angeles. I came to realize that we were only a small piece of a much larger puzzle, but without our piece, the puzzle could not have existed. Where are the Woodwards and Bernsteins of the world? I suppose after what happened to me and to Gary Webb (author of *Dark Alliance: The CIA, the Contras, and the Crack Cocaine Explosion*), I don't blame people from staying far away from this story. It makes you wonder how the media ever covers any story dealing with the CIA, unless it's fed to them.

Years later Box told me that Lourdes survived.